Working with Substance-Exposed Children

Strategies for Professionals

Edited by Cordelia H. Puttkammer, M.Ed., OTR/L

Foreword by Kathleen VandenBerg, M.A.

Contributing Authors:
Gale Berkowitz, Dr.P.H.
Deborrah Bremond, Ph.D.
Jean Gardner Cole, M.S.
Antoine K. Fomufod, M.D., M.P.H., FAAP
Kathleen Harp, M.H.S., PT, PCS
Shirley J. Jackson, M.S., OTR/L
Ellen Aronson Kaplan, M.S., PT
Robin Lindauer Lang, OTR/L
Diedra Mitchell-Wright, LICSW
Rebecca A. Parks, M.S., OTR/L
Diane E. Powell, Ph.D.
Anne Reynolds, M.S., CCC-SLP
Ila Sherman, OTR
Nika St. Claire, M.S.
Andrea Santman Wiener, PT, PCS
Davene M. White, RN, NNP

Therapy
Skill Builders®
a division of
The Psychological Corporation
3830 E. Bellevue / P.O. Box 42050
Tucson, Arizona 85733
1-800-763-2306

Reproducing Pages from This Book

As described below, some of the pages in this book may be reproduced for instructional or administrative use (not for resale). To protect your book, make a photocopy of each reproducible page. Then use that copy as a master for photocopying.

The Learning Curve Design is a registered trademark of The Psychological Corporation.

Therapy Skill Builders®
a division of
The Psychological Corporation
3830 E. Bellevue / P.O. Box 42050
Tucson, Arizona 85733
1-800-763-2306

ISBN 0761647600 Catalog No. 4760

10 9 8 7 6 5 4
Printed in the United States of America

For information about our audio and/or video products, write us at: Therapy Skill Builders, a division of The Psychological Corporation, P.O. Box 42050, Tucson, AZ 85733.

Contents

Foreword

The recent media coverage of the number of infants and children prenatally exposed to drugs led to a concerted effort on the part of many disciplines to approach this problem. In the last decade, emphasis on the pregnant drug addict has led to treatment programs which focus on the social, psychological, and developmental characteristics that place the mother and infant at risk. Underlying this effort has been an acknowledgment of the problem of substance abuse as a *disease.* Treating families with parent-focused efforts as well as child-focused efforts has facilitated hope in treating and supporting this difficult problem. It is a problem which touches not only medicine but education, psychology, society, and each one of us.

For these reasons, this book is excellent and timely. Representing several disciplines with a wide variety of experience, this book demonstrates that sensitivity for those facing this problem is possible and impressive. Readers of this book will experience, through these authors, an understanding of the complicated needs of this population which calls for persistent efforts to reach out and *keep reaching out* in a spirit of nonjudgment. These professionals have shown that they believe in these addicted parents, many of whom have infants who are irritable, fragile, and at risk. Moreover, they show that these efforts pay off!

These pages also bring out the stresses facing the professional who works in this challenging arena and who must deal with missed appointments, relapses, evaluating emerging disabilities, and brief periods of progress which may be wiped away by a return to abuse of drugs in the family. By viewing these children and infants as members of *families* who are searching their own attitudes about substance abuse, and by tapping into the hidden resources that intervention efforts can find, these professionals have demonstrated that working with parents toward recovery can be hopeful at times and even miraculous at others.

Read this book because it describes the scope of the problem and is multidisciplinary, realistic, sensitive, and thorough. It makes a definite contribution to helping us conceptualize how to approach the problem. It is a relief to see approaches offered in this book with optimistic prognoses and which integrate these young high-risk children into programs with children of the same age who have not been exposed to drugs. (These programs provide, among other things, early intervention and developmentally appropriate learning environments.) It points out our need to be patient and encourages us to believe that eventually interventions that are supportive, nonjudgmental, and persistent will pay off. Read this book because it focuses on the family and not just the child alone. Read this book because it has a developmental focus and treats addiction in parents as a disease.

The interventions described in this book will create the attitude that all is not lost and there are many opportunities for success with this population.

Kathleen VandenBerg, M.A.
Director, Infant Development Program
Stanford University Medical Center
Stanford, California

Acknowledgments

The editor would like to thank Howard University. This book grew out of a small faculty incentive grant given to Shirley J. Jackson and Cordelia H. Puttkammer in 1987. I would like to thank my coworkers and those involved in the original research, especially Shirley J. Jackson. Dr. Antoine K. Fomufod supported this project from the beginning. Thanks to Claudia Schildroth, Chief Occupational Therapist at Howard University Hospital, and Adrid Gadling, a staff occupational therapist who facilitated recruiting the original substance-abusing mothers so we could involve their neonates. Carole Brown and Pat Wilbarger were the two certified Brazelton assessors, and both donated many hours to this research. Cloene Taylor, head nurse in the NICU, helped us involve all the nurses in the NICU and contributed valuable time to this effort.

Ideas were exchanged with Alice Sapienza and Rose Cavelli from Children's Rehabilitation in Philadelphia, as well as with other therapists in audiences where Shirley J. Jackson and I have presented.

Marcia Coling contributed significantly through her encouragement and by reading the document and providing many valuable suggestions. Patricia Hartwell and Kathleen Hunter deserve untold thanks for their many hours of editing. Clayonnia Colbert-Dorsey typed and revised many pages. Shiu Wei Yin executed some graphics.

To my family, friends, colleagues; to our children, Eric, Nancy, Meta; and to my husband, Charles, who contributed many hours of patience, I want to say, "Thank you."

About the Editor

Cordelia H. Puttkammer, M.Ed., OTR/L, is an Associate Professor in the College of Allied Health Sciences, Howard University. Since 1978, she has focused attention on early intervention. She worked on a home-based infant team at Ivymount School from 1980 to 1988.

She has served on a number of advisory boards and was appointed by the District of Columbia Board of Education to the Advisory Panel on Special Education from 1983 to 1992.

Her interest in infants who have been substance-exposed began in 1985 with children on her case load, and then evolved through a research grant concerned with drug-exposed neonates in the neonatal intensive care unit at Howard University Hospital in 1987. She has made numerous presentations to occupational therapy groups locally and nationally.

Ms. Puttkammer has been involved since 1974 as an advocate for children with learning disabilities. In 1979 she coauthored *A Handbook for Helping Your Learning Disabled Child in the District of Columbia.* The latest revision was published in 1989.

Contributing Authors

Gale Berkowitz, Dr.P.H., received a B.A. degree in Psychology from Johns Hopkins University and the Master and Doctor of Public Health degrees from the University of California, Berkeley. She has been a policy research analyst and Evaluation Analyst in Public Health Issues since 1985. Until recently she was an Evaluation Analyst at the Center for the Vulnerable Child in Oakland, California, and a Senior Research Associate at the Institute for Health Policy Studies at the University of California at San Francisco. Her publications are in the area of maternal and child health, foster care, case management, and resiliency in children.

Deborrah Bremond, Ph.D., is a psychologist at Children's Hospital, Oakland, California. She has worked with medically fragile substance-exposed infants and toddlers, providing developmental assessment and early intervention. She is part of the Neonatal Follow-up and Parent-Infant programs administered through the Child Development Center. Dr. Bremond has been involved in designing developmental tracking systems for community-based programs serving mothers and infants in residential drug-treatment programs.

Jean Gardner Cole, M.S., is an Infant Developmental Specialist. Her training is in Special Education and Child Development, and her experience is in early intervention, infant assessment, teaching, consulting, and research. She is a Master Trainer in the Brazelton Neonatal Assessment Scale (BNAS) at the Child Development Unit, Children's Hospital, Boston; a faculty member at Wheelock College; and a Research Associate at Boston City Hospital where she is presently engaged in using the BNAS in two large studies assessing the effects of cocaine on newborns.

Antoine K. Fomufod, M.D., M.P.H., FAAP, was educated in Nigeria and completed his pediatric studies with a fellowship in Neonatology at Johns Hopkins University School of Medicine and Baltimore City Hospitals. He has coordinated the Howard University College of Medicine Pediatric Student Teaching Program at D.C. General Hospital in the past, and had been an Associate Professor of Pediatrics and Child Health at Howard University College of Medicine for several years. Since 1986 he has been the Director of Neonatology at Howard University Hospital, and since 1992 a Professor of Pediatrics. Dr. Fomufod has published more than 45 articles and abstracts in numerous national and international journals. He has presented locally, nationally, and internationally on various aspects of neonatology, high-risk infants, and perinatal substance abuse. He has received numerous honors and awards and provided valuable community service in the areas of infant mortality, boarder babies, and perinatal substance abuse.

Kathleen Harp, M.H.S., PT, PCS, is a pediatric physical therapist in private practice in the Washington, D.C., metropolitan area. She provides home-based services to children with neuromotor problems from birth to 15 years. Ms. Harp graduated from the University of Delaware in physical therapy and received the Master of Health Science degree from the Krannert Graduate School of Physical Therapy, University of Indianapolis. She has been practicing since 1987 and is a Pediatric Clinical Specialist.

Shirley J. Jackson, M.S., OTR/L, currently is pursuing the Ph.D. degree in Psychology. She has worked as both a clinician and administrator in mental health and physical disabilities. She has been on the faculty of the College of Allied Health Sciences at Howard University since 1980 and is the current Chair of the Occupational Therapy Department. She and Cordelia Puttkammer have collaborated in a number of local and national presentations regarding their research with substance-exposed infants and their families.

Ellen Aronson Kaplan, M.S., PT, has been involved with direct care for children from multirisk families since 1971. She is certified in neurodevelopmental treatment (NDT) and received an M.S. degree in Developmental Disabilities/Early Intervention. Ms. Kaplan has worked as a service provider and consultant at two University-affiliated programs: the Westchester Institute of Human Development affiliated with New York Medical College, and the Rose F. Kennedy Center of the Albert Einstein College of Medicine. She also has been an instructor for Ithaca College's program in Physical Therapy. Her professional presentations have included lectures, workshops, and poster presentations on such topics as motor development of infants and toddlers from multirisk families who have been exposed to cocaine in utero, adaptive parenting, therapeutic feeding, normal and abnormal motor development, and principles of therapeutic treatment. Ms. Kaplan is coauthor of the chapter on "The Role of Physical Therapy on an Interdisciplinary Team," in *Developmental Disabilities: Handbook of Interdisciplinary Practice,* edited by B. A. Thyer and N. T. Kropf (currently in press).

Robin Lindauer Lang, OTR/L, received the B.S. degree in Occupational Therapy from Towson State University. Presently she is an occupational therapist in the Anne Arundel County Public School System. Previously she worked with drug-exposed infants and toddlers at the Treatment and Learning Centers Infant Program, Rockville, Maryland. She is certified in neurodevelopmental treatment (NDT) for pediatrics. She has completed continuing education in both sensory integration and oral motor dysfunction.

Diedra Mitchell-Wright, LICSW, ACSW, received the M.A. degree in Social Work. Since 1977 she has been employed as a perinatal social worker at Howard University Hospital. Her area of expertise is working with obstetrical substance-abusing and other high-risk patients. She has authored and coauthored articles on high-risk infants and obstetrical patients, and she has made presentations at local conferences and workshops.

Rebecca A. Parks, B.A., M.S., OTR/L, has been a Peace Corps volunteer, a staff therapist in an acute rehabilitation center and in head injury, and has started the Occupational Therapist Department in two hospitals. She has been a clinical instructor of undergraduate and graduate students in occupational therapy, as well as medical coordinator and Director for the American Refugee Committee in Thailand. She was Associate Director for Health of Peace Corps/Thailand, and was Chief of Operations for the Pacific, Asia, Central Europe, and the Mediterranean Region of the Peace Corps in Washington, D.C. Ms. Parks is fluent in French and Thai. She is a commissioned officer with the Public Health Service, serving as Senior Pediatric Specialist at the National Institutes of Health in Bethesda, Maryland.

Diane E. Powell, Ph.D., is the Director of Project DAISY in the Early Learning Years Branch in the District of Columbia Public Schools. She also is responsible for the coordination of transition and integration programs for young children with disabilities who receive educational programming within the least restrictive environment. She is the former director of a Level 5 program for the seriously emotionally disturbed and learning disabled children, has served as specialist in the area of behavioral and emotional disorders, and is the former coordinator of programs for the seriously emotionally disturbed in the Montgomery County Public Schools. She has worked as a child development and parent-training specialist in the Division of Maternal and Child Health. She is currently on the adjunct faculty of Trinity College and the University of the District of Columbia. She has taught in both the private and public school sectors. She holds a doctoral degree from American University in the area of Emotional Disturbances and Learning Disabilities. Dr. Powell also has a Master's degree in Education as well as a Master's degree in the area of Clinical Psychology. She has provided expert testimony to the Senate Select Committee, the House Narcotics Committee on Children Prenatally Exposed to Drugs, Educational Implications, as well as to the Congressional Black Caucus.

Anne Reynolds, M.S., CCC-SLP, is a speech-language pathologist who has been working since 1978 with young children with multiple disabilities. While most of her career has focused on the two- to five-year-old population, she has expanded her area of expertise to include children from birth to 24 months, and to seven years of age. Her primary therapeutic interests are the development of early language and play skills and the assessment and treatment of oral motor and feeding skills. She operates a part-time private practice in Maryland and the District of Columbia, and is employed part-time at the Reginald S. Lourie Center in Rockville, Maryland, where she works with speech- and language-delayed children from birth to five years of age.

Ila Sherman, OTR, is an early intervention specialist who has worked with premature infants and their families since 1987. She is particularly interested in the effects of narcotics in utero and has participated in collecting research and has provided inservices to other professionals.

Nika St. Claire, M.S., currently is the program director of the Center of CARE (Chemical Addiction Recovery Efforts) at Children's Hospital, Oakland, California. She has worked in the field of perinatal addiction since 1980, and has worked in a variety of programs for pregnant and parenting addicts and their children. She has written, directed, and produced a video, "Treating the Pregnant Addict." Ms. St. Claire has served on the steering committee for the State of California task force on substance-exposed infants. As a founder and president of California Advocates for Pregnant Women, she has been active in the policy and research arena for substance-exposed infants and their families.

Andrea Santman Wiener, PT, PCS, is a pediatric physical therapist in private practice in Washington, D.C. She is president of Building Blocks Pediatric Rehabilitation Services and has been providing physical therapy to children since 1986. She graduated from Boston University, Sargent College of Allied Health Professions and received a Master's degree at the Krannert School of Physical Therapy, University of Indianapolis. She is certified in pediatric neurodevelopmental treatment (NDT) and is a Pediatric Certified Specialist.

Davene M. White, RN, NNP, has provided acute, chronic, and follow-up care to drug-exposed infants and children, many of whom required long hospital stays due to abandonment ("boarder babies") and many of whom were born to HIV-positive mothers. She serves on the Advisory Board of NAPARE (National Association of Perinatal Addiction, Research and Education), the District of Columbia's Pediatric AIDS Advisory Committee, is founder and director of POSSAE (Promoting Optimal Solutions to Substance Abuse and Exposure), and presently serves as a technical expert and consultant at the Center for Substance Abuse Prevention/Community Team Training Institute (CSAP/CTTI). Ms. White lectures nationally while continuing to contribute to the education and training of pediatric and obstetric residents, nursing, and social service students of Howard University. Since 1976 she has been on the neonatal staff of Howard University Hospital, and she joined the faculty of the Howard University College of Medicine in 1981.

Introduction

This handbook is intended as a guide to persons interested in becoming involved with substance-exposed infants as home caregivers, volunteer workers, teachers, medical staff members, students, or therapists. It represents a multidisciplinary team approach and is therefore a compilation of various professionals' thinking and experiences about working with substance-exposed infants and their families. It acquaints the reader with effective methods of management and treatment for difficult-to-manage substance-exposed infants and children. Contributors have worked in different parts of the country and within different service models; it is clear, therefore, that they all have had different experiences. Their exposure varies, and each chapter should be read with this in mind.

To gain an appreciation of the issues related to drug exposure and treatment, it is recommended that the book be read in its entirety. It is also recognized that caregivers and some specialists will read in depth those chapters specific to their interests; therefore, the book is designed to have each chapter stand on its own merit.

Although we constantly refer to the "substance-exposed" infant, there are many terms that can be used to describe this population, and various terms are used throughout the different chapters. Having said that, may we urge much caution in doing what we have had to do in this book–grouping children together and applying a label. Generalizations and labels may be acceptable in a handbook, but each infant is a unique individual and must be approached and treated as one.

Treating drug-exposed infants on a case-by-case basis is well advised because we do not know exactly how the brain is affected, and the range of responses to exposure is large indeed. Not all substance-exposed neonates will need the help of professionals. Some do not exhibit early signs of involvement when tested soon after birth. Likewise, infants who require early intervention may no longer need treatment upon entering first grade. Data regarding long-term neurological consequences are largely anecdotal. Research has been difficult to interpret. However, substance-exposed infants and neonates must continue to be considered "high risk" (Neuspiel and Hamel 1991) for the reason stated above–we do not know exactly how the brain is affected.

We give much attention in this book to the effects of illegal substances on the human body and on the infant/caregiver relationship. Our goal is to reach the family. We operate on the assumption that each mother can be involved and help her child. But much more research needs to be done, misconceptions must be clarified, and, especially, services for infants and families need to dramatically expand and improve. Public policies and some private institutions need to change for this last to happen. Caregivers, health-care professionals, and educators must become advocates for substance-exposed infants, children, and their families.

Reference

Neuspiel, D. R., and S. Hamel. 1991. Cocaine and infant behavior. *Developmental and Behavioral Pediatrics* 1:55-64.

Chapter 1

Understanding Drug Dependence

Rebecca A. Parks, M.S., OTR/L

People have always sought ways to change or escape their reality by chemical means. The desire to eliminate pain or to have intense experiences in sensation pushes people toward use of various agents from caffeine to heroin, from nicotine to cocaine.

Societies in all parts of the world have used substances that suppress pain and sorrow and also provide pleasurable sensations when consumed. The oldest are those obtained from the cannabis plant, the opium poppy, and the coca bush. Archeological evidence indicates that cannabis was cultivated as early as 6000 B.C.; religious and mystical use of cannabis in Indian societies was reported from about the seventh century A.D. By the end of the 19th century, drug abuse and addiction were being seen in many countries and were beginning to receive the attention of national governments as part of moves toward social responsibility (Gossop and Grant 1990).

Drugs such as opium and cocaine have had historically well-accepted use as painkillers during surgery, and agents like caffeine are ingested on a daily basis in social and routine situations around the world. Thus, defining *abuse* of chemical substances, and when use has become dependence, is not a straightforward task. Drug use and abuse must always be judged in their social context and by the impact they have on the user, the user's family, and the community.

Drug Dependence

In 1964, a World Health Organization (WHO) Expert Committee defined *dependence* as "a state, psychic and sometimes also physical, resulting from the interaction between a living organism and a drug, characterized by behavioral and other responses that always include a compulsion to take the drug on a continuous or periodic basis in order to experience its psychic effects, and sometimes to avoid the discomforts of its absence."

The original WHO definition was eventually seen as inadequate and developed further to include a variety of drug-dependence syndromes, with the characteristics of any specific syndrome produced by any drug then calling for precise description.

Elements of a dependence syndrome include tolerance (increasing habituation to ingestion of the drug), withdrawal symptoms (identifiable signs as the drug's effect leaves the system), withdrawal relief (disappearance of these signs when the drug is taken again), subjective awareness of compulsion (the user has some knowledge of the drive to use the drug), narrowing of repertoire (the user's routine around responding to the need for the drug becomes increasingly more focused and goal-oriented), salience (life's normal activities are sorted and trimmed down to those most germane to obtaining and taking the drug), and reinstatement (although the user may eliminate use for a considerable period, resuming even minimal contact with the drug will swiftly place the user back in a dependence) (Gossop and Grant 1990).

The social implications of drug abuse are less well quantified and documented than the health consequences, but they represent an equally serious problem (Gossop and Grant 1990).

The problems associated with alcohol and other drug abuse have continued to escalate, until today it is generally acknowledged that these problems represent one of the major threats to the health, welfare, and economy of the country. It now seems that alcohol and other drug abuse, and the myriad personal and social complications associated with it, has pervaded all strata of society and all aspects of life in the United States (Harrington et al. 1987).

In the *Alcohol and Drug Abuse Handbook* (1987), Harrington et al. estimated that nine to 12 million individuals are directly affected by alcohol and drug abuse in America, and that each individual usually affects four other persons in some negative, unhealthy, or destructive manner. They further pointed out that at least 15% of all hospital patients on any given day are being treated for one or more problems or complications that are the direct and/or indirect effects of alcohol or other drugs.

The Magnitude of the Problem

In 1990, the biennial National Household Survey on Drug Abuse of the National Institute on Drug Abuse (NIDA) reported that of the U.S. population surveyed (201 million people aged 12 years and older), 74 million had at some time used illicit drugs, 167 million had used alcohol, and 147 million had smoked cigarettes.

Overall, use of any illicit drug in the previous month was more common among young adults (18 to 25), males, blacks, residents of large metropolitan areas, and residents of the West. Prevalence of use of illicit drugs in the previous month was highest among those 18 to 25 years of age. Use of illicit drugs, alcohol, and cigarettes generally peaked during the late 1970s and declined thereafter. However, cocaine, along with its derivative, crack, has been of increasing concern in recent years. In the 1990 NIDA survey, about 11% of those surveyed (or 23 million people age 12 years and over) reported having used cocaine or crack one or more times in their lifetime; 6 million reported having used in the previous year; and 1.6 million reported having used in the previous month. Of these recent users, about one million were males and 600,000 were females.

The Effects of Cocaine

Although the number of persons initiating cocaine use has decreased since 1985, there remains a hard core of addicts who continue to use cocaine in an extremely destructive manner. Cocaine use by women of childbearing age poses a great risk to the fetuses of pregnant woman abusers (Schuster 1991).

Cocaine is the most powerful naturally occurring central nervous system stimulant. Employed as a street drug, users report euphoria with an enhanced sense of well-being, alertness, and friendliness. Regular abuse of the drug can produce an acute psychosis which is similar to and can be mistaken for paranoid schizophrenia or amphetamine psychosis (Benzer and Nold-Klett 1987).

A WHO Advisory Group Meeting on Adverse Health Consequences of Cocaine and Coca-Paste Smoking considered cocaine to be the most highly dependence-producing drug available (Gossop and Grant 1990). It is a potent stimulant whose popularity as a recreational mood-altering drug has increased dramatically during the last decade. It is erroneously perceived by most users as a status drug having minimal health consequences and as an activity in which members of a higher social class are involved. It is considered by many to be a daring chemical to experiment with; under federal law, illegal possession, manufacture, use, or sale of cocaine is a felony.

Tolerance to the mood-elevating effects of cocaine can develop after repeated use of the drug (Benzer and Nold-Klett 1987). The blood-brain barrier is particularly important with regard to the drugs of abuse, because they cross the blood-brain barrier quite rapidly. Drugs of abuse generally alter the function of neurons by influencing a receptor site between two neurons (Westermeyer 1986). One of NIDA's areas of concentration is the development of medications that will not only act as antagonists to block the reinforcing properties of drugs, but also will correct the chemical imbalances created in the brain by prolonged exposure to drugs of abuse. These neurochemical effects often last long after substance abuse has been discontinued, causing an intense craving (Schuster 1991).

Nationwide growth in the population of those who are probably addicted to crack justifies the declaration by William Bennett (former director, Federal Drug Policy) that crack is "our biggest and most immediate problem." Crack smoking has become widespread notwithstanding the myth propagated by the media that it is an inner-city, low-income, largely minority problem. Many middle-class communities are "still asleep" to the widespread local availability of crack.

Crack use by the middle class has been increasingly recognized. According to some estimates, as many as 70% of New York City's drug users may be affluent. Doctors, nurses, accountants, professors, Wall Street executives, air traffic controllers, all have fallen victim to the crack epidemic (Wallace 1991). In the same vein, poor minority women are overidentified in the obstetric community, while middle- to upper-class white women are underidentified; preconceived notions and expectations of health-care providers are a big factor in this skewing of statistics based on bias in screening procedures (Stallings-Sahler 1992).

Providers' misplaced expectations may account for spurious representations of the magnitude of the problem among poor and minority populations. Nonetheless, a great deal of substance abuse in the United States is the result of social dislocations—poverty, child abuse and abandonment, and discrimination against minorities (Schuster 1991). As Wallace (1991) says, Halfon (1989) reminds us not to neglect an important factor that may explain the motivation to develop a drug economy. For Halfon, inextricably linked to the evolution of booming cottage drug industries is the loss of services and the poverty that characterized the 1980s. He links his observations of the gap between rich and poor in the 1980s, and the gutting of our programs for the underprivileged, to the evolution of a drug economy centered on the packaging, marketing, and distribution of crack cocaine.

Lasch (1979) describes our contemporary society as one in which societal and family dynamics have combined to create a culture mainly composed of narcissists. The glamour of cocaine and its pharmacological effects coincide with the needs of the narcissist. For those who attempt to ameliorate painful feelings, emptiness, boredom, and low self-esteem, cocaine represents an attractive and seductive drug because of the feelings of euphoria, grandiosity, and confidence it provides—especially to those wishing to emulate the lifestyles of the rich-and-famous users of cocaine. As America's favorite new drug, it no longer remains the special toy of the media, stars, or even of those mostly middle- and upper-middle-class white males who were its initial users. Intranasal cocaine usage grew to include people of all races and backgrounds in clubs and bars and at parties, where anyone with the desire—and the money—could try the new drug (Wallace 1991).

Animal research reveals that cocaine is the only drug for which laboratory animals will continuously bar-press without stopping for food or rest, and for which they will pass up females in heat. Laboratory research shows cocaine to be the most reinforcing of drugs, with animals consistently self-administering it until they drop dead. This was not found to be true in heroin or alcohol studies.

In humans, users actually experience a neurochemically based need for more cocaine, which, after chronic use, manifests itself as an all-consuming cocaine craving (Wallace 1991).

The routes of administration of drugs carry certain risks for biomedical complications. Parenteral injection may lead to a wide variety of medical complications associated with viral, bacterial, and fungal infections (Westermeyer 1986). There is also the possibility that contaminated needles and syringes may be used and that adulterants may be added to illicit heroin, amphetamines, or cocaine (Gossop and Grant 1990).

The excess mortality and morbidity associated with cocaine are higher when cocaine is injected than when it is sniffed. In deaths from overdose, various causes have been identified, such as cerebral hemorrhage and cardiac arrest. Cocaine overdose deaths in the United States increased by about 300% over the period 1978-1982 (Gossop and Grant 1990).

Wallace (1991) points out that with regard to social implications of crack and cocaine use, the characteristics of crack smokers suggest the possibility that those who smoke experimentally and recreationally have risk factors that may have predisposed them to the development of the abuse and dependency syndromes. Psychological data on this sample provide evidence of exposure to dysfunctional family dynamics in childhood.

By the same token, the majority (54.3%) of crack smokers in the sample report some kind of familial discord that is directly related to their crack smoking. In the view of patients, compared with any pre-existing familial discord, crack either creates or exacerbates relationship problems, justifying the reporting of these events as crack-related.

According to Washton (1989), a dual addiction to sex and drugs is rampant among patients addicted to cocaine. Inciardi (1990) acknowledges the concern that with crack use in particular, the high level of sexual activity that may be resulting from the exchange of sex for the drug presents a greater potential for transmission of the human immunodeficiency virus (HIV) and other sexually transmitted diseases (Wallace 1991). Here, then, is the double-barreled threat of HIV infection related to crack and cocaine use: increased uninhibited sexual activity and intravenous injection of the drug. As Schuster points out (1991), of the more than 140,000 persons diagnosed with AIDS by September 1990, 31% of the cases were attributable to intravenous drug use. In addition, one to 1.5 million people are HIV positive; many of these cases are attributable to high-risk sexual behavior and sex-for-drugs exchanges.

Basis for Therapeutic Intervention

Despite the difficulty encountered by investigators trying to attribute cause, it is generally agreed that some combination of drug-exposure factors and sometimes chaotic and possibly dangerous home environments (Maloney 1992) have resulted in drug-exposed infants and young children who are at risk for inability to reach their full developmental potential in early life. As care providers and parents, we are not obliged to delay intervention until all causative factors are precisely sorted out and attributed to their direct effects. Such delay would be foolhardy and might result in our attempting finally to take action only when it is too late to prevent irreversible physical, emotional, or social damage to these children.

The best foundation to an intervention approach is parent training on providing an environment which aids the child's self-regulation and promotes normal development. Parental lack of awareness of these issues ultimately could become the child's biggest problem (Stallings-Sahler 1992).

It is always salient to take into account issues affecting the child which relate to low socioeconomic status or low education with or without the problem of drug use. All relevant and impinging factors must be considered in evaluating and intervening to treat these children.

References

Anthony, J. 1992. Epidemiological research on cocaine use in the USA. In *Cocaine: Scientific and social dimensions,* edited by G. Bock and J. Whelan, 20-39. New York: John Wiley and Sons.

Ashery, R., ed. 1991. *Training drug treatment staff in the age of AIDS: A frontline perspective.* Rockville, MD: U.S. Department of Health and Human Services/National Institute on Drug Abuse.

Benowitz, N. 1992. How toxic is cocaine? In *Cocaine: Scientific and social dimensions,* edited by G. Bock and J. Whelan, 57-80. New York: John Wiley and Sons.

Benzer, D., and M. Nold-Klett. 1987. Abuse of amphetamines, cocaine, and other stimulant drugs. In *Alcohol and drug abuse handbook,* edited by R. Harrington, G. Jacobson, and D. Benzer, 54-92. St. Louis: Warren H. Green.

Bock, G., and J. Whelan, eds. 1992. *Cocaine: Scientific and social dimensions.* New York: John Wiley and Sons.

Gossop, M., and M. Grant, eds. 1990. *Preventing and controlling drug abuse.* Geneva: World Health Organization.

Halfon, N. 1989. *Born hooked: Confronting the impact of perinatal substance abuse.* Statement presented in Hearing before House Select Committee on Children, Youth, and Families. 101st Congress, U.S. House of Representatives.

Harrington, R., G. Jacobson, and D. Benzer, eds. 1987. *Alcohol and drug abuse handbook.* St. Louis: Warren H. Green.

Inciardi, J. 1990. The crack-violence connection within a population of hard-core adolescent offenders. *NIDA Research Monograph* 103:92-111.

Kaplan, C., B. Bielerman, and W. Tenhouten. 1992. Are there "casual" users of cocaine? In *Cocaine: Scientific and social dimensions,* edited by G. Bock and J. Whelan, 57-80. New York: John Wiley and Sons.

Lasch, C. 1979. *The culture of narcissism.* New York: Warner.

Maloney, J. 1992. Crack babies: The myth and the reality. *Learning Disabilities Newsbriefs* January/February:15.

Musto, D. 1992. Cocaine's history, especially the American experience. In *Cocaine: Scientific and social dimensions,* edited by G. Bock and J. Whelan, 7-19. New York: John Wiley and Sons.

National household survey on drug abuse: Highlights 1990. Rockville, MD: U.S. Department of Health and Human Services/National Institute on Drug Abuse.

Rodning, C., L. Beckwith, and J. Howard. 1989. Prenatal exposure to drugs: Behavioral distortions reflecting CNS impairment? *Neurotoxicology* 10:629-34.

Schuster, C. 1991. *National conference on drug abuse research and practice: An alliance for the 21st century.* Rockville, MD: U.S. Department of Health and Human Services/National Institute on Drug Abuse.

Stallings-Sahler, S. 1992. *Workshop on sensory processing dysfunction in infants and young children: Crucial intervention for a critical period.* Tallahassee, FL: Intervention Horizons.

Wallace, B. 1991. *Crack cocaine: A practical treatment approach for the chemically dependent.* New York: Bruner/Mazel.

Washton, A. 1989. *Cocaine addiction: Treatment, recovery, and relapse prevention.* New York: Norton.

Westermeyer, J. 1986. *A clinical guide to alcohol and drug problems.* New York: Praeger.

Woolverton, W. 1992. Determinants of cocaine self-administration by laboratory animals. In *Cocaine: Scientific and social dimensions,* edited by G. Bock and J. Whelan, 149-164. New York: John Wiley and Sons.

Chapter 2

The Substance-Abusing Pregnant Woman

Antoine K. Fomufod, M.D., M.P.H., FAAP

Diagnosis, Recognition, and Intervention

Substance-abusing pregnant women are part of the current national epidemic of drug use in America. The fact that drug abuse or chemical dependence in childbearing women has been increasing just as explosively as is the case in men and teenage children may not be fully appreciated by the general population and to some extent by segments of health-care providers. Although overall drug use in pregnancy has been stated to be as high as 60% (Rayburn et al. 1982; Doering and Stewart 1978), substance abusers comprise about one-half or less of these. The incidence of substance abuse in pregnancy is currently estimated to be between 10% and 20% (Chasnoff 1989; Chasnoff et al. 1990; Gillogley et al. 1990). Drug-abusing childbearing women are encountered at any point in the spectrum of obstetric care (specifically, antepartum period, during labor and delivery, and on postpartum wards). Quite often the diagnosis is missed or made late during labor because that is when the patient first presents for care. The missed diagnosis also can result from the doctor's inadequate knowledge and experience in perinatal chemical dependence.

Recognition of Substance Use During Pregnancy

The diagnosis of perinatal drug abuse is based on history (if available), physical appearance or presentation, and laboratory testing. If the diagnosis is not to be missed, all three aspects must be kept in mind. A case in point is that in which there is denial of drug use by a pregnant woman whose physical appearance is lacking the classic signs described later.

Medical and Obstetric History

Health-care personnel must be aware that most pregnant substance users will not volunteer information about their drug habits; in fact, when asked casually, they are more likely to deny drug use. Those admitting usage often lie about its duration and frequency; their responses to questions are usually that they stopped using drugs as soon as they knew that they were pregnant or that use was curtailed to weekends or when in the company of other users, such as at parties. However, with careful attention to such medical complications of illicit drug use as sexually transmitted diseases, liver disease, pneumonia, complications of prior pregnancies such as unexplained spontaneous abortions, abruptio placentae (untimely placental separation), stillbirths, low birth weight and prematurity, fetal distress, and meconium-stained term deliveries, abuse can be suspected and a diagnostic approach instituted. Lack of prenatal care in previous and current pregnancies is fairly common (Chasnoff et al. 1985; Fulroth et al. 1989; Hadeed and Siegel 1989). Even when prenatal care is utilized, visits often are infrequent and numerically inadequate. This behavior has been attributed to either ambivalence about the pregnancy or effects of the drugs. Multiple-drug usage, including especially cigarettes and alcohol, should be explored during history taking. In the current epidemic of cocaine use, it has been observed that a strong association exists between concurrent use and abuse of alcohol and cigarette smoking respectively.

Physical Appearance

A classic appearance has been described for the typical drug abuser, especially one who administers the substance intravenously. Such an individual presents with a wasted or undernourished body appearance, looks physically exhausted and weak, is disoriented, and exhibits skin marks of both chronic and recent trauma. The eyes are frequently red and the pupils dilated. Skin marks take the form of needle tracks (scars), abscesses or boils, and fresh infections. They all result from injections of drugs through contaminated needles and syringes. See Table 2.1 for detailed listing of findings in substance users.

Table 2.1
Classical Physical and Clinical Profile of the Drug Abuser

General Appearance
- Look of exhaustion and tiredness
- Malnourished
- Anemic/pale

Skin
- Track/needle marks/thrombosed veins
- Abscesses or cellulitis
- Edema of hands or feet
- Sweating

Respiratory System
- Breathing difficulties
- Pneumonia/tuberculosis infections
- Cough, wheezing

Central Nervous System/Behavior
- Restlessness, anxiety, or depression
- Loss of employment
- Theft and incarcerations
- Paranoia or disorientation
- Convulsions
- Pupils very dilated or constricted

Abdomen and Genitalia
- Hepatomegaly (enlarged liver)
- Abdominal (stomach) pain
- Diarrhea
- Ulcers or growths on sexual organs (syphilis, herpes, warts)
- Foul, creamy discharges (gonorrhea, etc.)
- Painful urination

Others
- Tachycardia (fast heart rate)
- Heart murmurs
- Hypertension
- Rhinitis (nasal mucosae red, thickened, and discharging)
- Low-grade fever
- Jaundice (yellow discoloration of eyes)

In some women, bodily appearances may be so subtle and indistinguishable from the general population that substance use becomes overlooked. This type of presentation, while not limited to, is more likely to be encountered in middle-class and professional women. In these, careful and detailed past medical and obstetric histories, outcome of previous newborns and children, and appropriate laboratory testing are all necessary for the diagnosis.

Laboratory Testing for Diagnosis Confirmation

Maternal urine testing for presence of illicit drugs can be useful either in collaborating a history of substance use or when history is not forthcoming but the physician has a high index of suspicion. Also, in the case of a symptomatic newborn without a maternal diagnosis of drug abuse, testing of paired mother-infant urine specimens can contribute to management interventions. Because screening laboratory tests can give both false results (positive and negative), they must be interpreted in the overall context of the past and present histories and the presentation of the women and their newborns.

A treatise on maternal treatment interventions is beyond the scope of this chapter. Suffice it to state here that patient confrontation, education and counseling, inpatient treatment or community referral to chemical dependence programs, and, finally, follow-up by social worker, perinatal nurse specialist, or public-health nurse are the necessary ingredients of successful management outcomes.

References

Chasnoff, I. J. 1989. Drug use and women: Establishing a standard of care. *Annals of the New York Academy of Sciences* 562:208-10.

Chasnoff, I. J., H. J. Landress, and M. E. Barrett. 1990. The prevalence of illicit drug or alcohol use during pregnancy and discrepancies in mandatory reporting in Pinellas County, Florida. *New England Journal of Medicine* 322:1202-06.

Chasnoff, I. J., W. J. Burns, S. H. Schnoll, and K. A. Burns. 1985. Cocaine use in pregnancy. *New England Journal of Medicine* 313:666-69.

Doering, P. L., and R. B. Stewart. 1978. The extent and character of drug consumption during pregnancy. *Journal of the American Medical Association* 95:843-46.

Fulroth, R., B. Phillips, and D. J. Durand. 1989. Perinatal outcome of infants exposed to cocaine and/or heroin in utero. *American Journal of Diseases of Children* 143:905-10.

Gillogley, K. M., A. T. Evans, and R. Hansen. 1990. The perinatal impact of cocaine, amphetamine, and opiate use detected by universal intrapartum screening. *American Journal of Obstetrics and Gynecology* 163:1535-42.

Hadeed, A. J., and S. R. Siegel. 1989. Maternal cocaine use during pregnancy: Effect on the newborn infant. *Pediatrics* 84(2):205-10.

Rayburn, W., J. Wible-Kant, and P. Bledsoe. 1982. Changing trends in drug use during pregnancy. *Journal of Reproductive Medicine* 27:569-75.

Chapter 3

The Substance-Exposed Neonate

Antoine K. Fomufod, M.D., M.P.H., FAAP

Effects of Prenatal Drug Exposure

It is now well known that when a pregnant woman uses drugs, her unborn infant is also affected. During pregnancy, almost all drugs cross the placenta and enter the blood stream of the developing baby. This is in direct contrast to prevailing concepts in the preintensive-care period of the 1950s, when the placenta was viewed as a protective barrier that excluded from the fetus noxious substances consumed by the mother.

Infants born to substance-using mothers are at a higher rate of perinatal morbidity and mortality than infants in the general population (Rementeria and Nunag 1973; Naeye 1972).

The components of the perinatal morbidity are:

- Low birth weight and intrauterine growth retardation
- Central nervous system damage that affects and impairs neurobehavioral development
- Neonatal abstinence (withdrawal) syndrome
- Congenital malformations

Fortunately, not all babies show these negative effects of perinatal drug exposure. This is because the vulnerability of the unborn baby is determined by a variety of intrinsic genetic factors, maternal characteristics, and the mother's patterns of use. From the four broad groups, the infants can be subclassified clinically according to the period and type of presentation. (See Table 3.1.)

Table 3.1
Clinical Findings in the Immediate Newborn Period

Low birth weight
- Due to prematurity
- Due to intrauterine growth retardation which, in addition to decreased birth weight, includes:
  - Small head circumference
  - Short stature

Respiratory distress syndrome
- Immature lungs in prematurity
- Meconium aspiration
- Congenital pneumonia

Neonatal jaundice
- Central nervous system dysfunction
  - Feeding difficulties
  - Jitteriness, irritability, seizures
  - Abnormalities of tone and reflexes

Intrapartum Presentation of the Drug-Exposed Newborn

When recent perinatal drug ingestion by the mother is superimposed on chronic transplacental fetal exposure, the presentation of the baby in the delivery room is often an acute picture of central nervous system depression with only feeble or no spontaneous cry and generalized weakness. This picture is a dramatic contrast to the drug-free newborn who is vigorous, with an immediate and loud piercing cry which are the manifestations of an adequate establishment of independent extrauterine cardiorespiratory status. This well-adapted newborn has good Apgar scores, unlike the drug-exposed infant whose scores are low or abnormal because of neuromuscular depression and systems attenuation by the drugs. Furthermore, some drugs have direct vascular (blood vessel) effects which reduce both the blood and oxygen supplies to the baby, producing stress and agitation. In this situation, the unborn baby often passes meconium (accumulated stools of the unborn); and if gasping occurs before or upon delivery, the meconium is aspirated into the lungs, interfering with establishment of respiration after birth. The phenomenon of intrapartum meconium staining of babies of mothers addicted to drugs, particularly cocaine and heroin, has been well reported in the pediatric literature (Chasnoff et al. 1985; Fulroth et al. 1989; Hadeed and Siegel 1989).

Congenital Malformations

Various combinations of these abnormalities have been found during the initial assessment of drug-exposed infants. The combination of low birth weight due to intrauterine growth retardation and upturned nostrils, narrow eyelids, low-set ears and carp-shaped mouth in fetal alcohol syndrome is an example. On the other hand, some of the findings are not directly caused by the drugs or their metabolites but are the secondary effects of aberrant processes induced by drugs.

Even after allowance has been made for other causes of low birth weight, almost every study that has looked at drug-exposed infants has shown that drug abuse results in decreased mean weight, head circumference, and length at birth. The growth retardation, particularly microcephaly (very small head) has been especially reported with cocaine use, cigarette smoking, and alcohol abuse (Gross et al. 1983; Naeye 1981; Hadeed and Siegel 1989; Hanson et al. 1976). Several mechanisms are offered to explain why infants born to drug-abusing mothers become growth retarded. The mother's lifestyle interferes with obtaining a regular balanced diet, and therefore there is little or no weight gain during pregnancy. She may even experience a weight loss! Cocaine, in addition to being an appetite suppressant that results in decreased maternal energy intake, also competes for food dollars. Cocaine has a direct vasoconstrictive effect on the placenta (Sherman and Gautieri 1972), thus reducing blood flow and causing hypoxia (Woods et al. 1987). Alcohol consumption and tobacco have been shown to result in decreased intrauterine growth (Naeye 1978) through the same mechanisms just discussed. Because of chronic exposure to these noxious substances during periods of rapid growth, differentiation, and development, the interruption of head and/or somatic growth has caused both neurobehavioral impairment and delay in cognitive, motor, and perceptual performance (Villar et al. 1984; Harvey et al. 1982). Because of these, it is very important in the initial physical examination and assessment of these infants to document the presence and degree of intrauterine growth retardation as baseline for subsequent follow-up and interventions.

Neonatal Abstinence (Withdrawal) Syndrome

Approximately 85% of infants exposed to mothers using the narcotics cocaine, heroin, morphine, methadone, meperidine, codeine, pentazocine, and propoxyphene will have central nervous system symptoms and signs of withdrawal, also called neonatal abstinence syndrome (NAS) (Zelson 1975; Ostrea et al. 1976; Wilson 1989).

The onset of symptoms may be at birth or within three to five days of delivery. In some instances, depending on the drug and other factors, the symptoms may not become obvious until ten days of life. The nature of the drug exposure, the amount and frequency of use, and the interval between last use and delivery are all determinants of symptomatology. Acute manifestations are often easy to bring under control (as described later), but subacute symptoms of narcotic withdrawal may sometimes persist for four to six months. See Table 3.2 for the signs and symptoms of Neonatal Abstinence (Withdrawal) Syndrome.

Table 3.2
Signs and Symptoms of Neonatal Abstinence (Withdrawal) Syndrome

Central nervous system	***Skin***
High-pitched or shrill cry	Excoriation of knees and elbows
Restlessness and sleeplessness	Facial scratch (rub) marks
Irritability	Mottling
Hyperactive reflexes	Perspiration
Hypertonicity	***Other systems***
Poor state regulation	Lacrimation (tearing)
Tremors and seizures	Tachypnea
Gastrointestinal system	Yawning
Voracious sucking	Rhinorrhea
Vomiting	Weight loss/failure to gain weight
Diarrhea	Fever

It should be pointed out that not all infants show all the symptoms and there are great individual differences in the combinations of manifestations. A useful way to recount the symptomatology is to match each of the relevant terms with the letters in *withdrawal,* as shown in Table 3.3.

Table 3.3
A Mnemonic: Symptoms of Neonatal Abstinence (Withdrawal) Syndrome

Letter	
W	Wakefulness
I	Irritability
T	Tremors, tachypnea, temperature variation
H	Hyper -tonia, -reflexia, -activity; high-pitched cry
D	Diarrhea, disorganized suck
R	Rhinorrhea, rub marks, respiratory distress
A	Apnea, autonomic dysfunction
W	Weight loss/poor gain
A	Alkalosis (respiratory)
L	Lacrimation

Adapted from American Academy of Pediatrics, Committee on Drugs, 1982-83. Chairman, Albert W. Pruitt, M.D. *Pediatrics* 72:895-902.

Goals of Management and Therapeutic Interventions

The goals of treatment interventions in neonatal narcotic withdrawal syndrome are to:

- Normalize activity and behavior
- Establish and maintain efficient feeding patterns
- Achieve appropriate weight gain
- Reverse restlessness and sleeplessness

These goals can be achieved in 30% to 50% of symptomatic infants with only such supportive treatment measures as swaddling to decrease sensory stimulation, frequent small feeds of hypercaloric (24 cal./oz.) formula, and close monitoring of vital signs and weight. For infants not responding to the above measures and those initially manifesting very severe symptoms such as seizures, pharmacologic treatment is necessary.

In order to avoid unjustified pharmacologic treatment by physicians and nurses who become sympathetic with the jittery and tremulous activity in the mildly withdrawing infant, an abstinence scoring system (Finnegan et al. 1975; Lipsitz and Blatman 1974) should be adopted. See Appendix F for the score sheet currently used at Howard University Hospital.

The scoring approach is more objective in the therapeutic decision-making than dependence on a limited number of symptoms reported by more persuasive staff from a few shifts. This notwithstanding, it needs to be emphasized that the combinations of persistent vomiting and diarrhea, weight loss and dehydration, fever, sleeplessness, or seizures by themselves justify initiating medical therapy with or without scoring. The drugs commonly used in treating NAS are paregoric, phenobarbital, and diazepam. They are usually administered by mouth, are well tolerated, and are absorbed from the gastrointestinal tract. Decreasing scores and appropriate weight gain are objective criteria for tapering and finally discontinuing drug therapy. Irritability, tremors, and poor sleeping patterns may last for up to six months and should not be used as major criteria for continued drug administration.

Successful management outcome requires a team approach which includes a physician, nursing staff, social worker, and parents. Early involvement of the social worker is a necessary ingredient in establishing a relationship of confidence for subsequent psychosocial care. This involvement allows for assessment of parental abilities and support systems to care for the infant after hospital discharge. These infants are difficult to bond with and take care of, day in and day out; therefore, while still in the hospital setting, parents and caretakers should be provided the counseling and emotional support necessary to carry them through the difficult times ahead. During this period, the parents and caregivers should be taught to recognize and interpret symptoms, especially the previously mentioned subacute ones that do not require medicinal therapy. This is important because withdrawal symptoms may recur after hospital discharge. In such a situation, the parents need not feel guilty about the withdrawal recurrence and blame themselves for it, because this can result in failure to contact professional staff for discussions which can result in readmission for therapy.

Prognosis and Long-Term Outcome

Because of the neurobehavioral morbidity, compromised intrauterine growth, and continuing postnatal deviant performance, prognosis for these infants as a group is guarded. Individual improvements or deterioration can be determined only by careful follow-up; therapeutic interventions of the appropriate type must be an integral part of this follow-up.

Sudden infant death syndrome (SIDS) and acquired immunodeficiency syndrome (AIDS) have been observed in infants born to women who are substance abusers (Oleske et al. 1983; Chavez et al. 1979). A five- to tenfold increased rate of SIDS has been reported in children of heroin-abusing mothers (Chavez et al. 1979). A similar increase has been reported in infants born to cocaine-using women. The national incidence of positive HIV test results in the population of newborns prenatally exposed to drugs is not yet known. The long-term mortality rates also are unknown. A confounding variable that interferes with the long-term morbidity and mortality prognosis is the social and often chaotic environment in which the drug-exposed infants are raised. As the child matures and deficits become apparent, it is difficult to determine whether these are the evolutionary effects of the drugs or due to environmental influences.

Mental retardation, lowered intelligence, hyperactivity, shortened attention spans, learning and organizational disorders, impaired physical coordination, growth and developmental delays, and problems with social-interpersonal adjustment are seen with greater frequency in children prenatally exposed to drugs than those not. Community, medical, psychosocial, and economic resources must be identified and made available to these children and their families.

Experts generally agree that children of addicts have numerous school and behavioral problems (interestingly, whether they are born to drug-abusing mothers or raised by drug-using caregivers). This finding has important implications for interventions for two reasons: to improve the home surroundings and day-care opportunities for all drug-exposed youngsters, and to enhance the parenting skills of their caregivers.

References

Chasnoff, I. J., W. J. Burns, S. H. Schnoll, and K. A. Burns. 1985. Cocaine use in pregnancy. *New England Journal of Medicine* 313:666-69.

Chavez, C. J., E. M. Ostrea, Jr., and J. C. Stryke. 1979. Sudden infant death syndrome among infants of drug-dependent mothers. *Journal of Pediatrics* 95:407-09.

Finnegan, L. P., R. E. Kron, J. F. Connaughton, and J. Emich. 1975. Assessment and treatment of abstinence in the infant of the drug-dependent mother. *International Journal of Clinical Pharmacology* 12:19-32.

Fulroth, R., B. Phillips, and D. J. Durand. 1989. Perinatal outcome of infants exposed to cocaine and/or heroin in utero. *American Journal of Diseases of Children* 143:905-10.

Gross, S. J., J. M. Oehler, and C. O. Eckerman. 1983. Head growth and developmental outcome in very-low-birth-weight infants. *Pediatrics* 71:70-75.

Hadeed, A. J., and S. R. Siegel. 1989. Maternal cocaine use during pregnancy: Effect on the newborn infant. *Pediatrics* 84(2):205-10.

Hanson, J. W., K. L. Jones, and D. W. Smith. 1976. Fetal alcohol syndrome: Experience with 41 patients. *Journal of the American Medical Association* 235:1458-60.

Harvey, D., J. Prince, J. Burton, C. Parkinson, and S. Campbell. 1982. Abilities of children who were small-for-gestational-age babies. *Pediatrics* 69:296-300.

Lipsitz, P. J., and S. Blatman. 1974. Newborn infants of mothers on methadone maintenance. *New York State Journal of Medicine* 74:994-99.

Naeye, R. 1972. The epidemiology of perinatal mortality. *Pediatric Clinics of North America* 19: 295-310.

______. 1978. Effects of maternal smoking on the fetus and placenta. *British Journal of Obstetrics and Gynaecology* 85:732-737.

______. 1981. Influence of maternal cigarette smoking on the fetus and placenta. *Obstetrics and Gynecology* 57:18-20.

Oleske, J., A. Minnefar, and R. Cooper. 1983. Immune deficiency syndrome in children. *Journal of the American Medical Association* 249:2345-49.

Ostrea, E. M., C. J. Chavez, and M. E. Straus. 1976. A study of factors that influence the severity of neonatal narcotic withdrawal. *Journal of Pediatrics* 88:642-45.

Rementeria, J. L., and N. Nunag. 1973. Narcotic withdrawal in pregnancy: Stillbirth incidence with a case report. *American Journal of Obstetrics and Gynecology* 116:1152-56.

Sherman, W. T., and R. F. Gautieri. 1972. Effect of certain drugs on perfused human placenta: Norepinephrine release by bradykinin. *Journal of Pharmaceutical Sciences* 61:878-83.

Villar, J., V. Smeriglio, R. Martorell, C. H. Brown, and R. E. Klein. 1984. Heterogeneous growth and mental development of intrauterine growth retarded infants during the first three years of life. *Pediatrics* 74:783-91.

Wilson, G. 1989. Clinical studies of infants and children exposed prenatally to heroin. *Annals of the New York Academy of Sciences* 562:183-94.

Woods, J. R., M. A. Plessinger, and K. E. Clerk. 1987. Effect of cocaine on uterine blood flow and fetal oxygenation. *Journal of the American Medical Association* 257:957-61.

Zelson, C. 1975. Acute management of neonatal addiction. *Addictive Disorders* 2:159-68.

Chapter 4

Emotional Concerns

Cordelia H. Puttkammer, M.Ed., OTR/L

Substance-exposed infants not only are biologically vulnerable, but often receive inadequate caretaking. They are subject to frequent moves, out-of-home placement, and care given by numerous caregivers. It is a formidable challenge to foster a positive infant/caregiver interaction that is vital to the well-being of both. This chapter will describe some of the differences in reactions and interactions between typical infants and infants exposed to drugs in utero. Techniques for facilitating normal and productive interactions will be included when they are known.

Delayed Development

Some substance-exposed neonates are handicapped in emotional development because their physical development is delayed. To participate in subtle give-and-take interactions, infants need to be in an alert state, be able to establish eye contact, and be able to communicate through cries, frowns, and, eventually, smiles. A newborn suffering addiction, who is almost never in a quiet alert state, is clearly not available or accessible.

Normal neonates are capable of expressing a wide range of emotions including interest, distress, disgust, and pleasure. By the age of three months, they can distinguish among smiles, anger, and frowns from their caregivers. By six months, babies can express their own fear, anger, and shame, and not only recognize but respond to the mother's facial expressions (Termine and Izard 1988). By seven months of age, babies can readily distinguish between happy and fearful faces, even if the faces are unfamiliar. Substance-exposed infants often reach these milestones at a much later age.

Processing auditory stimuli, and connecting the visual with the auditory–rudimentary reading of social cues–is important for infants even in the early weeks of life. Normal neonates can distinguish between their mothers' and strangers' voices. By three or four months of age, they know the synchrony of voice with moving face; by five to seven months, they can match facial and vocal expressions (Acredolo and Hake 1982). Very often, drug-affected infants develop these skills quite late, too, and the delay costs them dearly.

When infants do not meet these milestones, they cannot follow their caregivers' clues and do not then read when the caregiver may be sad or angry or depressed, and begin to modify their behavior accordingly. The caregiver begins to feel frustration and interprets the inattentive behavior as the child not liking the caregiver. A strong bond is not established; rather, a fearful and tentative relationship exists. The trust an infant must feel is not there.

Purposeful Communication Is Difficult

Real communication, early on, is an important factor in establishing the relationship between neonate and caregiver. At best, it can be haphazard and easily derailed; it is even more so if infant and/or mother are laboring under the handicaps of drugs. The facial expression of an awake, healthy newborn is extremely labile: it changes every seven to nine seconds (Malatesa 1982). Substance-exposed neonates, however, have difficulty expressing a variety of internal feelings. Add to that condition the observation of researchers that most mothers usually respond in any fashion to infants' expressions only about 25% of the time, and you see how fragile the lines of communication can be (Malatesa 1982).

Most infants are adept at providing clear signals to the caregiver when expressing needs, but the caregiver also must be sensitive in reading and reacting appropriately to these signals. For example, when infants display high-intensity expressions, parents tend to engage in more stimulative interactions with them (DeGangi and Greenspan 1990). But overstimulation has adverse effects on drug-exposed babies (Source and Emde 1982). Similarly, parents of infants who appear less alert or less responsive may try to compensate for their infants' diminished emotional responsiveness by overstimulating them.

How much stimulation is too much is difficult to sense in advance, but easy to see after it is done—that is, when the infant's calm is shattered. With all good will and even with no physical problems, an adult caregiver can commit misreadings of this kind and then try to avoid making the same mistake again by being less responsive. In a troubled home situation, it is easy to see how the parent may go from one extreme to the other, from overstimulation to complete neglect. Again, uncertainty prevails, the child is not able to predict, and trust is not established and felt.

Difficult to Soothe, Averse to Touch

Distressed neonates need a great deal of help to arrive at "state organization," a stable emotional condition lasting for a period of time (more than a minute) during which they are neither crying nor deeply asleep (Brazelton 1984). Unfortunately for their caregivers and their own development, these infants seem never to be contented and thus available. Further, the usual soothing techniques that mothers employ to help their babies move toward state organization often do not have the desired effect on drug-affected babies, with the result that caregivers often feel frustrated and irritated by their inability to soothe their infants.

As healthy infants develop, they learn self-directed regulatory behaviors so that they can maintain state organization, continue interaction, and experience pleasure as a result. They begin to calm themselves by various means, such as thumb or finger sucking or looking away before resuming an activity. These learned regulatory techniques eventually help an infant to persist in purposeful behavior, such as reaching for a toy or working at a new motor skill (DeGangi and Greenspan 1990), or conveying a message to an adult–for example, wiggling that says, "I want to get down!"

But cocaine-exposed infants don't learn and enjoy interaction or its results at the usual ages (Neuspiel and Hamel 1991); they remain several stages back for a long time, because they can't learn unless they can be calm. It is therefore imperative that professionals working with these infants teach the caregivers calming techniques and means of "reading" the infants' responses. These babies need delicate parenting in order to learn to interact successfully.

Another crucial aspect of the interaction process between babies and caregivers is the babies' response to physical contact with the caregivers, especially during diapering and feeding. The infant does not want to be touched or held; as one professional expressed it, "One of the most consistent signs I see in the infants of cocaine-addicted mothers is that these babies do not cuddle well" (Cersonsky 1988, 186). Not being cuddly makes drug-exposed infants emotionally unavailable and less rewarding for their caregivers. Aversion to touch is easily interpreted as, "The baby doesn't like me." The results are decreased holding and cuddling, the infant not getting those needs met, and further alienation. Again, use of calming techniques that are likely to work, including certain ways of holding these very distressed infants, can help to reverse this downward spiral. (See Chapter 10 on general principles and intervention techniques.)

Some success in easing the frantic state will make life less stressful for both mother and child, but it will not change that part of the addicted baby's nervous system; that is, it will neither transform the baby into a cuddler nor teach the child how to cope with built-in aversions. For example, when healthy infants experience aversive events, such as face washing, they learn to control their crying and to avert their heads to avoid the noxious stimuli. This is constructive adaptation. But with infants or toddlers who exhibit real tactile defensiveness, the daily experience of face washing can trigger tantrums (Royeen 1990).

Development of Sleep-Wake Cycles

Normal neonates also constructively adapt their sleep-wake cycles to the demands of the world outside the uterus. In utero, the infant is subject to regular rhythms of sleep-wake cycles through cross-placental transmission. Sleep-wake patterns are already rhythmical at birth (Pierce 1990). Over the first few months after birth, these periods of sleeping and waking gradually lengthen. By the twentieth week of life outside the womb, infants begin to achieve true synchrony to the day and night; that is, they begin to sleep when it is dark and be alert and awake during the light. They have responded to training to light and dark and to social cues (Moore-Ede et al. 1982).

Substance-affected infants take much longer to achieve true synchrony for a number of reasons. Their internal rhythms may never have been established in utero if the mothers did not have reasonably regular schedules during pregnancy. Also, intensive-care units and hospital nurseries do not provide the cues that help to establish normal circadian rhythms (Pierce 1990); the noise, the ever-present lights, and the around-the-clock procedures all do a real disservice to this population.

Beyond Infancy

As these neonates develop from infants into toddlers and into school-age children, the effects of the mothers' substance abuse persist. It is not unusual for these infants and toddlers to experience more hospitalizations–especially, according to one pediatric researcher, as a result of pneumonia and diarrhea (Gordon 1989). The same expert says that "new medical evidence suggests that many will grow up with lasting intellectual, medical, and social problems."

As infants and toddlers, these children may be "explosively impulsive" (Gordon 1989) and have difficulty concentrating on tasks and completing them. They often fail to show emotion, and they relate poorly to other people. Their motor milestones (holding up head, sitting, crawling, walking, talking) are often delayed. Later, they score significantly lower in overall intelligence testing (Gordon 1989). They are seriously hampered by being unable to filter out foreground from background visual and auditory information; they are at the mercy of all incoming stimuli. They may become just as upset by a passing siren or a telephone bell in the next room as by a harsh voice. Similarly, outdoor light, electric light overhead, or a dog moving in the room may be equally distracting. Drug-affected toddlers seem to lack the capacity that healthy, normal preschoolers have of becoming wrapped up in–really attentive to–what they are looking at or listening to. Perhaps they are shut out of some of the most engaging of the experiences of early childhood, such as watching carefully until the cat pounces or until the caterpillar reaches the end of the twig; or doing the same motor task until the sand pail is full or the tower of blocks is so high.

Sometimes substance-exposed infants seem to be able to accomplish a task one day, only to forget the skill the next day. Toddlers can pick up their toys when told to on Tuesday, and yet by Thursday there is no carryover. They may need to be retaught each time. They are frequently diagnosed as hyperactive and learning disabled, some with acute conditions.

Prospects for the futures of many of these substance-exposed infants are equally sobering. Researchers at the University of California recently have "isolated" brain damage in areas of the brain associated with behaviors typical of a learning disabled child in more than a third of a group born addicted to cocaine (Dixon 1989). However, many patterns of behavior can't be measured until the children reach school age. A director of a study offers judgments that parallel the outlook of the Head Start consultant quoted above: "The older the group of children we study, the more the average performance declines. . . . I think we are going to see children with very confusing and complex patterns of learning disabilities and behavior problems. They will have difficulty succeeding in school" (Dixon 1989).

The community of professionals who work with babies and children can only hope that the number of infants born drug-addicted or substance-exposed declines. Meanwhile, both professional and lay communities must turn their best efforts to intervention on as many fronts as possible, and as early as possible.

References

Acredolo, L., and J. L. Hake. 1982. Infant perception. In *Handbook of developmental psychology,* edited by B. B. Wolman, 224-283. Englewood Cliffs, NJ: Prentice Hall.

Ainsworth, M., and S. M. Bell. 1975. Mother-infant interaction and the development of competence. In *The growth of competence,* edited by K. J. Connolly and J. Bruner. New York: Academic Press.

Als, H. 1982. The unfolding of behavioral organization in the face of the biological violation. In *Social interchange in infancy: Affect, cognition, and communication.* Edited by E. Z. Tronick. Baltimore: University Park Press.

Anderson, C. 1979. *Informing mothers about behavioral characteristics of their infants: Mother-infant interaction.* Paper presented at the meeting of the Society for Research in Child Development. San Francisco, March.

Bakeman, R., and J. Brown. 1980. Early intervention: Consequences for social and mental development at three years. *Child Development* 51:437-47.

Barnard, K., and H. Bee. 1983. The impact of temporally patterned stimulation on the development of preterm infants. *Child Development* 54:1156-67.

Brazelton, T. B. 1984. *Neonatal behavioral assessment scale* 2d ed. Philadelphia: J. B. Lippincott.

Cersonsky, J. 1988. Cocaine abusers as mothers. *Pediatrics* 82:136-37.

Cole, J. 1991. *Drugs and babies: A dangerous mix.* Boston: March of Dimes pamphlet published by Boston City Hospital. (Available for $2.00 from Cole Consultants, 78 High Street, Leominster, MA 01453.).

DeGangi, G. A., and S. I. Greenspan. 1990. Affect/Interaction skills. In *Neuroscience foundations of human performance,* edited by C. B. Royeen, 1-30. Rockville, MD: The American Occupational Therapy Association.

Dixon, S. 1989. Generations of crack kids about to plague schools. *San Francisco Chronicle,* April 24.

Emde, R., R. Harmon, D. Metcalf, K. Koenig, and S. Wagonfeld. 1971. Stress and neonatal sleep. *Psychosomatic Medicine* 33:491-97.

Flax, M. 1987. Maternal life events stress and neonatal behavioral organization. *Dissertation Abstracts International* 48:3702.

Gordon, B. 1989. New disability impacts preschools. *Special Edge* 16.

Herson, M., and D. Barlow. 1978. *Single case experimental designs: Strategies for studying behavior change.* New York: Pergamon Press.

Izard, H. 1980. The young infant's ability to produce discrete emotional expression. *Developmental Psychology* 16:132-40.

Klaus, M., and J. Kennell. 1982. Human maternal behavior at first contact with her young. *Pediatrics* 46:187-92.

Kron, R., S. Kaplan, L. Finnegan, M. Litt, and M. Phoenix. 1975. The assessment of behavioral change in infants undergoing narcotic withdrawal: Comparative data from clinical and objective methods. *Addictive Diseases* 2:257-75.

Malatesa, H. 1982. Learning display rules. *Child Development* 53:991-93.

Marcus, J., S. Hans, and R. Jeremy. 1982. Patterns of one-day and four-month motor functioning in infants of women on methadone. *Neurobehavioral Toxocology and Teratology* 4:473-76.

Moore-Ede, M. C., B. Sulzman, and A. Fuller. 1982. *The clocks that time us: Physiology of the circadian timing system.* Cambridge, MA: Harvard University Press.

Neuspiel, D. R., and S. Hamel. 1991. Cocaine and infant behavior. *Developmental and Behavioral Pediatrics* 1:55-64.

Pierce, D. 1990. Cognition: Temporal orientation and organizational capacity. In *Neuroscience foundations of human performance,* edited by C. B. Royeen, 1-40. Rockville, MD: The American Occupational Therapy Association.

Rodning, C., L. Beckwith, and J. Howard. 1989. Prenatal exposure to drugs: Behavioral distortions reflecting CNS impairment? *Neurotoxology* 10:629-34.

Royeen, C. B., ed. 1990. *Neuroscience foundations of human performance.* Rockville, MD: The American Occupational Therapy Association.

Sostek, A. 1978. Infant scales in the pediatric setting: The Brazelton neonatal behavioral assessment scale and the Carey infant temperament questionnaire. *Journal of Pediatric Psychology* 3:113-21.

Source, M., and A. Emde. 1982. The meaning of infant emotional expression. *Journal of Child Psychology and Psychiatry* 2:145-58.

Strauss, M., J. Lessen-Firestone, R. Starr, and E. Ostrea. 1975. Behavior of narcotic addicted newborns. *Child Development* 46:887-93.

Strauss, M., R. Starr, E. Ostrea, C. Chavez, and J. Stryker. 1976. Behavioral concomitants of prenatal addition to narcotics. *The Journal of Pediatrics* 89:842-46.

Termine, N., and C. Izard. 1988. Infants' responses to their mothers' expressions of joy and sadness. *Developmental Psychology* 24:223-39.

Chapter 5

HIV-Positive Infants

Rebecca A. Parks, M.S., OTR/L

No book on the effects of drug exposure during infancy and childhood would be complete without in-depth exploration of HIV infection. HIV/AIDS initially appeared in the early 1980s as a disease of homosexual and bisexual men, with a relatively smaller number of cases reported following transfusion of contaminated blood and blood products to newborns or hemophiliacs. In the 1990s, HIV infection in large urban centers has become primarily a disease of heterosexuals. Some areas of New York City have identified that over 60% of the total 4,145 AIDS cases reported through July 1990 were persons with histories of intravenous drug use (IVDU) and/or sexual contact with IVDUs (Schoenbaum and Webber 1992). Numbers of new cases are steadily decreasing among the transfused and hemophiliacs and among the homosexual population, but drug abusers are now the primary risk group for HIV infection, and it is they who will in future cause propagation of the infection among the heterosexual population (Boschini et al. 1992).

Socioeconomic and Emotional Concerns

Transmission of HIV among drug users is much more complicated socioeconomically and emotionally than a simple story of contaminated needles. With the advent of crack use and its instant widespread popularity, additional factors, including prostitution to acquire the drug and consistent high-risk sexual behaviors among intravenous drug users (IVDUs) and nonIVDUs (with no use of barrier contraception) also must be considered as contributing to the alarming increase in HIV transmission among heterosexuals.

As of June 1990, the World Health Organization (WHO) estimated that worldwide eight to ten million people were infected with HIV, of whom over three million were women of childbearing age (Dickens 1992). The increasing rate of infection among women means that more babies will be born with HIV infection; it is estimated that an infected woman has a 20% to 60% chance of passing the infection to her child (Wofsky 1987). Both symptomatic and asymptomatic women can transmit HIV to their infants via transplacental passage of the virus in utero, exposure to maternal blood and vaginal fluids during labor and delivery, and postpartum ingestion of breast milk containing the virus (Rogers 1987).

Because vertical transmission from infected mothers to their infants accounts for 80% of all childhood cases of AIDS, current and future efforts clearly must emphasize early diagnosis of mothers and infants, early treatment, and, above all, prevention through education regarding modes of transmission, especially among high-risk populations.

Ninety percent of children with maternally transmitted HIV are black and Hispanic, very often living in vulnerable, impoverished, IV-drug-using communities where the interconnectedness of drugs and childbearing makes interruption of sexual and IV-drug transmission impossible without a public willingness to bear a considerable cost (Walker 1991). In cultures of poverty, childbearing is often essential to self-respect and self-definition: dreams for the children's future are essential where success in the present is blocked. Therefore, education concerning birth control is sometimes seen as a racist kind of minority population control (Walker 1991).

To the individual HIV-infected woman considering bearing a child, the percentage of risk of giving birth to an infected child may seem reasonable, although the additional concern for the effect of a pregnancy on disease progression in an infected woman must be considered. These effects are still in dispute, but the possibility that pregnancy worsens health status in the infected mother has been documented by some authors (Brettle et al. 1992).

Early Diagnosis and Differences between Pediatric and Adult HIV/AIDS

The major difficulty in diagnosis of HIV infection in newborns and infants is the inability to differentiate between passively transferred maternal antibody to HIV infection and actively produced antibody from the infant (Ammann 1987). Because antibody testing may not accurately determine infection in infants before age 18 months, the diagnosis may depend on the appearance of clinical symptoms (Walker 1991).

HIV has many presentations in infants, and the clinical manifestations and severity of disease may vary, suggesting that the time at which infection occurred (sometimes as early as 20 weeks gestation), amount of viral inoculum, and any preexisting immunodeficiency are important variables (Rogers 1987). Failure to thrive due to a variety of etiologies is one of the major features of pediatric HIV (Rubinstein 1987). Clinical symptoms usually occur within two years, but infection may be clinically silent for up to 5½ years. Some children may be HIV antibody positive but not have the clinical features of AIDS or ARC (AIDS-related complex) (Vinters and Anders 1990).

Groups of infants and young children identified with HIV infection show an incubation for AIDS and a whole disease course that is shorter than for adults: the median incubation period for perinatally acquired or transfusion-associated AIDS is about two years. Pediatric and adult groups are also susceptible to different types of opportunistic infection: severe bacterial infections are more common in childhood, although *Pneumocystis carinii* pneumonia (PCP) and thrush, the most common opportunistic infections in children, are common to both groups. The most important differences between children and adults with HIV is that infants and children are still developing (Weiss and Mazade 1990). The process of growth and development is predictable and well described, so any changes occurring secondary to disease or to treatment can be noted more quickly in infants and children than in adults.

Loss of appetite, wasting, and neuropsychological impairment (detectable in 40% to 95% of HIV-infected children) are hallmarks of pediatric HIV infection. Consequently, measurements of linear growth and weight gain and assessments of neurobehavioral function through tests of motor skills and cognitive ability can be used to evaluate the disease progression and, by the same token, the effects of clinical intervention and drug therapy.

Infants who are symptomatic early in life following intrauterine infection or from infection after transfusions in the neonatal period will have more devastating courses than those who are asymptomatic in early infancy or who acquire infection through later transfusions or administration of blood factors. Opportunistic infections presenting in the first year of life are associated with a higher mortality. *Pneumocystis carinii* pneumonia (PCP) and *Candida esophagitis* are the most common opportunistic infections (Scott 1987).

The particular type of opportunistic infection developed by a child also may be a key to the rate of disease progression. In general, children who present with AIDS at less than one year of age have a shorter median survival than those who present after one year. The type of clinical disease with which the child presents also appears to predict prognosis: for example, survival following PCP is dismal (Weiss and Mazade 1990).

In a life-table analysis of 64 children with AIDS reported to the New York City Department of Health, 59 of whom were presumed vertically infected, two distinct courses were distinguished:

1. Children with a history of *Pneumocystis* pneumonia, in whom the onset of symptoms occurred at a mean age of 5.5 months (range: birth to 29 months) and in whom pneumonia was diagnosed at a mean of 11 months (range: 2 to 53 months)
2. Children with other opportunistic infections whose mean age at the onset of symptoms was 14.3 months (range: 1 to 60 months) with opportunistic infection presenting at a median of 31.4 months (range: 3 to 77 months)

The children with *Pneumocystis* pneumonia had a median survival time of nine to 12 months after birth, whereas children without this infection had a median survival time of 31.5 months. The survival after opportunistic infection was similar for both: median of less than 3 months with 75% dead within one year (Pizzo and Poplack 1989).

Syndromes Associated with Pediatric HIV Infection

- Wasting syndrome
- Lymphoid interstitial pneumonitis
- Recurrent bacterial infection
- Encephalopathy
- Lymphadenopathy syndrome
- Cardiomyopathy
- Hepatitis
- Renal disease

Children transfused in the newborn period who subsequently developed AIDS were first reported in 1983 by Ammann et al., who found that symptoms appeared six months to three years post-transfusion. The incubation period from transfusion to the appearance of symptoms seems shorter in those transfused as very small premature babies when compared to the older child, where the incubation period may be the same as in the transfused adult (Hilgartner 1987).

Problems with the Central Nervous System (CNS)

In infants with HIV infection, there can be chronic encephalopathy, as well as primary HIV infection of the central nervous system with failure to thrive and loss of developmental milestones.

Common Neurologic Findings

- Developmental delay; loss of developmental milestones
- Chronic encephalopathy
- Seizure disorders
- Motor dysfunction
- Microcephaly
- Abnormal CT Scan findings: cortical atrophy, calcifications (Oleske 1987).

Both static and progressive encephalopathy are seen. Delays are predominantly in speech and language and acquisition of motor skills; some infants have lost milestones previously achieved. It is often difficult to specify the exact cause of a developmental delay, because sociocultural factors, recurrent opportunistic infections, and primary invasion of the central nervous system may all play causative roles (Boland 1987).

Neurologic sequelae are seen in a higher proportion of pediatric patients than in the adult population. Only a minority of pediatric AIDS patients are neurologically normal, and up to 50% present with a progressive encephalopathy, with an additional 25% having a mild nonprogressive brain deficit. The encephalopathy may have slow or fulminant clinical course and appears to be caused by direct HIV infection of the central nervous system, analogous to the AIDS dementia complex (ADC) described in adults.

Progressive encephalopathy is characterized by intellectual deficits with diminished IQ and occasional progressive dementia, loss of developmental milestones, microcephaly, and progressive weakness. It is associated with a poor prognosis, with death occurring on average in about eight months after onset of neurologic symptoms (Vinters and Anders 1990).

Clinical Intervention

One must optimistically look to the future for the ultimate solution to HIV infection in infants. At some ideal future time when prevention through vaccination has been mastered, all women at risk for infection may be vaccinated prior to attaining the virus and prior to conception, so that no new cases of infant infection will occur. Those infections not occurring in utero someday will be preventable by intervention at birth, perhaps with a combination of vaccine and immune globulin (Quinnan 1987).

With ongoing drug trials, it is conceivable that infant infection not prevented before or at birth eventually will be curable, given the appropriate drug therapy.

Although a definitive cure is still elusive, it has been demonstrated that chemotherapy is effective in curing intercurrent opportunistic infections and often in affecting the rate of disease progression. Changes have been reported following AZT therapy in tests of both gross and fine motor skills and cognitive function. Therapy may not have actually improved the status of some, but very few children continued to show declines in development while on chemotherapy. In summary, the well-documented failure to grow normally that is found in infants and young children with HIV infection is clearly altered with antiretroviral therapy (Weiss and Mazade 1990). Administration of AZT, for example, has been associated with such improvements as weight gain and more normal distribution in measures of growth, cognitive function, and decrease of neurological impairment.

The evolving success with drug therapy, although not total, has gradually caused a change in the character of pediatric HIV infection. Whereas the appearance of the disease a decade ago was seen as a "death sentence" because length of survival following diagnosis was characteristically short, clinical intervention by chemotherapy and better overall management has turned HIV infection into a life-threatening but chronic process which has the potential to destroy an entire family. Parents are often confronted by their own health status as well as that of their children. Both parents and children are disenfranchised and need health-care providers who are sensitive, knowledgeable, and willing to advocate (Boland 1987).

Although popular understanding of AIDS has increased significantly thanks to mass education campaigns, the diagnosis still carries a stigma. Parents are afraid to go public, because they have seen the reaction in neighborhoods not ready to accept an infected child among them. Despite clear needs, parents are afraid to enroll their children in special school programs because they hope things will get better and they are afraid of what will happen to an older sibling when the diagnosis becomes known to the community (Boland 1987). Mothers of HIV-infected children who attend school often avoid other mothers, because they fear that somehow the secret of their children's sickness will be revealed. Parents' close guarding of their terrible secret can inadvertently put HIV-infected children at risk of undesirable exposure to common childhood illnesses often caught from classmates. Since children are not identified to school personnel as having HIV infection, mothers may not be aware that there has been an outbreak of, for example, chicken pox until their children have already become ill (Walker 1991).

Infected infants and children and their families have been subject to discrimination and barred from basic services. Although children acquire AIDS as a consequence of adult behavior, they nevertheless have shared the general public opprobrium frequently cast on affected patients (Koop 1987). Despite their devastating illness and uncertainty about the future, these children must be afforded a normal and dignified life; they must be nurtured, helped to grow and develop, allowed to interact with peers, attend school, and encouraged to enjoy and participate in all activities of childhood, notwithstanding the likelihood of a shortened life span.

The most effective approach to case management is by team with excellent coordination among the hospital, the home, and the community. HIV-infected people and their families need help with a wide range of issues. These issues include adjusting to a life-threatening diagnosis, obtaining concrete services, organizing to meet needs for care, managing the reactions of children to a parent's or sibling's illness or death, future planning for loss and bereavement, and reorganizing family functioning following loss. Because of the progressive nature of HIV infection, a variety of medical, rehabilitation, social, and educational services need constant readjustment to suit the needs and capabilities of the child and family. Diagnosis and service provision require a team of professionals in immunology, epidemiology, pediatrics, rehabilitation, social services, and education (Harris 1991).

Problems related to the diagnosis of HIV infection in infants are complex and often overwhelming, necessitating a multidisciplinary approach and adoption of a chronic childhood illness model, as the children are living longer. A range of physical, occupational, and speech therapy services indicated for these children may include parent education on handling, positioning, feeding, and language stimulation; preschool and special education referral; behavioral intervention; and nutrition counseling. General parental counseling, ongoing medical followup, and intervention during acute episodes should be part of the specialized services for these children and their families (Harris 1991).

Privacy and informed consent are basic issues to case management, since most families have suffered the effects of isolation and discrimination when their friends and communities learned that they were caring for an HIV-infected child. How a family manages an illness depends both on the nature of family organization and on the belief systems that govern the family's response to illness. HIV disease not only makes extraordinary demands on family organization, but also carries an extraordinary burden of social stigma (Walker 1991).

For health-care professionals, infants with HIV infection will not be foreign to previous case management experience, because the complications due to direct effects of the infection and an immunocompromised state often lead to conditions commonly seen in a rehabilitation setting (Mukand et al. 1991). Although there is no one typical picture of an HIV-infected infant, presenting conditions commonly correspond with AIDS-related neurological syndromes. They reflect a variety of primary and opportunistic diseases which may result from diffuse or focal involvement of the brain or spinal cord or development of increased intracranial pressure due to hydrocephalus (Levy and Berger 1991).

As an example, infected infants often present with signs of abnormal central nervous system function: abnormally increased or decreased muscle tone, primitive reflexes, posturing, impaired oromotor function, swallowing difficulties, cognitive or perceptual deficits, and inappropriate developmental level for chronological age. The picture is reminiscent of other syndromes and has much in common with infantile cerebral palsy, congenital hydrocephalus, and conditions such as Menke's Disease, which result from genetic defects.

Regarding therapeutic approach, the clinician is well armed to plan treatment on the basis of principles appropriate with other more traditionally seen newborn and infantile conditions. Tonal abnormalities are commonly seen in HIV-infected infants, and therapeutic intervention would involve provision of suitable seating, such as Tumble Forms™ seats,* to inhibit extensor tone and facilitate a more nearly normal sitting position with flexed hips, knees, and ankles. Custom-made ankle-foot orthoses, often used as night resting splints, can be provided to prevent permanent deformities in the case of excessive extensor tone causing abnormal plantarflexion of the feet.

Assessment of oral motor function may reveal abnormalities secondary to neurological involvement of this system, which will naturally contribute to the tendency toward poor nutrition. Techniques for oral motor desensitization and feeding can help to ameliorate the function of oromotor structures and improve oral intake. To the greatest extent possible, caregivers should teach simple, replicable techniques for proper handling, feeding, positioning, and play activities by the foster parent, siblings, and other family members so as to maximize function (Harris 1991).

While application of traditional treatment approaches to the HIV-infected infant is broadly useful, the most important difference is that HIV is progressive, and sudden, unexpected changes may occur at any time. Achieved developmental milestones may disappear like vapor with the onset of an acute PCP infection, a bout with *Mycobacterium avium intracellular* (MAI), or a negative reaction to side effects from what previously had appeared to be a well-tolerated chemotherapy regimen.

Rehabilitation of HIV-positive infants begins with a thorough evaluation of physical, developmental, and functional status. Family social and emotional issues also should be considered to the extent that they will bear on attempts at ongoing clinical intervention. Muscle tone, strength, and developmental milestones should be assessed and documented, both to provide the starting point for therapy and to help monitor changes over the long term as the infant is followed by the team.

---

*Tumble Forms, P.O. Box 89, Jackson, MI 49204.

Abnormalities in tone, strength, and functional movement as it is reflected in developmental milestones are treated with range-of-motion exercises, proper positioning, and specific stimulation activities designed to elicit desired performance and age-appropriate skills (see Harris 1991). Parents and caregivers should be involved as collaborators and instructed in ways that they can be therapeutic by following up on their infants' care when at home.

Appropriate seating for table-top activities, such as feeding, and well-designed strollers must be provided so as to maintain physiologically optimum positions conducive to normal tone and achievement of milestones (see Harris 1991). Feeding difficulties should be assessed by experienced clinicians, who can offer suggestions for remediation of oral motor problems which unavoidably contribute to the ever-present possibility of malnutrition.

See Appendix E (page 191) for Universal Precautions for Prevention of HIV and HBV* in a Health-Care Setting.

*Hepatitis B

References

Ahmed, P., ed. 1992. *Living and dying with AIDS.* New York: Plenum Press.

Ammann, A. 1987. The immunology of pediatric AIDS. In *Report of the Surgeon General's workshop on children with HIV infection and their families,* edited by B. Silverman and A. Waddell, 32-37. Washington, DC: U.S. Department of Health and Human Services.

Ammann, A. J., M. Cowen, D. Ware, and P. Weintraub. 1983. Acquired immunodeficiency in an infant: Possible transmission by means of blood products. *Lancet* 1:956-958.

Boland, M. 1987. Management of the child with HIV infection. In *Report of the Surgeon General's workshop on children with HIV infection and their families,* edited by B. Silverman and A. Waddell, 41-43. Washington, DC: U.S. Department of Health and Human Services.

Boschini, A., D. Carlini, P. Ballarini, C. Ghira, D. Ferlini, C. Smacchia, and M. Benigni. 1992. Social rehabilitation of drug addicts and its influence on HIV transmission. In *AIDS and human reproduction,* edited by F. Melica, 84-91. Basel: Karger.

Brettle, R. P., L. MacCallum, and F. Johnstone. 1992. Interaction of HIV, drug use, and pregnancy. In *AIDS and human reproduction,* edited by F. Melica, 102-107. Basel: Karger.

Dickens, B. 1992. Ethical and legal issues in HIV infection and pregnancy. In *AIDS and human reproduction,* edited by F. Melica, 162-168. Basel: Karger.

Galantino, M. L., ed. 1992. *Clinical assessment and treatment of HIV.* Thorofare, NJ: Slack.

Harris, M. 1991. Physical therapy in pediatric HIV infection. In *Rehabilitation for patients with HIV disease,* edited by J. Mukand, 343-357. New York: McGraw-Hill.

Hilgartner, M. 1987. HIV transmitted by blood products. In *Report of the Surgeon General's workshop on children with HIV infection and their families,* edited by B. Silverman and A. Waddell, 26-28. Washington, DC: U.S. Department of Health and Human Services.

Koop, C. 1987. Excerpt from keynote address. In *Report of the Surgeon General's workshop on children with HIV infection and their families,* edited by B. Silverman and A. Waddell, 3-5. Washington, DC: U.S. Department of Health and Human Services.

Levy, R., and J. Berger. 1991. Neurologic complications of HIV infection: Diagnosis, therapy, and functional considerations. In *Rehabilitation for patients with HIV disease,* edited by J. Mukand, 55-76. New York: McGraw-Hill.

Marcil, W., and K. Tigges. 1988. *Terminal and life-threatening illness.* Thorofare, NJ: Slack.

______, eds. 1992. *The person with AIDS.* Thorofare, NJ: Slack.

Mukand, J., E. Starkeson, and J. Melvin. 1991. Public policy issues for the rehabilitation of patients with HIV disease. In *Rehabilitation for patients with HIV disease,* edited by J. Mukand, 1-20. New York: McGraw-Hill.

Oleske, J. 1987. Natural history of HIV infection II. In *Report of the Surgeon General's workshop on children with HIV infection and their families,* edited by B. Silverman and A. Waddell, 24-25. Washington, DC: U.S. Department of Health and Human Services.

Pizzo, P., and D. Poplack, eds. 1989. *Principles and practice of pediatric oncology.* Philadelphia: J.B. Lippincott.

Pizzo, P., and K. Wilfert, eds. 1991. *Pediatric AIDS.* Baltimore: Williams and Wilkins.

Quinnan, G. 1987. Current developments and future prospects for AIDS vaccines. In *Report of the Surgeon General's workshop on children with HIV infection and their families,* edited by B. Silverman and A. Waddell, 44-46. Washington, DC: U.S. Department of Health and Human Services.

Rogers, M. 1987. Transmission of HIV infection in the U.S. In *Report of the Surgeon General's workshop on children with HIV infection and their families,* edited by B. Silverman and A. Waddell, 17-19. Washington, DC: U.S. Department of Health and Human Services.

Rubinstein, A. 1987. Supportive care and treatment of pediatric AIDS. In *Report of the Surgeon General's workshop on children with HIV infection and their families,* edited by B. Silverman and A. Waddell, 29-31. Washington, DC: U.S. Department of Health and Human Services.

Scherr, L. 1991. *HIV and AIDS in mothers and babies.* London: Blackwell Scientific Publications.

Schoenbaum, E., and M. Webber. 1992. Heterosexual transmission of HIV infection. In *AIDS and human reproduction,* edited by F. Melica, 42-46. Basel: Karger.

Scott, G. 1987. Natural history of HIV infection in children. In *Report of the Surgeon General's workshop on children with HIV infection and their families,* edited by B. Silverman and A. Waddell, 22-23. Washington, DC: U.S. Department of Health and Human Services.

Vinters, H., and K. Anders. 1990. *Neuropathology of AIDS.* Boca Raton, FL: CRC Press.

Walker, G. 1991. *In the midst of winter.* New York: W.W. Norton.

Weiss, R., and L. Mazade, eds. 1990. *Surrogate endpoints in evaluating the effectiveness of drugs against HIV infection and AIDS.* Washington, DC: National Academy Press.

Wofsky, C. 1987. Transmission of HIV infection in the U.S. In *Report of the Surgeon General's workshop on children with HIV infection and their families,* edited by B. Silverman and A. Waddell, 32-37. Washington, DC: U.S. Department of Health and Human Services.

Chapter 6

Nursing and the Substance-Exposed Neonate

Davene M. White, RN, NNP

Alcohol- and drug-exposed infants are a large and ever-growing population requiring treatment in newborn nurseries, neonatal intensive care units, and early intervention programs.

There are many forms of perinatal substance use. Improper or abusive use of legal substances such as alcohol and cigarettes is common and legally tolerated. The misuse of controlled substances such as sedatives, cocaine, amphetamines, marijuana, and narcotics is frequently encountered and appears to be increasing. The use of illegal (street) drugs (those with no medically sanctioned uses) such as crack cocaine, crystal amphetamine, PCP, and LSD has been less apparent during pregnancy until the past decade.

The problems of drug- and alcohol-exposed infants and their families are affecting practitioners and presenting difficulties and increased strain on already overburdened programs. The problem of HIV infection in young children is threatening the foster-care system now and with increasing numbers for the future. Of all the HIV-infected children under 13 years of age in the United States, about 80% have a parent with AIDS (Falloon et al. 1989). The foster-care system also is being overwhelmed with children abandoned in hospitals or removed from homes due to poor parenting practices associated with maternal crack cocaine abuse.

Screening Newborns

At present, we do not know how many women use drugs during pregnancy or how many infants born alive in the United States have been exposed to drugs in utero. One method of detection is to test the neonate's urine for drugs. However, this procedure has its limitations because the successful detection of drug metabolites in the neonate's urine is dependent on the time of the last drug intake by the mother or when after birth the neonate's urine was collected. The accuracy of urine screening is also debatable because dilute urine can give negative results and a 24-hour urine collection is needed to provide more accurate data. For the analysis of PCP in neonatal urine, the data are conflicting because of the rapid disappearance and the instability of the drug (Gillogley et al. 1990).

Most studies report that urine screening is not sensitive enough to improve the detection rate of substance abuse in pregnancy (McCalla et al. 1992; Rahbar et al. 1993). Neonatal urine collection is a useful tool for detection of the tissue concentration of illicit drugs, if there is intact skin and the collection bag stays in place for the sample.

Another process generally employed to assess substance abuse is the interview. Interviewers must assure confidentiality, ask about past drug use, and establish a good relationship with the woman. Interviews should uncover whether the woman may be passively exposed because she lives with someone who smokes marijuana or crack (although it is not known whether enough can be consumed passively to significantly affect the fetus). This information also can be obtained with the use of self-report tools.

Alcohol and other drug use during pregnancy has negative physical and psychological consequences for both the mother and the child. Addicted mothers are less likely than other expectant mothers to obtain appropriate prenatal care and nutrition, resulting in high-risk pregnancies as well as low-birth-weight babies who are more at risk of infant mortality and childhood disability. There also is a strong correlation between alcohol and other drug dependence and a number of social problems such as child abuse and neglect, domestic violence, sexual abuse, and homelessness.

Punitive Sanctions

Punitive sanctions by many federal, state, and local officials are being imposed, ranging from maternal criminalization if an infant tests positive on toxicology at birth, to placement of the infant and other siblings in the custody of the state. Such measures often do not take into consideration the medical, psychological, and economic needs of women and their children. These measures may delay the development of alcohol and drug treatment programs that address their needs. A survey of existing drug treatment programs in New York City (Chavkin 1990) found that 54% refused to treat pregnant addicted women; 67% refused to treat pregnant addicts on Medicaid; and 87% denied treatment to pregnant women on Medicaid who were addicted to crack cocaine. Fewer than half of the programs that did accept pregnant women made arrangements for prenatal care, and only two programs provided child care.

In 1981, Beschner and Thompson identified 25 programs nationwide serving 547 women. Few programs were making any attempt to serve the children of drug-abusing women. These programs were not providing family counseling and the skills the women would need to provide successful parenting potential. Women entering programs were likely to be given a therapeutic regimen designed for men, with little or no attention paid to their special need for mothering skills and coping mechanisms. Child development and child behavior were seldom included in drug rehabilitation programs. Weston reported that "no preventive intervention programs have been located which are specifically on (drug abusing) women and prenatal care" (Weston et al. 1989). The challenge to change the design of drug and alcohol treatment programs to focus on a comprehensive design involving prenatal care, drug treatment, infant-parent support, and child-care skills, is an established unmet need.

What Can a Nurse Do?

- Identify the unmet needs of the drug-exposed infant (for example, through services such as developmental assessment, accessible pediatric health services, therapeutic day care, and early education)
- Identify service capacity to provide rehabilitation services, public health and community nurses, adequate nutrition, and Medicaid for drug-exposed infants
- Identify elements and barriers present in the health-care system that thwart recognition of drug- and alcohol-exposed infants
- Identify elements and barriers related to family stability, utilization of foster care as a temporary measure, and full application of kinship care for long-term parental separation
- Establish local and regional interagency agreements to ensure provision and monitoring of services to infants and families at risk due to alcohol or drug abuse
- Make specific financial recommendations on the cost of services needed

Practitioners are seeing a wide range of problems presented by drug- and alcohol-exposed infants. These problems are straining already overburdened health and social service programs. The increasing numbers of infants with chronic illness resulting from poor maternal prenatal health habits, coupled with in utero exposure to substances, is creating a new set of demands (Weston et al. 1989). At the same time, fiscal policies have caused budget limitations for programs designed to support families and promote healthy child-rearing practices. With limited funding, services and staff are being challenged to implement models such as case management. For families whose poverty levels preclude any financial resources to provide home care and follow-up management, there may be no services at all.

The Role of Nursing

The nurse's major responsibility in the newborn care area is to prepare an infant for discharge to a home that is physically prepared for the arrival. The parents have accepted the baby as a person, understand their feelings toward their child, and are prepared for the special care of the baby. The current challenge in addressing the needs of infants exposed to substances in utero is to focus comprehensively on prenatal care, drug treatment, infant-parent support, education, and child-care skills. The success of infant care will involve this comprehensive approach by all team members engaged in a creative and productive exchange of ideas. The challenge extends to identification of grant-funding services and potential contracts to add or initiate services that optimize the medical, social, educational, and psychological growth and development of the child as well as the family.

Any assessment should follow the guidelines established by the Accreditation Manual of the Joint Commission Accreditating Health Care Organizations. The scoring guidelines for standards addressing medical care, nursing care, monitoring, and evaluation of alcohol and other drug-dependence services provides an excellent guideline from which to establish a case management plan for each infant born to a perinatal substance abuser.

Staff at all levels in the health and child-welfare system need significant training to undertake the provision of optimal and effective care of drug-exposed infants and drug-abusing mothers. The numbers, the complexities of their problems, and the difficulties of their life situations are daunting to even the most experienced and sensitive care providers.

The daily care of the child must move toward reality-based acceptance by the parent that the child may have long-term effects of prenatal exposure to substances. The parents must be helped to sort out, identify, and deal with their guilt, fear, and anger, and to recognize that their child needs support and attention.

Recognition of quality care for the infant also includes daily management and care of the family. The importance of involvement of the family (parents, significant others, siblings) in the care of newborns prenatally exposed to drugs is impossible to overemphasize. From the beginning, the parents and infant must be thought of together and treated as a family. If parents are willing and ready, they must be incorporated into the care team.

Family care conferences with the medical staff, nursing staff, and social workers assure that the team is coordinated in their plans and decisions. The social worker is a principal person to whom the parents can turn for support of their financial, emotional, and other needs. The medical staff members often rotate; therefore, the nurse becomes the unchanging member of the team, available to both the infant and parents on an ongoing basis. Thus, the nurse becomes the key person in coordinating the health-care services.

Audiovisuals and other educational materials are critical to instruct mothers on the care of substance-exposed newborns. The nurse must have a full knowledge of the population from which the patients are drawn; the socioeconomic status and racial and ethnic characteristics of the parents; the content of prenatal care; and the home environment and preparations made for the child after birth.

Pamphlets, handouts, and posters orient the mother to the unit's expectations of her involvement in the care of the newborn and the potential effects of substance abuse on the neonate. (See Tables 6.1, 6.2, and 6.3 for sample handouts.)

Team meetings should focus on assessment and service delivery needs. For example:

- Review of the program and service policies, procedures, and data collection with regard to perinatal substance abuse
- Review of the staff demonstration and response to the biopsychosocial and cultural antecedents affecting perinatal substance abuse
- Review of the criteria utilized in determining the treatment needs and discharge planning needs for infants exposed to substances in utero, in recognition of the mothers' coping skills and parenting practices
- Review of the services available for follow-up of these infants and mothers
- Recognition of appropriate resources or referrals to optimize compliance with the discharge plan

Through increased knowledge and cooperation among professionals, there can be an impact on perinatal substance abusers and their infants. Health care providers need to maintain consistent identification and intervention practices for all women to assure that effective treatment is provided for substance-exposed neonates.

References

Abel, E. L. 1982. Consumption of alcohol during pregnancy: A review of effects on growth and development of offspring. *Human Biology* 54:421-53.

Abel, E. L., and R. J. Sokol. 1987. Incidence of fetal alcohol syndrome and economic impact of FAS-related anomalies. *Drug and Alcohol Dependence* 19:51-70.

Beschner, G., and P. Thompson. 1981. *Women and drug abuse treatment: Needs and services.* Department of Health and Human Services Publication No. (ADM)84-1057. Services Research Monograph Series. Rockville, MD: National Institute on Drug Abuse.

Bingol, N., M. Fuchs, V. Diaz, R. K. Stone, and D. S. Gromish. 1987. Teratogenicity of cocaine in humans. *Journal of Pediatrics* 110:93-96.

Briggs, G. G., J. H. Samson, and D. J. Crawford. 1976. Lack of abnormalities in a newborn exposed to amphetamines during gestation. *American Journal of the Disabled Child* 129:249-50.

Chasnoff, I. J., R. Hatcher, W. J. Burns, and S. H. Schnoll. 1983. Pentazocine and tripelennamine (Ts and Blues): Effects on the fetus and neonate. *Development Pharmacology Therapy* 6:162-69.

Chasnoff, I. J., W. J. Burns, S. H. Scholl, and K. A. Burns. 1985. Cocaine use in pregnancy. *New England Journal of Medicine* 313:666-69.

Chavkin, W. 1990. Drug addiction and pregnancy: Policy crossroads. *American Journal of Public Health* 80:483-487.

Clarren, S. K., and D. W. Smith. 1978. The fetal alcohol syndrome: A review of world literature. *New England Journal of Medicine* 298:1063-67.

Falloon, J., J. Eddy, L. Wiener, and P. Pizzo. 1989. Human immunodeficiency virus infection in children. *Journal of Pediatrics* 114:1-30.

Gillogley, K. M., A. T. Evans, and R. Hansen. 1990. The perinatal impact of cocaine, amphetamine, and opiate use detected by universal intrapartum screening. *American Journal of Obstetrics and Gynecology* 163:1535-1542.

Jones, K. L. 1988. *Smith's recognizable patterns of human malformation.* 4th ed. Philadelphia: W.B. Saunders.

Kandall, S. R., S. Albin, L. M. Gartner, and J. Lowinson. 1977. The narcotic-dependent mother: Fetal and neonatal consequences. *Early Human Development* 2:159.

Little, B. B., L. M. Snell, V. R. Klein, and L. C. Gilstrap. 1989. Cocaine abuse during pregnancy: Maternal and fetal implications. *Obstetrics and Gynecology* 73:157-60.

MacGregor, S. N., L. G. Keith, I. J. Chasnoff, M. A. Rosner, G. M. Chisum, P. Shaw, and J. P. Minoque. 1987. Cocaine use during pregnancy: Adverse perinatal outcome. *American Journal of Obstetrics and Gynecology* 157:686-90.

McCalla, S., H. L. Minkoff, J. Feldman, L. Glass, and G. Valencia. 1992. Predictors of cocaine use in pregnancy. *Obstetrics and Gynecology* 79:641-644.

Naeye, R. L., W. Blanc, W. Leblanc, and M. Khatamee. 1973. Fetal complications of maternal heroin addiction: Abnormal growth, infections and episodes of stress. *Journal of Pediatrics* 1055.

National Institute on Alcohol Abuse and Alcoholism. 1983. Fifth special report on alcohol and health from the Secretary of Health and Human Services. Washington, DC: Government Printing Office.

Rahbar, F. 1975. Observations on methadone withdrawal in 16 neonates. *Clinical Pediatrics* 14: 369-71.

Rahbar, F., A. Fomufod, and D. White. 1993. Impact of intrauterine exposure to phencyclidine (PCP) and cocaine on neonates. *Journal of the National Medical Association* 85(5):349-352.

Senay, E. C. 1985. Clinical experiences with Ts and Blues. *Drug and Alcohol Dependence* 14:305-12.

Weston, D., B. Ivins, B. Zuckerman, C. Jones, and R. Lopez. 1989. Drug exposed babies: Research and clinical issues. *Zero to Three* 9(5):1-7.

Young, M. 1989. Perinatal HIV transmission. Paper presented at Symposium on Perinatal Substance Abuse, "The Cry of the City." Howard University, March 29.

Table 6.1
Strategies Needed to Care for Children Who Were Exposed to Drugs and Substances Before Birth

Davene M. White, RN, NNP

The home is an essential part of the child's development.
The emphasis of parenting and home life should be to establish a close relationship with the child.

Strategies	How to Help Correct Behavioral Problems for Your Baby	Notes
Respect	Do not expect your baby to understand your needs. Expect the baby to cry and be demanding and unpredictable. Slow your life down, and do not expect the baby to be happy to come along. Expect your baby to cry and be upset when you are not around.	
Ritual and Routines	Provide regular meal times, bed times, and play times. This will help your child develop self-control and a sense of comfort with your home environment.	
Regulated Limit-Setting	Rules should be based on the baby's safety. Give your baby a safe place in your home in which to explore and be active.	
Flexible Room Environment	Remove and add toys and play materials for your baby to use. Clean those items often, and inspect them for torn edges and loose pieces.	
Attachment	Help your child learn self-trust by smiling and giving approval often. Help your child to depend on others by responding to the child's needs, and make the child feel important. Harsh, loud words cause the child to mistrust, have fear, insecurity, and anger toward you and others.	
Transition Time Plans	Time between activities is a must. Each activity needs a clear beginning, a middle, and an end. This is how to teach your child to prepare for change and be able to cope with it.	
Feelings	Help your child to recognize that feelings are real, important, and normal. When a child misbehaves, find out what the child wanted, and talk about what the child did before dealing with the problem.	
Mutual Discussion	Talking about behavior and feelings (with concern rather than judgment) makes the child's experiences real and sets up an accepting atmosphere for communication. Permission to have feelings helps the child to recognize wishes and fantasies on one hand and reality on the other. Talking allows the child to express feelings and gain self-control.	
Role Model	The parent must understand that establishing individual trusting relationships leads to the parent becoming an important person whose behavior is more likely to be imitated.	
Peer Sensitivity	The parent must be aware that high-risk children become sensitive and aware of the needs and feelings of others only by repeatedly having their own needs met.	
Decision-Making	Freedom to choose and to take responsibility for choices (gradually expanded as the child's abilities develop) promotes self-esteem, problem-solving mastery, and moral values.	

Table 6.2
Newborn Symptoms of Substance-Exposed Infants
Davene M. White, RN, NNP

Symptoms	Related Problems	Notes
Irritability	Seizures	
Restlessness	Scraping of knees and elbows Disturbed sleep patterns	
Poor feeding	Frantic sucking Vomiting Diarrhea	
Crying	Not relieved by holding High pitched	
Tremors	Hyperactive reflexes Stiffness	
Rapid breathing	Sneezing Runny nose	
Small for age	Low birth weight Smaller head than nonexposed infants Shorter birth length	
Rapid heart rate	High blood pressure	
Reduced response to people and the environment	Turning away from the parent Sensitive to touch	

Table 6.3
How to Comfort Your Baby
Davene M. White, RN, NNP

Behavior	Comforting Techniques	Notes
Irritability	*Handling* For the first few weeks, your baby may need to be swaddled while being held. The warmth and closeness of a tightly wrapped blanket calms the baby. In time, the baby will learn to be calm without help. *Rocking* Slow rocking in an up-and-down motion may help your baby stop crying. The baby may need this kind of help before making face-to-face, eye-to-eye contact with you. *Calming* When your baby becomes calm, hold the baby in a face-to-face position. Look at your baby, and encourage your baby to look at you. Talk to your baby as you play together.	
Restlessness	*Positioning* Place the baby on one side, with a rolled-up blanket supporting the baby's spine. Place rolled-up cloth diapers between the baby's legs. Let the baby's legs bend a little. This will help the baby to move the legs freely, and the baby will be less stiff. Change your baby's position often—every half-hour, if needed. *Bathing* Bathe your baby every day. Use warm water and a mild soap such as Neutrogena or Dove. Dry your baby well, and don't use too much lotion or baby oil. Apply any medicines, ointments, or creams that your doctor has prescribed or recommended.	
Poor Feeding	*Feeding* Feed your baby small amounts of formula every three hours. Later, when the baby is stronger, you can give more formula. The time then can be lengthened by a few minutes until it is four hours between feedings. For the first four months, give your baby nothing but formula. Do not switch from formula to whole milk until your baby is one year old. Be sure to gently and slowly burp the baby after every feeding. *Burping* If the baby has been crying for more than a few minutes before feeding, take time to calm the baby. Place the baby against your chest, and gently pat the baby's back to release excess air caused by crying. Feed the baby three or four ounces of formula. Then burp the baby. Burping can be done while holding the baby in a sitting position with one hand on the baby's stomach and the other hand gently rubbing and patting the baby's back.	

(continued)

Table 6.3
How to Comfort Your Baby (continued)

Behavior	Comforting Techniques	Notes
Crying	*Baby is not able to sleep* Reduce the stimulation around the baby. Turn down the lights, and reduce noises or music. Pat your baby on the back, and talk to the baby in a soft humming voice. *Pacifier* When the baby has been fed and still tries to suck the fists or the clothes, a pacifier may help the baby to relax.	
Breathing Problems	*Sneezing, runny nose* If mucous or formula is in the nose, clean the baby's nose with a bulb syringe. *Trouble breathing* If your baby is uncomfortable lying on the stomach after feeding and burping, place the baby on one side. Roll up a blanket and place it against the baby's back for support. When your baby is awake, active, and alert, let the baby sit up in an infant seat. If the baby's color is pale or appears blue, call 911 immediately.	
Play positions	Place your baby on the stomach to play. Put colorful, stimulating toys beside the baby. This will encourage the baby to turn from the waist and reach for the toys.	
Carrying	Carry your baby facing forward, supported by your arm under the baby's thighs. In this position, the baby's arms can be kept forward. This makes it easier for the baby to bring the hands together. This position also helps the baby strengthen the muscles needed for reaching and grasping.	
Handling	Drug-exposed babies are sensitive to quick, rough movements. They may respond by stiffening their bodies or crying. Slow, gentle swinging is better for these babies. Watch to see how your baby reacts to being handled. The baby will look distressed when the handling is too rough or uncomfortable.	
Exercise	Your baby's muscle development needs to be evaluated when the baby is four months old. If any problems are discovered at that time, the doctor will recommend a physical therapist or occupational therapist. These specialists can start an exercise routine to help your baby overcome any problems. Some babies are given exercise routines even before they come home from the hospital. If you have been given an exercise routine for your baby, follow the schedule strictly. The exercises will help your baby loosen up and prepare for active movement.	

Chapter 7

The Perinatal Social Worker

An Interview with Diedra Mitchell-Wright, LICSW, ACSW

The social worker plays a vital role in coordinating discharge planning, discharge placement, and follow-up of babies born to drug-addicted mothers. Often it is the social worker who must develop a strong bond with the mother in order to get the sensitive information needed for this planning. The social worker assesses the needs of both mother and baby, and initiates phone calls and paperwork for necessary services.

The task begins as soon as the pregnant mother seeks prenatal care or when she enters the hospital. The social worker begins collecting vital information which alerts the medical team as to whether the mother will be unable to make appropriate plans for her infant or whether she will participate responsibly in the support and care of her baby. It is the social worker who labors to address the mother's multiple and perhaps desperate needs and those of her infant, by assessing dwindling and oversubscribed social resources.

This chapter outlines the roles and functions of the perinatal social worker in responding to the competing demands of drug-addicted mothers, the needs of their drug-exposed infants, and the requirements and standards of the medical and legal professions. This description of the job is presented in a question/answer format to help the reader appreciate the tone and sensitive nature of the information managed by the social worker.

The Social Worker's Role

Q. *What is the role of a perinatal social worker?*

A. The job is multifaceted. First, it involves completing a thorough initial assessment as soon as the mother is admitted to the hospital. Sometimes this means interviewing the mother in the labor and delivery rooms. As you know, many mothers have not been seen for prenatal care and there has been no opportunity for assessment and intervention.

Second, my job includes monitoring all contacts and visits to mother and baby in order to establish a contact file in the interest of the neonate. Sometimes these mothers leave their babies in the hospital and we have no way to contact the mothers or any interested parties. Phone calls and visits are closely monitored and documented, including name of the caller or visitor, time, nature of the call, phone number, and address.

My main role is to remain in contact with the mother from intake through discharge, and to design and carry out an effective discharge plan for both mother and baby, keeping the two together if possible. In essence, the social worker's role involves assessing needs, identifying and accessing resources, and making referrals. Throughout this process, the social worker provides counseling and emotional support as needed, and monitors any changes in the family situation that might affect successful discharge and follow-up of both mother and baby.

Q. ***How long is your initial interview with the mother?***

A. A minimum of 20 minutes, depending upon the mother's physical and emotional state and the nature of the infant's medical condition.

Q. ***What is the average hospital stay for these mothers?***

A. With today's insurance regulations, the hospital stay has been shortened. It is common for patients to be discharged in two days, and sometimes in 24 hours. This can make timely assessments and screenings difficult.

Q. ***What is your average caseload of substance abusers?***

A. From a total caseload of approximately 70 mothers per month, roughly one-third to half are substance abusers.

Profile of the Substance-Abusing Mother

Q. ***What are the most common problems the mothers present?***

A. There are several:

1. No prenatal care. Most of the mothers have no history of prenatal care. When they enter the hospital for delivery, that is the only medical care received during the pregnancy.
2. No Medicaid registration or other source of medical payment. Most mothers do not receive Medicaid support and, therefore, have no means of health-care payment. This is often the rationale given for failure to get prenatal medical attention—no Medicaid. However, even when application forms are provided, mothers often fail to follow through.
3. No home to return to upon discharge. Placement for mother and baby upon discharge is often a major concern, since many mothers come "right off the streets." Others live with extended family, usually with the mother's mother or an aunt and other children and siblings. Sometimes the prospect of the new baby coming into such a strained environment is just too much for the family to handle.
4. Leaving the hospital against medical advice (AMA). Some mothers sign out of the hospital early, sometimes taking their babies with them.
5. Difficult follow-up. Frequent moves make postdischarge follow-up difficult. Sometimes we are unable to provide the services and monitoring often needed by the infant because there is no way to contact the mother by address or phone.

Q. ***What about work history?***

A. Most mothers report a very spotty work history. Working in unrewarding menial jobs is commonly reported. Most mothers report being totally dependent on other people, often moving from place to place, living with friends. They report "hustling" for a living. Some mothers report not staying at one place too long for fear of being kicked out and told never to return. It is obviously much easier to hustle and to live from place to place without a baby.

Q. ***What is the average age of substance-abusing mothers you see?***

A. The range is from 15 to 35 years of age. The majority are between 21 and 25.

Q. ***How reliable is the mother's information?***

A. Most mothers are open to sharing information. Many of them take the opportunity to vent. Some of them are defensive, as you can imagine, and many of them deny having a drug problem.

Q. ***How do you think mothers view the social worker?***

A. Many of them view us as agents working for the establishment trying to take their babies. Once they understand that the role of the social worker is to help plan for the baby and help them keep the baby, they relax and are more receptive to intervention. Some are defensive because they are already known to Protective Services and may have had other children removed from their care.

Q. ***What proportion of your caseload is made up of first pregnancies? How many are repeat cases?***

A. Approximately one-third are first pregnancies. Many of the repeaters already have more than one child being cared for by the grandmother, other family members, or an unrelated caretaker.

Q. ***Is there any evidence of family planning?***

A. Rarely. Many mothers make statements such as, "It just happened"; "If only I had gone to the clinic"; or "I had no Medicaid so I couldn't sign up for tubal ligation." Many report that they were trying not to get pregnant because they didn't want any more children.

Q. ***Are most of the mothers aware of when they became pregnant and by whom?***

A. Yes. They report knowing when they became pregnant. They report being fully aware that they were not using any form of birth control. Most mothers report knowing who the baby's father is. Occasionally, the father comes to the hospital to see about the baby and may make arrangements to take the baby home to be cared for by him or by his family. But more often, the mother reports that the father is not going to be involved. Sometimes the baby is the result of drug activity and prostitution.

Q. ***How do most mothers report becoming addicted to drugs?***

A. Most say that it came about by being "with the wrong crowd," or that the baby's father got them involved. Many indicate that their downward slide was caused at least partly by depression and feelings of hopelessness. As one mother said, "I can get drugs when I can't even find food to eat." Drugs are a means of escape and, unfortunately, addiction goes hand in hand with low self-esteem.

Q. ***What is the drug most commonly used by the mothers you see?***

A. Crack cocaine is by far number one. Consistent with the national picture, cocaine is often used in combination with other (legal and illegal) drugs, especially alcohol and heroin, or perhaps methadone. Cigarettes are part of the scene; they do not pose the same threats as alcohol or illegal drugs, but they are detrimental to the infant both before and after birth.

Q. ***For mothers who have already been in drug rehabilitation, what is the major cause for their return to drug use?***

A. By far, the major cause of recurring drug use is returning to the same hopeless, drug-infested environment which the mother left. There are not enough community outreach programs to pick up where drug rehabilitation services leave off. The mothers are simply not strong enough to return to the same environment and withstand the temptation of drugs.

Social Work Intervention

Q. ***What does the social worker hope to accomplish while the mother is in the hospital or before her infant's discharge?***

A. The social worker will focus on:

1. Gathering pertinent psychosocial data to assess overall needs.
2. Making referral for drug rehabilitation for the mother.
3. Encouraging postpartum follow-up for mother and infant.
4. Encouraging the mother to return to the hospital after she is discharged to visit the baby.
5. Counseling the mother on stress-reduction techniques—how to handle the stress that she might encounter after she takes the baby home.

Q. ***What can the social worker plan with the mother?***

A. Discharge planning begins with the initial interview and includes examination of matters such as:

1. What additional medical attention will the mother and infant require? Where will they receive services, and how will the care be financed?
2. Is there a family support system? Will the mother or someone else be the primary caretaker? What resources does the mother have? What does she need to provide proper care?
3. What does the mother know about routine care of the drug-exposed infant? How, and how quickly, can she be taught? Are there resources for support?

4. When and where should the infant have clinical follow-up? Are transportation and day care needed?
5. Does the mother need drug rehabilitation placement? When and where?

Q. ***What advice do you give to methadone- and heroin-addicted mothers who wish to take their babies home?***

A. Mainly, I encourage compliance with their drug counselor who would recommend detoxification at the appropriate time. Mothers who do detoxify before the baby goes home complain of the terrible side effects of the methadone, which render them ineffective for mothering. The infant requires a lot of energy and attention for routine care, and mothers in detox become lethargic, sleepy, and less available and tolerant of the infant's needs and behaviors. This situation could easily lead to abuse of the infant.

Q. ***What steps do you take when a mother is either unavailable or deemed unfit to take her baby home?***

A. We contact the Youth Division of the Police Department to get a "hold" in order to keep the infant in the hospital until the Department of Human Services Protective Service agents make final plans for the infant.

Q. ***Under what other specific conditions might you call the Police Youth Services Division?***

A. A police hold is requested:

1. When a mother returns to the hospital to take the infant home and is obviously under the influence of alcohol or illicit drugs.
2. When a mother chooses to sign the infant out of the hospital against medical advice (AMA) and the condition of the child is obviously life threatening.
3. When the social worker's home assessment determines that the home environment is unfit or unsafe and that discharge would place the infant in imminent danger.

Q. ***At what point do you declare the drug-exposed infant a "boarder baby"?***

A. When the infant is medically stable and ready for discharge but cannot be released from the hospital to a responsible parent due to any of the following:

1. Inability to locate the mother or next of kin.
2. Lack of parental permission to make alternative plans.
3. Continued conviction that the home is unfit and/or the mother is unable to provide adequate care.

According to law in the District of Columbia, the city agency with the authority for child placement is to recognize the "boarder baby" status and implement an appropriate placement ten days after medical clearance.

Q. ***How are HIV-positive infants handled for discharge?***

A. Here at Howard University Hospital, there is a separate Chronic Care Services Clinic (CCSC) where HIV-positive neonates are followed by a team of specialists. The mother is contacted and counseled by a physician, and the team social worker provides education and supportive intervention. The perinatal social worker simply alerts the CCSC social worker of the case and follows up to ensure that transfer is complete.

Q. ***What would an ideal program look like from your perspective?***

A. It would establish a means of reaching mothers and getting them into the medical system prior to delivery. Perhaps an early detection outreach team could routinely rotate to apartment buildings, community centers, neighborhoods, and churches, providing pregnancy screening. Small rewards could be offered to motivate pregnant women to attend clinics.

In such a program, the lack of insurance would not be a deterrent to treatment. The system should be made into a motivator rather than a deterrent for treatment. An improved system would provide, most immediately:

1. Accessible medical treatment for both mother and infant.
2. Available and appropriate drug treatment programs allowing for easy access.
3. Services for other children in the home, including day care, medical, and developmental assessment.
4. Parenting education, support groups, and individual counseling.
5. Assistance with housing alternatives.
6. Assessment of vocational/educational and other training needs.

The perinatal social worker would still have to address multiple and urgent needs of both mother and drug-affected neonate, which involves the task of initiating connections to ready sources of help and support.

Chapter 8

Assessment Issues and Concerns

Deborrah Bremond, Ph.D.

Multiple Substances, Multiple Effects

The short-term effects of substance exposure during pregnancy have been well documented; effects on the fetus can range from first trimester abortion to cerebral infarcts and premature labor (on one end of the continuum) to afflictions including tachycardia vasoconstriction, and temporary increases in blood pressure. Drug-affected (cocaine) infants have a higher rate of intrauterine growth retardation (IUGR), lower birth weights, and smaller head sizes than infants born to nonusing women (DeStefano-Lewis et al. 1989).

Measuring the effects of substance exposure is difficult enough, and it is compounded by the fact that many women use more than one drug during pregnancy. Substances taken during pregnancy could be classified, as they were in a 1989 study, into three categories:

- Drugs, such as heroin, that are addictive and may cause addiction in the newborn
- Drugs that are considered toxic and may result in behavioral changes in the infant without addiction
- Drugs that are teratogenic; that is, drugs that may cause physical abnormalities in the infant (Weston et al. 1989).

The numerous possible combinations make it all but impossible to identify specific outcomes related to specific substances. It is safe to say that developmental outcomes for substance-exposed children are varied and fall along a continuum of risk.

Compounding the problem even further is the constellation of environmental factors into which substance-exposed children are born. Many of these children are born into unstable-caregiving environments, where family dysfunction and chronic, even intergenerational, drug use is common. It is worth noting that an increasing number of drug-exposed children are the product of suburban and rural families who, in addition to all the above problems, are often isolated from the support of agencies and extended family.

The racial background and the most-used substances may vary according to geography. A report on substance-exposed infants in San Diego, California, concluded that while the majority of cocaine users came from inner city African-American and Latino populations, the majority of methamphetamine users were

Caucasian and came from rural and semirural areas (Dixon 1989). Information on the kind of home an infant is born into, or even information on what drugs were taken during pregnancy, do not by themselves constitute a profile of the substance-exposed child. But data on such matters is gathered by the professional in the course of a complete examination.

Recent Research

More research has been done on the effects of prenatal substance exposure on neonates and infants than has been done on children at toddler and preschool ages. The lack of research with older children is related to the comparative ease of hospital-based research, the follow-through provided by postpartum care, and the short period that research has been done on developmental outcomes for substance-exposed children. There is some research on substance-exposed toddlers and preschoolers, however. Commonly cited studies have been generated from the University of California at Los Angeles, Department of Pediatrics, and the Center for Perinatal Addiction at Northwestern University, Evanston, Illinois.

One study conducted by Carol Rodning et al. (1989) at UCLA compared 18 substance-exposed with 57 high-risk preterm toddlers. The two groups were compared at age 18 months on measures of intellectual functioning, quality of play, and security of attachment to primary caregiver. In addition to externally structured, standardized developmental tests, unstructured play sessions were videotaped and scored. Although the substance-exposed toddlers had significantly lower scores on the structured tests of development, they were still within the low-average range. This finding was in contrast to the unstructured free-play session, which revealed difficulties that the substance-exposed toddlers had with self-initiation, motor planning, and organization without the assistance of the examiner.

The Center at Northwestern University has followed more than 200 infants who were exposed to substances in utero (Chasnoff et al. 1992), and results of the two- and three-year follow-up appear to concur with those of the researchers at UCLA. The toddlers demonstrated normal cognitive and motor development as measured by the *Bayley Scales of Infant Development* (1969, 1992) and the Stanford-Binet, but examiners documented that 30% to 40% experienced language delays and behavioral difficulties. These last were manifested in the form of poor tolerance for frustration, distractibility, and difficulty with sensorimotor integration. And still another study (Bremond 1992) appeared to confirm the incidence of attentional and social-emotional difficulties. Bremond's work, a doctoral dissertation, examined infant/parent pairs in a controlled environment, and concluded that developmental outcomes are influenced by the quality of infant/parent interaction—one more confirmation of a belief already firmly held by most of the medical community and other professionals who work with infants, including those who do assessments.

Assessment: A Close and Careful Portrait

The advent of the implementation of Part H of the Americans with Disabilities Act (PL 99-457) has caused professionals who are working with at-risk infants and families to take a closer look at the process of assessment in order to define criteria for eligibility and ascertain the level of needed intervention services. At the 1993 Biennial Training sponsored by Zero to Three, National Center for Clinical Infants' Programs, Dr. Sam Meisels reminded the audience that the Latin root for assessment is defined as to "sit alongside" (Meisels 1993).

Assessment is a process by which information is gathered about a child's competencies and areas of challenge in the acquisition of developmental functioning. Domains of functioning included in an assessment are the child's emotional and social capacities; cognitive, language, motor, and sensory abilities (Greenspan and Meisels 1993). The developmental projectory of these domains of functioning must be understood in the cultural context of the family. A comprehensive assessment should point the way toward helping children acquire age-appropriate developmental skills. Early assessment is important because it has been demonstrated that identification of developmental difficulties and intervention are most effective when accomplished during the toddler and preschool years. Assessment should not be used to label a child as substance exposed. Exposure is only one of many risk factors that can contribute to developmental delay. The ultimate goal of assessment is to assist the child and the family as a unit in understanding the specific areas of strength and difficulty experienced by the preschooler.

An assessment protocol for toddlers and preschool children should consist of:

1. Caregiver interview and developmental history
2. Administration of developmental measurements
3. Observation of play
4. Observation of general behavior

Caregiver Interview

The parent/caregiver interview is important because, ideally, the caregiver is being asked to participate as a partner in evaluating the child's strengths and weaknesses. Teachers, diagnosticians, and other child-care workers need to treat caregivers with respect and consideration; an atmosphere of mutual confidence is likely to help along the flow of information and cooperation. Primary focus of the interview with the caregiver will be on gathering development information: birth information, developmental milestones, and ongoing current concerns.

Also during contacts with parents or caregiver, the evaluator will be making notes and observations to become part of the comprehensive portrait. The assessment will take into account the child's familial context, socioeconomic status, ethnic group, culture, developmental history, relationship functioning, and observable behaviors. During this process, the professional must be aware—and beware—of personal biases brought to the interview and the assessment process.

There are times when caregivers may not be good reporters. This is generally associated with the individual's lack of historical information, as in the case of a foster parent or a relative who recently gained custody or guardianship of a child. A biological parent who is involved in substance abuse may be an unreliable reporter because abusers tend to spend little or no time with their children. Thus, the professional's interview with the caregiver will provide an important source of information about the family context and the child's role in the family.

Administration of Developmental Measurements

There is much confusion about the difference between the use of screening and in-depth assessment. Screening is used on groups of children to get an indication of their development as compared to other groups of children in their age bracket. Developmental screening serves as a basis for identifying children experiencing difficulties in age-appropriate functioning. Developmental screening should never be used as the sole basis for labeling or diagnosing a child with developmental delay (Meisels and Provence 1989). Screening measures are usually normed and standardized and let an examiner know whether a child may require a more in-depth developmental evaluation. The *Denver Developmental Screening Test–II* (Frankenburg et al. 1990) and *The Early Screening Inventory–3* (Meisels et al. 1991) are examples of developmental screening measures.

An in-depth developmental assessment utilizes several sources of information to determine the extent and degree to which a child is experiencing developmental delay. Developmental testing will incorporate such information as medical, psychosocial, cultural history, and current circumstances into the process, along with behavioral and observational data collected from parents and teachers. Developmental tests are usually administered by a professional after a screening has raised questions about a child's functional development. The *Bayley Scales of Infant Development* (Bayley 1969, 1992) and the *McCarthy Scales of Children's Abilities* (McCarthy 1972) are examples of developmental measures that look at a child's abilities across several domains. The results from an in-depth assessment will provide the family and professionals with recommendations and strategies for intervention.

A good developmental evaluation will be reliable and valid with norms based on diverse populations. It will sample a range of functional capabilities. In addition to standardized instruments of measurement, less structured methods of assessment are used to supplement the evaluation process. These include checklists and observations of quality of interaction with caregivers and general behavior.

Observation of Play

Behavior during play can provide a wealth of information about the child's development–physical, cognitive, and imaginative. As the child matures, increasingly sophisticated themes, often of mastery, will dominate. But very early on, the concrete–the world of touch, taste, and sight–is dominant.

Children's play follows a set developmental pattern emerging during the second half of the first year (Piaget 1962; McCune-Nicolich 1981; Fein 1981; Belsky and Most 1981). The quality of a child's play progresses from simple object manipulation to complex object/toy manipulation. Simple play is characterized by reaching, holding, and attending to an object. Complex object manipulation includes exploring, poking, and turning objects in space. The child seeks information about the object in order to utilize it in a functional manner.

Symbolic play emerges during the second year, 12 to 24 months. Children begin using objects to represent other objects; a comb is used as a spoon, or a child can pretend to pour tea from a teapot. The length and complexity of pretend-play sequences become more pronounced with the child's maturation. The absence of symbolic play behaviors can be an indicator that the child is experiencing difficulties in cognitive, language, or social-emotional functioning.

Observation of General Behavior

Behavioral observations provide information in several domains of functioning that are not usually measured by assessment instruments. Relationship functioning, a child's sense of self, coping, and adaptation skills are not easily measured, and are best reported by the caregiver or observed by the evaluator.

Tapping into a child's internal structure of thoughts and emotions through play, storytelling, and picture drawing are nonstandardized and informal methods of obtaining a sense of how a child is feeling about the world. Does the child's story always end negatively or unresolved? Are picture of the self or others fragmented and distorted all of the time? If the answers are yes, then the child may be experiencing problems in social-emotional functioning. The child may be experiencing the world as unsupportive and nonresponsive. The child's ability to cope may be taxed and eventually be a cause of behavioral outbursts (Bremond 1993).

Results: Presenting the Portrait

Results should be presented to parents in a simple manner. Standard scores and developmental age-equivalent scores provide comprehensible information for the nonprofessional. More subjective observations also can be presented, assuming that the clinician brings empathy, support, and realism to the caregiver, as well as respect for the needs of the child.

Most important, intervention strategies should be developed and implemented. This, too, is done with due care for the parent/caregiver, since the professional is building a partnership for helping the child. Incidentally, there are times when a developmental evaluation will produce more questions than answers; and when this occurs, a more appropriate referral needs to be generated in order to ascertain a better picture of the child's functioning. Perhaps a more complete neurological examination is in order, or perhaps an undiscovered physical condition has distorted development.

Most often, however, a careful assessment does present a valid portrait of a child's developmental status. The more comprehensive the assessment, the smaller the possibility of misinterpreting a child's behavior. If the child is experiencing difficulties in the acquisition of abilities and skills, there will be evidence and indications for intervention and remedies. And if the child exhibits strengths, as all children do to some degree, caregivers and therapists can make plans to use these skills to the fullest.

There are many factors which contribute to the course and outcome of child development. Substance exposure is but one risk factor. The fact that children have been exposed does not automatically doom them to lower developmental functioning. Thorough assessment as early as possible, while there is maximum time for intervention, is an important first step toward remediation. After assessment, there might be therapy, help in the home, early and intensive childhood education, or all of these. The substance-exposed child can be helped in coping with developmental delays and acquiring necessary skills.

References

Bayley, N. 1969, 1992. *Bayley scales of infant development.* New York: The Psychological Corp.

Belsky, J., and R. K. Most. 1981. From exploration to play: A cross sectional study of infant free-play behavior. *Developmental Psychology* 17:630-39.

Bremond, D. A. 1992. Developmental outcomes for substance-exposed infants: Observations of mother/infant interaction during the first year of life. Ph.D. dissertation, The Wright Institute.

______. 1993. Assessment. In *Just kids: A practical guide for working with children prenatally substance exposed.* Sacramento: Shasta County Department of Education, California Department of Education, 43-51.

Chasnoff, I. J., D. R. Griffith, C. Freier, and J. Murray. 1992. Cocaine/polydrug use in pregnancy: Two-year follow-up. *Pediatrics* 89(2):284-89.

DeStefano-Lewis, K., B. Bennett, and N. Hellenger Schmeder. 1989. The care of infants menaced by cocaine abuse. *Maternal Child Nursing* 14:324-329.

Dixon, S. D. 1989. Effects of transplacental exposure to cocaine and methamphetamine on the neonate. *The Western Journal of Medicine* 150:436-42.

Fein, G. G. 1981. Pretend play: An integrative review. *Development* 52:1095-118.

Frankenburg, W. K., J. Dodds, P. Archer, P. Bresnick, P. Maschka, N. Edelman, and H. Shapiro. 1990. *Denver developmental screening test–II.* Denver: Denver Developmental Materials, Inc.

Greenspan, S., and S. Meisels. 1993. Toward a new vision for developmental assessment of infants and young children. Distributed to participants in Zero to Three, National Center for Clinical Infants' Programs, 8th Biennial National Training Institute. Dec. 3-4, Washington, DC.

McCarthy, D. 1972. *McCarthy scales of children's abilities.* New York: The Psychological Corp.

McCune-Nicolich. 1981. Toward symbolic functioning: Structure of early pretend games and potential parallels with language. *Child Development* 52:785-97.

Meisels, S. 1993. *New visions for the developmental assessment of infants and young children.* Washington, DC: Plenary Session, Zero to Three, National Center for Clinical Infants' Programs, 8th Biennial National Training Institute.

Meisels, S., L. Henderson, D. Mardsen, K. Browning, and K. Olson. 1991. *The early screening inventory–3.* Ann Arbor: University of Michigan, Center for Human Growth and Development.

Meisels, S., and S. Provence. 1989. *Screening and assessment: Guidelines for identifying young disabled and developmentally vulnerable children and their families.* Washington, DC: National Center for Clinical Infants' Programs.

Piaget, J. 1962. *Play, dreams, and imitation in childhood.* New York: Norton.

Rodning, C., L. Beckwith, and J. Howard. 1989. Characteristics of attachment organization and play organization in prenatally drug-exposed toddlers. *Development and Psychopathology* 1:277-89.

Weston, D., B. Ivins, B. Zuckerman, C. Jones, and R. Lopez. 1989. Drug-exposed babies: Research and clinical issues. *Zero to Three* 9(5):1-7.

Chapter 9

Theoretical Approaches to Treatment

Shirley J. Jackson, M.S., OTR/L

Effective response to the problems presented by substance-exposed infants and children requires all therapists to have a thorough knowledge of both the philosophical bases and the principles of two major theories: developmental theory, and sensory integration. When confronted with signs of abnormality that signal multiple problem areas (oral motor, muscle tone, social and behavioral responses, attention and state control, and central nervous system responses), the occupational, physical, and speech therapists are educated to provide evaluation and treatment to this population. Occupational therapists are highly trained in the use of sensory integration with high-risk infants and children. Therapists experienced in sensory integration can readily identify and distinguish abnormal responses and quickly adapt evaluations and treatment to elicit the infant's or child's best response.

Theory in practice, however, must always be governed by a sensitivity of cultural differences. Likewise, therapists, educators, and medical caregivers whose practice incorporates the principles of the cultural difference (CD) approach recognize that effective treatment strategies embody the values, beliefs, and expectations of the culture which they serve. For a practice to be effective, it must be in harmony with the belief system and cultural behaviors of the families of the substance-exposed infants and children.

The broad overview of the theories which follow provides a philosophical foundation for evaluation and treatment by occupational and physical therapists. These themes of developmental theory, sensory integration, and consciousness of cultural difference provide effective, meaningful, reality-based treatment to substance-exposed children and their families.

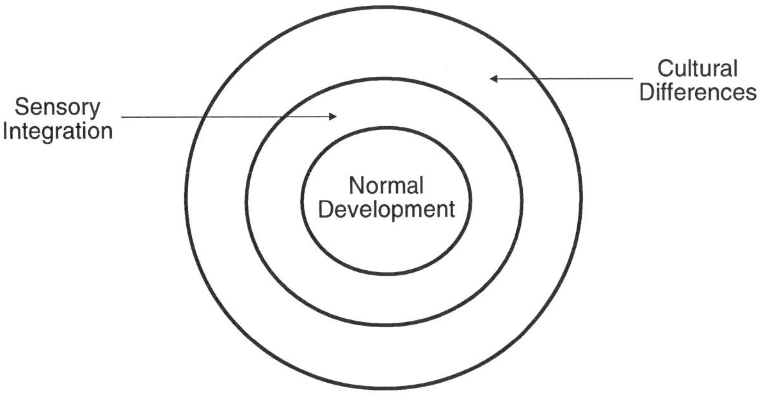

Theoretical Approaches to Treatment

Developmental Theory

Normal development as described by Piaget (1932) is a stage-specific sequence of how intelligence develops. The first stage in the development of cognition, according to Piaget, occurs during the first two years of life and is known as the sensory motor period. This stage of development is heavily dependent on nurturing issues of mother-infant bonding in order for the infant to develop a sense of trust and emotional security for life. It is a time when almost all learning is processed directly through the sensory and motor systems (Coling 1991).

Based on developmental theory, therapeutic intervention with infants and children must be introduced through the tactile channels of the sensory system. Tactile input, including touching, rubbing, massaging, holding, applying firm pressure along with tight body wraps, and use of warmth or selected water baths, can soothe, calm, relax, and comfort an irritable, agitated infant or child. When tactile input alone fails to calm the child, the vestibular system must be activated through movement such as controlled rocking. A state of calm is necessary before learning and meaningful interaction can take place.

Understanding developmental theory provides a basis for recognizing how the normal infant learns and behaves. Understanding how to elicit normal behaviors is a necessary requisite for understanding and applying the treatment principles of sensory integration.

Sensory Integration

Occupational therapy with substance-exposed infants and children is heavily dependent upon the principles of sensory integration as described by A. Jean Ayres (1979). According to the Ayres theory, the primary function of the central nervous system is to organize sensation for functional use. The central nervous system is made up of three major subsystems: the vestibular, tactile, and proprioceptive systems.

The primary function of the vestibular system is to orient one's body to the environment. This system must be operating properly in order for sensory stimuli to be meaningful. The vestibular system is addressed through the dynamic interaction of the tactile and proprioceptive systems. Vestibular system disturbances do not allow the body to interact or adaptively respond to environmental stimuli. In other words, if the infant's adaptive response system is dysfunctional and out of control, it becomes the therapist's responsibility to externally control the infant and the environment. The therapist dims the lights in the nursery to reduce the intense brightness and overstimulation to the infant's eyes, and holds the infant close, using a combination of deep pressure, slow stroking, and rocking. These techniques help the infant begin to orient, calm, and gain control of the central nervous system reactions.

Proprioceptive techniques are more appropriately used to address the central nervous system symptoms of irritability, being difficult to calm, and jittery excessive movements, as commonly seen in drug-exposed infants. For example, treatment might include tightly swaddling the infant in a blanket (proprioception) with the baby's hands near the face and mouth to encourage hand sucking as a self-calming sensory feedback technique (Hyde and Trautman 1989). Further, the therapist may firmly and closely hold the baby and slowly rock while applying deep pressure. These techniques help calm and orient the vestibular system. Before other treatment goals can be achieved, the vestibular system must be addressed.

This theoretical approach emphasizes working on one bodily system at a time: vestibular system work before visual system work. Control of the vestibular system will allow a fussy baby to be taken home by an insecure and fearful mother or guardian.

Cultural Difference Approach

Boykin (1985, 1983) described what has come to be known as a very powerful and popular paradigm for therapists working with people from varying ethnic, racial, and family backgrounds. The cultural difference (CD) approach was developed out of a need to recognize and respond effectively to ethnic and racial diversity among children in the classroom. Historically, the American school curriculum reflected only the Euro-American style of learning and its standards and values as the norm. The cultural difference theory recognizes that people from different cultures have different lifestyles, value systems, and, perhaps, learning styles which are not inferior or abnormal, but different. The beauty of this approach is that it acknowledges various cultures without ranking any one culture as good or bad in relation to other cultures.

The cultural difference approach is a theoretical notion which alerts therapists that people of color—blacks, Hispanics, Asians, and Native Americans—have different values and lifestyles from Europeans, even though they might have grown up in the same neighborhoods and attended the same schools. This alert is important since many of the therapeutic principles of sensory integration require environmental changes such as a quiet, isolated, subdued environment and a high demand for one-on-one adult attention and supervised input. These requirements may run contrary to many childbearing cultural practices. In addition, major home environmental changes such as quiet and isolation may be virtually impossible to achieve. Therapists will need to find creative ways to adjust the therapeutic demands to the client's family culture and lifestyle. The therapist's role is to help integrate the drug-exposed child into the family milieu.

Consciousness of cultural difference alerts the therapist to watch for clues as to accepted cultural family behaviors. The therapists may note, for example, that an infant's father or mother visits the infant in the hospital on what appears to be a haphazard, irregular basis and usually when no therapists are around. The hospital staff, depending on ethnic and cultural difference backgrounds, may interpret these visits as showing little interest in the child. In reality, the parents may be concerned that more frequent visits may get in the way of expert care for the child, especially during prime treatment hours. Levine (1987) noted that knowledge of culture can make therapy more meaningful and influence therapeutic outcome.

Family members' interactions with the medical staff may be affected by cultural differences that relate to many different matters: a sense of time, sense of personal space, ideas of family and medical roles, sources of social and emotional support, education, age, style of dress, style of communication, expectations, and methods of expressing caring and respect. An awareness of these values, beliefs, and methods of expression may lead to establishing good rapport and effective treatment, with an excellent outcome.

Therapists need to explore involving the parent in the care of the child in a positive and rewarding way, and on the parent's own terms. Often caregivers from non-European cultures feel that hospital care, including therapy, is exclusively the province of hospital staff (experts), and that there is no expectation of their contributing as parents while the child is in the hospital. This difference in belief needs to be addressed in a positive way. Even if a parent comes to the hospital smelling of alcohol or obviously drunk, it is important to involve the parent in the concerns of the child, such as through an observational discussion. A parent who obviously may have been drinking may not be drunk. Perhaps the parent felt the need to drink in order to have the courage to visit. Scolding or ignoring the parent is not useful. It is important to involve the parent, if nothing more than with positive conversation about the infant. If the entire family comes to visit the child, staff must find ways to allow each family member to express an interest in the child. In many home environments, children are intimately involved in the direct care of younger children. Home programs should involve the family if that has been the response of the family to the child in the hospital. When striving to integrate the child into the home and family lifestyle, the therapist must be sensitive to economic conditions and demands on the family. Therapy is effective when the family achieves success at home with the substance-exposed child. The medical staff and the therapists must work together in a team effort to promote positive cultural interactions for the effective treatment of the infant.

The other critical cultural difference issue which underscores the power of cultures is that of the drug culture. The drug-addicted mother will display behaviors which might be more reflective of the drug culture than of the family culture. Know the hallmarks of the drug personality, and recognize that because drugs have power over the individual, the therapist cannot expect the mother to effectively respond to the child's needs and demands unless the mother's needs are professionally addressed and resolved.

The mother's needs and the child's needs are often the same, making the two of them highly incompatible. However, many an untreated mother will insist on taking the baby home, promising that she can and will take care of the infant. Sometimes this means that the infant provides a new source of money which may be used for drugs, and the infant's needs go unmet. Follow-up and home-care programs are sometimes serious failures primarily because therapists and medical caregivers accept the mother's word, underestimating the power of drugs over the individual. Untreated mothers are simply incapable of responding to the demands of the infant and of the well-intended therapist or medical caregiver.

When the mother underestimates the power of drugs in her life, she simply cannot reliably tell the therapist or the social worker this information in an interview format. In fact, the mother might think that she has the power to overcome the drug habit for the good of the baby simply by willing herself to do so. She truly believes that she has the power to stop. The staggering statistics of drug rehabilitation failures constantly remind us that a mother returning to the same home environment, without intervention or support, is destined for failure. Therapists and other team members must pay attention to the warning signs and develop realistic home-based follow-up programs. The therapists must be nonthreatening models and mentors for the drug-addicted mother. Recognizing and attending to the nurturing needs of the mother is more important than attending to the nurturing needs of the infant. Therapy must be a source of enjoyment and successful practical intervention which can be replicated by the mother at home. Know the treatment approaches, and adapt them to the lifestyle needs of the mother and baby.

References

Ayres, A. J. 1979. *Sensory integration and the child.* Los Angeles: Western Psychological Services.

Boykin, A. 1983. The academic performance of Afro-American children. In *Achievement and achievement motives,* edited by J. Spence. San Francisco: Freeman.

______. 1985. The triple quandary and the schooling of Afro-American children. In *The school achievement of minority children,* edited by U. Neisser. Hillsdale, NY: Erlbaum.

Coling, M. C. 1991. *Developing integrated programs: A transdisciplinary approach for early intervention.* Tucson, AZ: Therapy Skill Builders.

Hyde, A., and S. Trautman. 1989. Drug-exposed infants and sensory integration: Is there a connection? *Sensory Integration Special Interest Section Newsletter* (American Occupational Therapy Association) 12(4):1-6.

Levine, R. 1987. Culture: A factor influencing the outcome of occupational therapy. *Occupational Therapy in Health Care* 4:3-16.

Piaget, J. 1932. *The moral judgment of the child.* London: Routledge and Kegan Paul.

Chapter 10

Intervention Techniques with Substance-Exposed Infants

Cordelia H. Puttkammer, M.Ed., OTR/L

Because of the direct and indirect effects of maternal drug use on the embryo and fetus, drug-exposed neonates do not react normally to familiar parenting techniques. Their reactions are not uniform, either; each one is a distinct individual with damaged, or at least affected, sensory systems. Each infant needs to be evaluated to determine areas of strength and areas of need. It is not an easy task to understand these complicated neonates.

Similarly, each infant/caregiver pair needs to be evaluated for strengths and weaknesses. Some caregivers may be able to take each suggestion or behavior model and follow through, while other families may be able to do very little to modify their environment or their behavior. Professionals can try to take advantage of strengths in the caregiver, and perhaps minimize the impact of negative conditions that cannot be changed.

The most important thing that anyone can do when intervening with a family with a drug-exposed infant is to support positive aspects of the parenting. Parents want to do a good job with their children, and they need to be told that they're doing something right. When first going into a home, try to find one or two positive things, and point them out immediately. For example, any sign that the infant is glancing at the caregiver can be occasion for an approving remark such as, "It is so nice to see that Sarah is watching you." Perhaps the only positive thing you can note is that the infant is not screaming or seems well fed. Indeed, a contented, well-fed infant is cause for celebration.

The professional must approve of and hope to reinforce the positive, while overlooking that which may be unchangeable. If the house looks like a disaster area and everyone's clothes are dirty, but the baby is being held in a loving manner, rejoice! If the house is tidy and the clothes clean, but the infant is being held at arm's length, praise what is tidy and clean. Letting a family know that you notice and that you care can make a big difference. A supportive, confidence-building atmosphere can enhance the work of the professional and thus the effectiveness of the caregiver.

General Principles

Each neonate will have to be evaluated individually, but some general rules are useful when planning intervention.

1. Work or stimulate only one system at a time. For example, if you want a neonate to attend visually, do not use motion, sound, or light touch at the same time.
2. Start with the tactile system, which is the most highly developed at birth. But because there is a high incidence of tactile defensiveness in this population, watch for signs of distress.
3. The vestibular system has direct connections with stomach innervation. Stimulation of this system must be approached with great care; stomach upsets are particularly costly for these infants, many of whom already need to gain weight. Any time that regular steady movement (vestibular input) takes place, monitor for nystagmus (rapid, rhythmical movements of the eyes, which show that the infant is dizzy).
4. Because of the supersensitivity of many of these neonates, it is imperative to decrease light and noise.
5. When holding the infant, use firm contact on as much of the body surface as possible.
6. Calming is accomplished through simulating a womb-like environment—relatively dark, quiet, and confined, with gentle movement.
7. Have a large supply of clothing available for both the neonate and the caregiver, because of regurgitation, diarrhea, and perspiration.
8. Keep alert for signs of overstimulation: yawns, hiccups, sneezes, grimaces, changes in skin color, changes in respiration, and eye aversion or tightly closing the eyes.
9. Use normal patterns of motion, and try to elicit normal patterns of stimulation and response so that there will be less chance of abnormal development.

Five areas of infant care will show how intervention techniques can be used to facilitate development and to enhance infant-caregiver interaction. The techniques focus on the sensory system—the primary system affected by maternal drug use. The five areas discussed are: calming, interaction and play, feeding, holding and carrying, and dressing.

Calming

It is highly important and very basic that caregivers be able to calm their frantic infants. Inability to do so can lead to frustration, hostility, and a feeling of being rejected by the infant. These feelings can lead to the caregiver's rejection of the infant and, ultimately, to child abuse. By learning how to calm their infants, mothers begin to feel competent.

The first item to introduce at birth is a pacifier. It should be the smallest possible, soft and pliable, and of one-piece construction. Drug-exposed neonates have a frantic quality to their suck, and a rubber nipple that becomes detached from plastic mounting can all too quickly and easily become stuck in the trachea, with fatal results. Feeding nipples designed for preemies can be adapted as pacifiers by stuffing them with packing, such as cotton, and taping the opening that would cover the formula bottle. The pacifier then can be taped to a soft board (such as is used on elbows with IVs to hold the arm extended) and kept in place constantly for the infant's use. Two feeding nipples of appropriate size are the #339-03 Enfamil™ Premature Nipple (manufactured by Mead Johnson, Evansville, Indiana) and the blue twist-on Special Care™ Nipple Unit (by Ross Laboratories, Columbus, Ohio).

Equally important for calming is satisfying the infants' need for containment. In a hospital nursery, these are the newborns often seen huddled in a corner of their incubators. Keep them swaddled almost continually. Wrapping their hands near the face encourages self-calming by means of hand sucking (Sherman 1990).

Holding to calm and quiet an infant is natural. Some special techniques for holding can satisfy the universal need for comforting, and can provide the proprioceptive input (firm, deep pressure into the joints, muscles, and body) which is organizing for drug-afflicted neonates (Ayres 1979; Slavik et al. 1984).

Two positions seem to work best for calming and organizing. The first is the football hold, or anterior-posterior position. Hold the infant prone, with your hand and arm under the length of the stomach and chest. Your spread fingers can support the head, and the infant can be held close to your body, with the baby's left or right side pressed against your stomach and chest. Your other hand provides firm pressure on the infant's back. For the infant who spits up, a vertical hold is effective. Place the infant against your chest with both your hands providing deep proprioceptive input all down the neonate's back and buttocks. Also, a gentle rocking motion—shifting your weight from side to side—is helpful. Steady, firm rocking "bores the central nervous system" (Wilbarger and Royeen 1987) and helps the infant fall asleep.

In general, substance-exposed infants need to have as quiet and darkened a place as possible, because frequently they are supersensitive to sound and light. A blanket placed over the nursery incubator or crib can muffle the continual noise of the nursery as well as noise in most homes. The blanket also will decrease the amount of light the infants are exposed to in both nursery and home.

Respond quickly—within the first few minutes—to crying and distress. Once drug-affected neonates begin to cry, they become inconsolable and frantic. Because they will cry until they vomit or collapse into deep sleep, it is important to employ calming techniques as soon as possible. Unfortunately, these infants seem to find other infants' crying contagious. Since it's difficult to prevent this from happening, it is doubly important that the caregiver respond promptly and know many means of soothing the neonate. The more strategies available, the better are the chances of success.

For some neonates, a warm bath is calming and soothing, probably because it may simulate the feeling of being in the womb. But the dressing and undressing aspects of this activity are upsetting unless approached slowly and quietly. No one can be in a hurry with these infants. Movement at a deliberate pace and maximum skin-to-skin contact between baby and caregiver can make the bath a beneficial experience.

Oil massages are soothing for some substance-exposed neonates. Stimulation of the muscles is of general benefit, and the deep proprioceptive input is both organizing and calming. Constant pressure contact with the skin is important. Work from the center of the body out to the extremities. Most infants do not like their palms or soles of the feet massaged. Constant warmth is important, so keep the undressed infant near a radiator, register, or other source of heat.

Mechanical devices that simulate the vibrations and sounds experienced in utero promote a quiet state in newborns. Several soft, cuddly toys are marketed that have battery-operated heartbeat devices inside. Century Products manufactures both a Cuddle Clinic™ and a hammock with a "heart" that beats at about the optimum 72 times per minute. Similarly, a woman's voice between 24 and 84 decibels has been found to ease these agitated neonates. Soft and slow repetition of the child's name, quiet singing, and rhythmic speech are all effective.

Vocal or instrumental music can facilitate peacefulness, provided it is soft and repetitive. A tape recorder placed under or near the crib can help the infant fall asleep. Unfortunately, many families prefer much louder music that is stimulating to adults, but which is absolutely contraindicated for substance-affected infants.

In short, the best environment for these neonates is relatively dark and very quiet, without radio, TV, or noisy adults or children present. It is not possible to provide these conditions at all times; but if caregivers are aware of the consequences of overstimulation, they can make adjustments and accommodations. Professionals interacting with families can model optimal situations and make appropriate suggestions.

Interaction and Play

It is extremely difficult to elicit a quiet and alert state in these neonates. They are usually either in a deep sleep or awake and irritated. In addition, many receive sedation for up to 45 days with paregoric, phenobarbital, or diazepan. But a quiet, alert state is what permits an infant to be aware of the environment and receptive to interaction. Professionals and caregivers must take on the frustrating task of trying to calm down the affected infant and wake up the child's senses at the same time.

An infant learns a great deal about the world from birth onward through the visual system. Each day the neonate does not open the eyes is a day that the child falls behind normal peers. But the substance-affected newborn finds it natural to keep the eyes closed, especially in bright or direct light. There is a greater concentration of pain receptors and sensors in the eye than anywhere else in the body; the extrasensitive newborn needs a great deal of help and encouragement to look around.

The calming techniques described above should be useful in soothing general irritation. The mother should make it a practice to hold the infant close to her body with firm contact over as much of the baby's skin as possible to increase the feeling of containment. The pacifier is important, too, because the non-nutritive suck seems to help the infant achieve an alert state. Soft music and, especially, a mother's gentle voice will encourage the neonate to open and widen the eyes. Keeping the light dim, and turning the infant away from sources of light, are essential.

Once eye opening—or at least squinting—is achieved, a high-contrast figure can be presented about seven or eight inches away from the neonate's face. A small, white paper plate with circles inked in with a black marker is a suitable object. The Brazelton Neonatal Assessment Scale uses a two-inch-diameter red ball. Objects that are large and reflect light, such as a foil balloon or a foil-covered paper plate, are attractive to a neonate with immature vision. Since peripheral vision develops first, begin at about a 45° angle with a moving stimulus. Slowly move the item toward the midline, or from ear to nose. The sequence to follow in presenting moving objects is:

1. Slow movement from left to right
2. Movement from right to left
3. Movement in an arc
4. Movement in a circle
5. Later, movement on the diagonal

Ordinarily, only one sensory system should be stimulated at a time with these infants; noise and movement should not be paired with vision. But touch, as well as slight vestibular input, often helps to integrate vision in the slightly older infant. For example, one could gently rock the infant while giving encouragement to look at an object.

Slightly older infants can benefit from interaction using other sensory systems. Guiding the motions of their hands and feet is useful and rewarding. Not until about 12 weeks of age do infants voluntarily feel one hand with the other hand. At about 16 weeks, babies spontaneously touch their hands to their knees. At about 19 weeks, they touch hands to feet. This is soon followed by bringing a foot to the mouth. Facilitating babies' ability to perform these motions before they are able to do so spontaneously can be a satisfying game for both infant and caregiver.

Other ways to play with these infants are equally simple—touching, imitating (including sticking out the tongue or opening the mouth wide), singing, or the rhythmic touching and cheerful "conversation" often encouraged by families. Avoid sudden movement or the light touch which irritates hypersensitive infants. With older infants, play baby games such as peek-a-boo. Using the familiar slow and calm manner, place a light cloth on the baby's face, then help the baby grasp it and pull it down, while you speak a soft, gentle "boo." Then place the cloth over your face and repeat the actions. Using hands to cover the face will come later.

Feeding

Because these neonates often have a low birth weight or are small for gestational age (SGA) (MacGregor et al. 1987), intake is even more important than for typical newborns. Their diarrhea and constant spitting up or active vomiting contribute to intake and retention problems. Also, their active sweating means that intake needs are increased. But despite their voracious appetites, they have poor feeding skills (Priestly 1973; Young 1989), and often are poor or slow weight gainers.

Holding an infant at a 45° angle for feeding seems to be best for the majority. A prefeeding cheek massage seems to increase lip closure and decrease the loss of milk from the sides of the mouth. Gently rub the soft part of the newborn's cheeks in a circular pattern. With an older infant, try intra-oral stimulation with the pad of your finger. Gently stroke from the back of the gums forward to the center; this seems to facilitate a more normal and efficient suck and decrease liquid loss. (Some of these infants test HIV positive, so use precautions when feeding and changing.)

Most of these babies are not breast fed, so bottle and nipple selection must be addressed at once. During at least the first 48 hours, a hard preemie nipple with a small hole works best. Continue to use a preemie nipple for as long as the infant exhibits frantic sucking. When feeding skills improve, a softer nipple is appropriate.

During feeding, place the infant's hands on the warm bottle or on the breast. For increased soft tactile input, put a cloth cover on the bottle; a tube sock with both ends cut off will do very well. Most neonates enjoy the feel of a bottle cover as they suckle.

The normal burping posture and heavy pats on the back are not good for these neonates, because this technique promotes spitting up and vomiting. Instead, hold the infant upright on your lap. While exerting slight pressure on the abdomen, support and rub the infant's back. When the burp is felt or heard and the feeding is complete, place the infant prone (on the stomach). Use an angle or 45° wedge so that the baby's head is higher than the feet. Sometimes just placing the baby in this position facilitates the burp.

Small, frequent feedings are best for drug-affected neonates. Mothers need to be reminded that these infants will require larger amounts of formula. Their inefficiency in sucking, their voracious appetites, and their spitting up and vomiting add up to large requirements. A demand-feeding schedule is recommended unless there is a problem of weight gain; in that case, adhere to a schedule as much as possible. It is almost always best not to waken these infants to feed them.

Holding and Carrying

There are two keys to holding and carrying the substance-exposed neonate: slow movement, and contact with as much of the child's body surface as possible. Infants can sense very quickly and easily who is confident, comfortable, and firm in carrying them. Cuddle the infant close to your body to increase a sense of security. A "snuggly" for carrying, positioned facing the mother's front, is effective. For the older infant, a carrier strapped or tied to the mother's back is beneficial. These means of carrying provide maximum contact while providing a constant temperature, calming heartbeat, and the vestibular input which facilitates early motor competence (Ayres 1979).

There are other devices for positioning the infant while the mother goes about her tasks. A hammock tied to the crib is a good holding device. Comfort pads and cradle bouncers are calming. Water beds or pillows partially filled with warm water provide gentle, soothing vestibular input.

Placing the infant in a prone position during wakeful moments provides a change. Putting a rolled-up washcloth under the chest at about the armpits with the arms over the roll helps facilitate a head-lifting position (extension). A firm hand on the buttocks will help decrease excess extension in the infant's torso during this activity.

Dressing

Because most substance-exposed neonates perspire profusely, all-cotton garments are best. Cotton absorbs perspiration well and allows the body to regulate its own temperature. Cotton can be bleached easily and is less allergenic than manmade fibers.

Because of the frequent bouts of diarrhea that substance-affected infants experience, their diapers need very frequent changing. Also, these babies often have very sensitive skin and are more prone to skin irritations than "normal" neonates. Disposable diapers seem to aid the formation of skin rash; cotton diapers "breathe" and are therefore less likely to cause rash or irritation.

The autonomic nervous system of a substance-exposed neonate may remain unstable, and body temperature and skin color will be poorly regulated. The infant's extremities may get cold and blue. Simple pull-on booties and tube caps are useful; garments with attached hoods are ideal. Long gowns with drawstring bottoms ensure that the infant's feet aren't entirely unprotected.

But beware of anything tight-fitting, or anything that is tight when pulled over the head. These infants become frantic when a garment is pulled tightly over the head. Loose-fitting garments with simple fasteners work best. Examine clothing for ease of getting on and off as well as ease of laundering. Often a complete change is needed when diapering. These infants use lots of clothing, so it should be easy to use and easy to care for.

Keep a number of cotton-flannel receiving blankets on hand. Wrapping the neonate snugly with the hands close to the mouth provides contact and comfort. These infants show real distress when undressed and left nude. Clothing helps provide the organization and control that these infants desperately need.

Holding and feeding a newborn, dressing and playing with the baby, and soothing the child to a state of peace and calm are the essential tasks of infant care. They also must be the means of easing substance-exposed newborns into a jarring, uncomfortable, probably painful world and helping them toward normal development.

References

Alroomi, L. G., J. Davidson, T. Evans, P. Galea, and R. Howat. 1988. Maternal narcotic abuse and the newborn. *Archives of disease in childhood* 63:81-83.

Amiel-Tison, C., and A. Grenier. 1986. *Neurologic assessment within the first year of life.* New York: Oxford University Press.

Anderson, J. 1986. Sensory intervention with the preterm infant in the neonatal intensive care unit. *American Journal of Occupational Therapy* 40:19-25.

Ayres, A. J. 1979. *Sensory integration and the child.* Los Angeles: Western Psychological Services.

Cassel, Z., and L. Sander. 1975. Neonatal recognition process and attachment. Paper presentation, Society for Research in Child Development, Denver.

Chasnoff, I. J., W. J. Burns, and S. H. Schnoll. 1984. Perinatal addiction: The effects of maternal narcotic and non-narcotic substance abuse on the fetus and neonate. *National Institute of Drug Abuse Series* 49:220-25.

Chasnoff, I. J., W. J. Burns, S. H. Schnoll, and K. A. Burns. 1985. Cocaine use in pregnancy. *New England Journal of Medicine* 313:666-69.

Chasnoff, I. J., D. R. Griffith, C. Freier, and J. Murray. 1992. Cocaine/polydrug use in pregnancy: Two-year follow-up. *Pediatrics* 89(2):284-89.

Chaze, B. A., and S. Luddington-Hoe. 1984. Sensory stimulation in the NICU. *American Journal of Nursing* 1:68-71.

Chouteau, M., P. Namerow, and P. Leppert. 1988. The effects of cocaine on birth weight and gestational age. *Obstetrics and Gynecology* 72:351-54.

Condon, W., and L. Sander. 1974. Neonate movement is synchronized with adult speech. *Science* 183:99-101.

Dennis, W., and Y. Sayegh. 1965. The effects of supplementary experiences on the behavioral development of infants in institutions. *Child Development* 36:81-90.

Dubowitz, L. M., and V. Dubowitz. 1981. The neurological assessment of the preterm and full-term normal infant. *Infant Clinics in Developmental Medicine* 79. London: Spastics International Medical Publications.

Finnegan, L., R. E. Kron, J. F. Connaughton, and J. Emich. 1975. Assessment and treatment of abstinence in the infant of the drug-dependent mother. *International Journal of Clinical Pharmacology* 12:19-32.

Finnegan, L., R. Kron, J. Connaughton, J. Emich, and W. Wieland. 1973. Comprehensive care of the pregnant addict and its outcome on maternal and infant outcomes. *Contemporary Drug Problems* 1:795-809.

Ghodse, A. H., J. L. Reed, and J. W. Mack. 1977. The effects of maternal narcotic addiction on the newborn infant. *Psychology Medicine* 7:667-75.

Goodfriend, M., L. Shey, and M. Klein. 1956. The effects of maternal narcotic addiction on the newborn. *American Journal of Obstetrics and Gynecology* 71:29-31.

Gorski, J., D. Lewkowicz, and L. Huntington. 1987. Advances in neonatal and infant behavioral assessments. *Journal of Developmental and Behavior Pediatrics* 8:39-50.

Hill, R. M., and M. Desmond. 1963. Management of the narcotic withdrawal in the neonate. *Pediatric Clinics of North America* 10:67.

Howard, J. 1988. Developmental and behavioral concerns for infants of drug dependent mothers. Paper presentation, Developmental Interventions in Neonatal Care, San Diego, CA.

Hume, L. 1989. Observation of fetal behavior state with cocaine. *American Journal of Obstetrics and Gynecology* 161:685-90.

Kahn, E., L. Neuman, G. A. Polk, L. Finnegan, R. Kron, J. Connaughton, and J. Emich. 1969. The course of the heroin withdrawal syndrome in the newborn treated with phenobarbital or chlorpromazine. *Journal of Pediatrics* 75:495-500.

Kandel, D. B. 1989. Cessation of illicit drug use in young adulthood. *Archives of General Psychiatry* 46:109-16.

Klenka, H. M. 1986. Babies born in a district general hospital to mothers taking heroin. *British Medical Journal* 293:745-46.

Krammer, L., and M. E. Pierport. 1976. Rocking waterbeds and auditory stimuli to enhance growth of preterm infants. *Journal of Pediatrics* 88:297-99.

Lane, S. 1991. Fetal and neonatal consequences of in utero cocaine exposure. American Occupational Therapy Association Conference, Cincinnati, OH.

LeBlanc, M. 1987. Effects of intrauterine exposure. *American Journal of Diseases of Children* 141: 937-38.

Levy, J. 1975. *The baby exercise book–The first 15 months.* New York: Random House.

Linn, S., S. Schoenbaum, P. Stubblefield, R. Mason, R. Rosner, and K. Ryan. 1983. The association of marijuana use with outcome of pregnancy. *American Journal of Public Health* 73:1161-64.

Lipton, E. L., A. Stenschneider, and J. B. Richmond. 1965. The autonomic nervous system in early life. *New England Journal of Medicine* 273:201-08.

Little, B. B., L. M. Snell, V. R. Klein, and L. C. Gilstrap. 1989. Cocaine abuse during pregnancy: Maternal and fetal implications. *Obstetrics and Gynecology* 73:157-60.

MacGregor, S. N., L. G. Keith, I. J. Chasnoff, M. A. Rosner, G. M. Chisum, P. Shaw, and J. Minoque. 1987. Cocaine use during pregnancy: Adverse perinatal outcome. *American Journal of Obstetrics and Gynecology* 157:686-90.

Madden, G. 1986. Maternal cocaine abuse. *Pediatrics* 77:209-11.

Marcus, J., S. Hans, and R. Jeremy. 1984. Differential motor and state functioning in newborns of women on methadone. *Neurobehavioral Toxicology and Tetralogy* 4:459-62.

Meisels, S., and J. Shonkoff, Eds. 1990. *Handbook of early childhood intervention.* New York: Cambridge University Press.

Miller, J. E. 1988. *The language of toys: Teaching communications skills to special needs children–A guide for parents and teachers.* Rockville, MD: Woodbine House.

Mori, A. M. 1983. *Families of children with special needs: Early intervention techniques for the practitioner.* Rockville, MD: Aspen Publications.

Myers, B. J. 1982. Early intervention using Brazelton training with middle-class mothers and fathers of newborns. *Child Development* 53:462-71.

Neuspiel, D., and S. Hamel. 1991. Cocaine and infant behavior. *Developmental and Behavioral Pediatrics* 1:55-64.

Palmquist, H. 1975. The effect of the heartbeat sound stimulation on the weight development of newborn infants. *Child Development* 46:292-95.

Pinto, F., M. Torrioli, G. Casella, E. Tempesta, and C. Fundaro. 1988. Sleep in babies born to chronically heroin-addicted mothers: A follow-up study. *Drug and Alcohol Dependence* 21:41-47.

Priestley, B. L. 1973. Drug addiction and the newborn. *Developmental Medicine and Child Neurology* 15:200-201.

Robson, B. 1989. *Special needs in ordinary schools: Preschool provision for children with special needs.* London: Artillery House.

Robson, K. S. 1967. The role of eye-to-eye contact in maternal-infant attachment. *Journal of Child Psychology and Psychiatry* 8:13-25.

Roland, E., and J. Volpe. 1989. Effect of maternal cocaine use on the fetus and newborn: Review of the literature. *Pediatric Neuroscience* 15:88-94.

Rosen, T., and H. Johnson. 1988. Drug-addicted mothers, their infants, and SIDS. *Annals of the New York Academy of Sciences* 533:89-95.

Rossetti, L. M. 1990. *Infant-toddler assessment: An interdisciplinary approach.* Boston: Little, Brown.

Salk, L. 1973. The role of the heartbeat in the relationship between mother and infant. *Scientific American* 24-29.

Semmler, C. (Ed). 1989. *A guide to care and management of very low birth weight infants: A team approach.* Tucson, AZ: Communication Skill Builders.

Sherman, I. 1990. Early intervention and drug-exposed infants: A case study. *Occupational Therapy Forum* 5:1-4.

Shore, M., P. Brice, and B. Love. 1992. *When your child needs testing.* New York: Crossroads Publishing.

Slavik, B., P. Danner, J. Green, and A. Ayres. 1984. Vestibular stimulation and eye contact in autistic children. *Neuropediatrics* 15:33-36.

Smith, I., C. Coles, J. Lancaster, P. Fernhohh, and A. Falek. 1986. The effects of volume and duration of prenatal ethanol exposure on neonatal physical and behavioral development. *Neurobehavioral Toxicology and Teratology* 8:375-81.

Strauss, M., M. Andesko, J. Stryker, J. Wardell, and L. Dunkel. 1974. Methadone maintenance during pregnancy: Pregnancy, birth and neonate characteristics. *American Journal of Obstetrics and Gynecology* 120:895-900.

Strauss, M., M. Andesko, J. Stryker, and J. Wardell. 1976. Relationship of neonatal withdrawal to maternal methadone dose. *American Journal of Drug and Alcohol Abuse* 3:331-45.

Strauss, M., R. Starr, E. Ostrea, C. Chavez, and J. Stryker. 1976. Behavior concomitants of prenatal addiction to narcotics. *Journal of Pediatrics* 89:842-46.

Soloway, I., and D. Walters. 1976. Neonatal drug dependence: Developmental and bio-cultural considerations. *Addictive Diseases* 2:673-68.

Termine, N., and C. Izard. 1988. Infants' responses to their mothers' expressions of joy and sadness. *Developmental Psychology* 24:223-39.

Van den Daele, L. D. 1987. Modification of infant state by treatment in a rockerbox. *Journal of Psychology* 74:161-65.

Villarreal, S. F., L. E. McKinney, and M. H. Quackenbush. 1992. *Handle with care: Helping children prenatally exposed to drugs and alcohol.* Santa Cruz, CA: ETR Associates.

Weston, D., B. Ivins, B. Zuckerman, C. Jones, and R. Lopez. 1989. Drug exposed babies: Research and clinical issues. *Zero to Three* 9(5):1-7.

Wilbarger, P. 1984. Planning an adequate "sensory diet" application of sensory processing theory during the first year of life. *Zero to Three* 5:7-12.

Wilbarger, P., and C. B. Royeen. 1987. Tactile defensiveness: Theory, research, and treatment of sensory affective disorders. Workshop sponsored by Sensory Integration Special Interest Group of the District of Columbia Occupational Therapy Association, Bethesda, MD.

Wilbarger, P., and J. Wilbarger. 1988. Sensory affective disorders: Beyond tactile defensiveness, a new view of sensory defensiveness, hyper-responsiveness, and related emotional and social eccentricities. Professional Development Program, May 21-22, Philadelphia.

Wilson, G., M. Desmond, and W. Vernlaud. 1973. Early development of infants of heroin addicted mothers. *American Journal of Disease Child* 126:457-59.

Young, M. 1989. Presentation at Symposium on Perinatal Substance Abuse, March 29, Howard University, Washington, DC.

Zelson, C., E. Rubio, and E. Wasserman. 1971. Neonatal narcotic addiction: Ten-year observation. *Pediatrics* 48:178-89.

Zuckerman, B. 1991. Heavy drug users as parents: Meeting the challenge. Paper presentation, Protecting the Children of Heavy Drug Users. Williamsburg, VA.

Zuckerman, B. 1992. Crack kids: Not broken. In *Pediatrics.* Boston: American Academy of Pediatrics. (Reprints from B. Zuckerman, Boston City Hospital, Talbot 214, 818 Harrison Ave, Boston, MA 02118.)

Zuckerman, B., and K. Bresnahan. 1991. Developmental and behavioral consequences of prenatal drug and alcohol exposure. *Pediatric Clinics of North America* 38(6):1387-1406.

Zuckerman, B., D. A. Frank, R. Hingson, H. Amaro, S. M. Levenson, H. Kayne, S. Parker, R. Vinci,. K. Aboagye, L. E. Fried, H. Cabral, R. Timperi, and H. Bauchner. 1989. Effects of maternal marijuana and cocaine use on fetal growth. *New England Journal of Medicine* 320(12):762-68.

Chapter 11

Occupational Therapy with Substance-Exposed Toddlers and Preschool Children

Robin Lindauer Lang, OTR/L

Evaluation

Evaluating drug-exposed infants and toddlers can be a challenging task. Most of these children have very short attention spans, requiring frequent refocusing to task and the need for formal testing to be broken into segments. Formal evaluation tools might have to be adapted in order to provide useful information, since the child also may have cognitive deficits. This makes their norms invalid. In addition, many standardized tests do not look at the quality of the child's skills, which is an area of great importance for the drug-exposed child. However, by using standardized measures along with other assessment tools and observations, the evaluator can develop an overall picture of the child's level of functioning.

A great deal of information can be obtained with a caregiver interview. The interviewer might ask questions about the child's sleep patterns, eating habits, schedule, and temperament. Having the caregiver complete a sensorimotor history might be helpful. (See, for example, Wilbarger in Coling 1991, 43-44.) It is important to obtain the child's medical history, especially if intervention is not being given in a medical facility where this information is readily available. This background can provide therapists with information about events that occurred (seizures, reflux, bleeds in the brain, and other information) or procedures that were performed (for example, G-tube or shunt). The drug-exposed infant may experience apnea and reflux and may need supplemental oxygen and an apnea monitor, but typically does not need more serious medical intervention. However, if other intervention occurs, by reading the medical record and birth history the therapist can be alert to any condition that could impact on the course of therapy.

It can be beneficial to videotape the initial assessment for future reference and skill comparison. However, the evaluator needs to recognize that the camera may intimidate either the child or the caregiver. In that case, the evaluator could forego taping until a later session to avoid interfering with establishing rapport.

Depending on which disciplines are involved with a child and the type of setting in which intervention is provided, the definition and requirements of the therapist's role will change. Generally, the occupational therapist may be responsible for the evaluation of fine motor, sensory functioning, and visual perceptual skills. The occupational therapist also may be responsible for or only assist in assessing gross motor, oral motor and feeding skills, play, cognition, and behavior.

See page 82 for a list of commonly used evaluation tools. For a more complete list of evaluation tools, see Coling 1991, pages 107-120.

Here are some additional questions to ask when observing a child:

Sensory

1. How does the child respond to handling, touch, and movement?
2. What is the child's overall temperament?
3. If fussy, how easily is the child calmed, and by what method?
4. Does the child tolerate being undressed? How does the child respond to different textures of clothes?
5. How does the child respond to movement on or with different types of surfaces?
6. Will the child play with textured mediums (clay, rice, foam)? Does the child avoid particular textures (sticky, dry, prickly, others)?
7. Is the child hypersensitive to light or noise?
8. How does the child respond to textures and temperatures of food during feeding?

Motor

1. Does the child move easily or stiffly?
2. What is the child's overall muscle tone? Muscle tone in the extremities? In the trunk?
3. Does the child have difficulty with transitions (going from quadruped to sitting, half-kneeling, kneeling, and other positions)?
4. Does the child move only in straight planes (forward and back), or does the child use some trunk rotation (moving around the longitudinal axis of the body, being able to separate the hips from the shoulder girdle by twisting)?
5. Can the child move slowly and show control over the movement, or does the child propel self and use momentum?
6. Are there any asymmetries, or differences, between the left and right sides?
7. Does the child avoid one side or extremity or "posture" it (for example, hold one arm retracted and flexed in the air where it cannot be used to assist in a functional activity or when holding a toy in one hand); or does the child forget that the toy is there and try to grasp another one without releasing the first?

8. Is the child's base of support so wide that it prevents moving into another position?
9. Is the child "fixing" anywhere to try to maintain stability? (Notice especially the shoulders, neck, pelvis, and toes.)
10. How much support does the child need to sit in a chair or upright on the floor? Does the child prop on anything? What's the best position for the child to have active upper-extremity use?
11. From testing, what is the child's skill level in gross and fine motor skills?
12. What is the quality of those skills? Must the child sacrifice anything to achieve it? What kinds of compensations are made?
13. Does the child exhibit tremors (especially in the upper extremities and mouth)? Do they interfere with function?

Intervention

After the assessments are completed and the child's strengths and weaknesses are determined, intervention can begin. First, the team must meet with the child's family or caregiver and determine the goals of treatment and who will work on them. This is usually done by writing an Individualized Education Program (IEP) or an Individualized Family Service Plan (IFSP). The type of plan used is determined by the age of the child. Intervention can take various forms, depending on the needs of the child, the family, and the facility where the intervention is being provided. Professionals from various disciplines may work with the child. The child may receive intervention in a small group or in an individual setting. Depending on the child's age and needs, these services may be provided in a school or clinic, or in the home.

A general picture of an involved child may include the following:

- Abnormal muscle tone (usually, tight extremities and a low-tone trunk)
- Delayed motor milestones
- Poor quality of movements
- Tremors, particularly in the upper extremities and jaw
- Poor feeding skills; many also have reflux or other gastrointestinal problems, and may have inadequate weight gain
- Over- or underactive sense of touch
- Short attention span
- Distractibility
- Poor play skills
- Poor social skills
- Low frustration level
- Difficulty in calming self

Occupational therapy intervention can take various forms. An eclectic approach utilizing both NDT (neurodevelopmental treatment) and SI (sensory integration) theory has been helpful, since the child will have needs in many areas.

Part of the occupational therapy intervention will involve ongoing consultation with other team members and the caregiver in order to establish effective lines of communication. Enabling the caregiver to have successful interactions with the child is extremely important. Helping the caregiver to understand why certain positions are better than others for the child to use and modeling ways to encourage desired skill development can make a major impact on the effectiveness of therapy. Team members can help provide continuity of skills from one discipline to another. For example, the occupational therapist can help the speech-language pathologist be aware of positioning the child and of activities during the session to further reinforce the occupational therapist's goals of symmetry and bilateral coordination. The speech therapist can share play and cognitive goals with the occupational therapist, so the occupational therapist can incorporate cause/effect awareness, object permanence, or turn taking into the fine motor activities.

Areas of Treatment

Sensory

Drug-exposed children have problems with the sensory system from the very beginning. Their inability to perceive hunger, to regulate a sleep/awake cycle, and to calm themselves are all symptoms of difficulty with sensory processing. As these children become older, some of these problems are still apparent in other forms. These children may be oversensitive to touch. Soft touch may feel "ticklish" to them. They have difficulty screening out sensory information that is not important. For example, they need a quiet room in order to focus, and even background noises may be too distracting.

When providing therapeutic touch or massage to these children, it may be less aversive if you hold one of the child's hands and let the child perform the activity independently. Working in front of a mirror, so they can more easily see where they are being touched, may also help these children accept the tactile input.

Sometimes a child may have difficulty dealing with sensory input from more than one sense at a time. For example, it may be too difficult to find a toy hidden in the bowl of dried beans because the child cannot process the tactile input and interpret the visual stimulation as well. Adapt the activity. Initially, have the child just dig in the beans, then fill containers with them and dump them or cover the feet or hands with beans. At another time, play with hiding and finding the toy from under a bowl or a cloth. Once the child can accept these activities and appears successful with them, then ask the child to find the toy hidden in the beans. By breaking the activity into smaller and easier tasks, you can be sure not to overload the child's sensory system and cause frustration.

Many drug-exposed children need to be taught to play. They may learn a skill in one area of development or with one toy and may not be able to generalize it to another area or toy. For example, a child may learn to release a peg into a hole in the lid of a can, but must relearn when asked to release a poker chip into a slot in the lid. Drug-exposed children have a difficult time motor-planning novel tasks, and they appear to have a limited ability to utilize trial-and-error to solve problems. Each activity needs to be taught and practiced over and over again until it becomes part of their repertoire of skills.

Be aware of auditory distractions in the treatment area. If it is a noisy place, move to another room, put up a barrier to block the distraction, or play soft, soothing music or Hemi-Sync metamusic in the background. (See Morris in Coling 1991, 121.)

Here are some treatment strategies to help remediate the child's difficulties with processing sensory information. (See Ayres 1979 for more information on sensory processing deficits.)

- Brush the extremities and back with soft bristled brushes (surgical scrub brushes work nicely) and textured clothes (Wilbarger and Royeen in Coling 1991, 45).
- Massage with lotion or powder.
- Play with a vibrating toy or pillow (make one by using a vibrator inside a hand puppet), or use Tiger Paw™, available from Suzanne Evans Morris's catalog.*
- When rocking or swinging the child, be alert to how changes in position affect different parts of the vestibular system. A child may tolerate rocking front to back but may have difficulty with side-to-side movement, or may tolerate swinging while sitting upright but not while prone. Watch for autonomic changes (sweating, skin color, and so on) during vestibular activities.
- Use textured mediums. Rub whipped cream or foam soap on a mirror or table. Hide toys in tubs of uncooked beans, rice, water, or foam chips. Let the child sit in these media. (Watch that children don't put these things in their mouths.)

Oral Motor Feeding

This may be an area where the occupational therapist and the speech-language pathologist work together. (See Chapter 13.)

Motor

Many drug-exposed infants and toddlers have motor problems. Some of these problems may be subtle. Here are some things you may observe:

- Extremely elevated shoulders. These children appear to have no neck due to "fixing" in their shoulders to maintain postural control.
- Protruding abdomens due to inactive abdominal muscles
- Little dissociation between the lower extremities (inability to have legs in different positions); or the legs may mirror each other (with both extended or both flexed), making transitional movements very difficult

*New Visions, Route 1, Box 175-S, Farber, VA 22938. Tiger Paw™ is available at $10.00.

- Little trunk rotation, tending to move in a front/back plane, or to pull self with arms to propel movement
- Inability to control and grade movements to slow down, moving quickly to use momentum instead of control
- Inability to tolerate upper-extremity weight bearing on elbows, with elbows directly under shoulders or on hands with shoulders directly over hands, or in prone or puppy prone. (These children tend to use increased flexion to "escape" direct weight bearing.)
- Walking on the toes, or curling the toes when trying to keep balance
- Posturing one or both arms; or both arms may not be used simultaneously

These children usually have difficulty using mature movement patterns due to hypotonicity of the trunk and poor postural stability. They tend to "fix" in the shoulder girdle and pelvis. They need work on weight shifting, trunk rotation, dissociation between their lower extremities, transitional movements, and upper-extremity weight bearing. The therapist may also need to help adapt highchairs, strollers, car seats, or table and chairs so the child can have appropriate seating for optimum functioning. The best seating position for these children is to sit with the back resting against a surface, with hips, knees, and feet at about 90° flexion, and with feet resting solidly on the floor or a footrest.

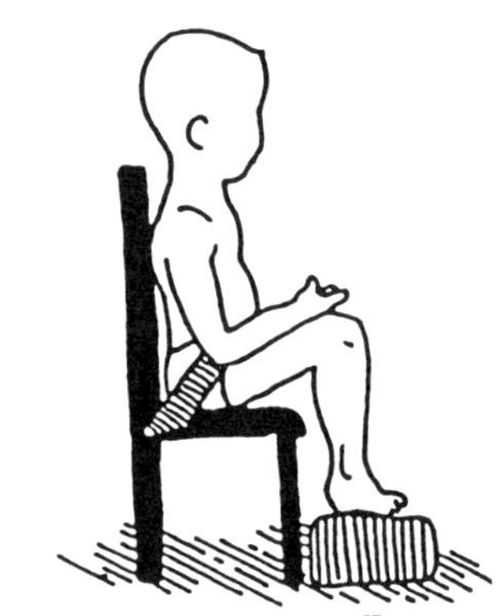

A child who does not have to expend energy to remain sitting can better perform required tasks such as eating or fine motor activities. It is important to discuss positioning with the caregiver. It also may be helpful to demonstrate one or two positions the caregiver can use when holding, playing with, and feeding the child.

Treatment Strategies

WORKING AT OR ON BENCHES

1. For kneeling, half-kneeling, and squatting
2. For pulling to stand and cruising (holding onto furniture while taking steps)
3. Sitting on and rotating trunk to play with a toy at one side

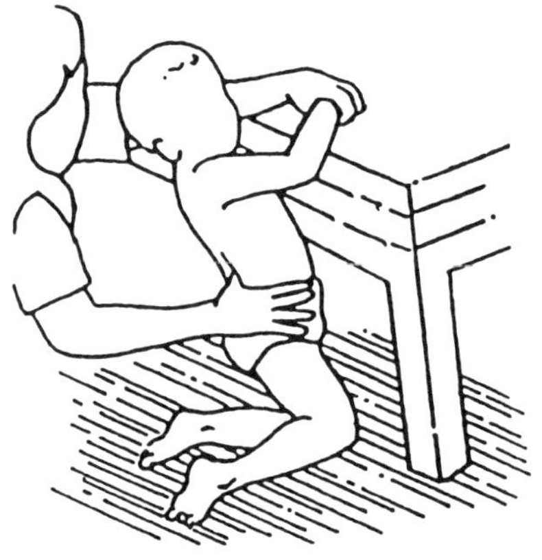

*The illustrations on pages 78-81 are reprinted from *Developing Integrated Programs: A Transdisciplinary Approach for Early Intervention* by Marcia Cain Coling. © 1991 by Therapy Skill Builders, a division of Communication Skill Builders, Inc., P.O. Box 42050, Tucson, AZ. Reprinted by permission.

4. Using the bench as a table, with a smaller bench to sit on
5. Prop a roll from the floor to the bench. Straddle the roll with both feet touching the floor.
6. For sitting on the edge with feet on the floor while working on upper-extremity exercises or reaching activities

THERAPEUTIC BALLS

1. Vestibular input: Rocking or bouncing in sitting, prone, or supine
2. Transitional movements: On top of ball in prone, sidelying, supine, sitting, and other positions
3. For righting head and neck and for lateral flexion
4. To improve equilibrium and balance reactions
5. Weight bearing on upper extremities in prone, shoulder girdle in supine and side

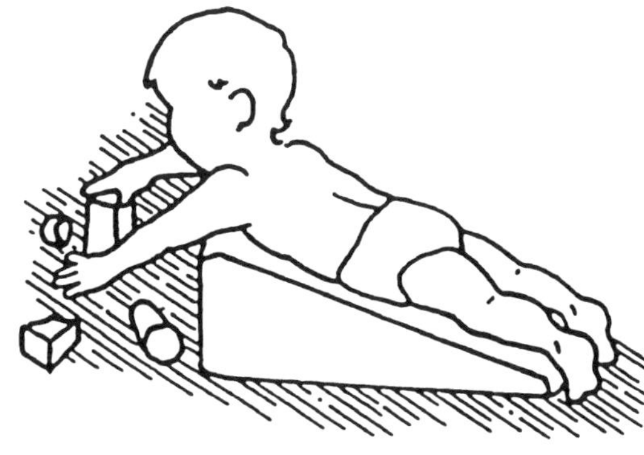

WEDGES

1. Prone over a wedge for upper-extremity weight bearing of fine motor tasks
2. Supine on a wedge to encourage reaching into the air
3. Sitting on the wide end, with a bench for a table (helps child to maintain flexion in hips)

ROLLS

1. Under chest and arms, for upper-extremity weight bearing with support
2. Sitting on (straddling or as a seat), to assist in facilitating weight shifting
3. Straddling while one end is elevated on a bench

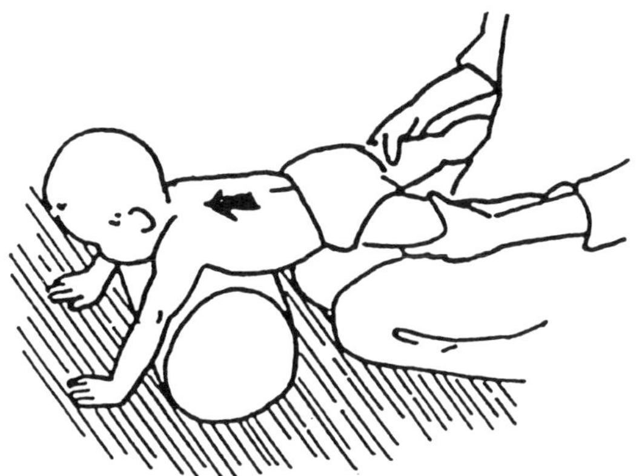

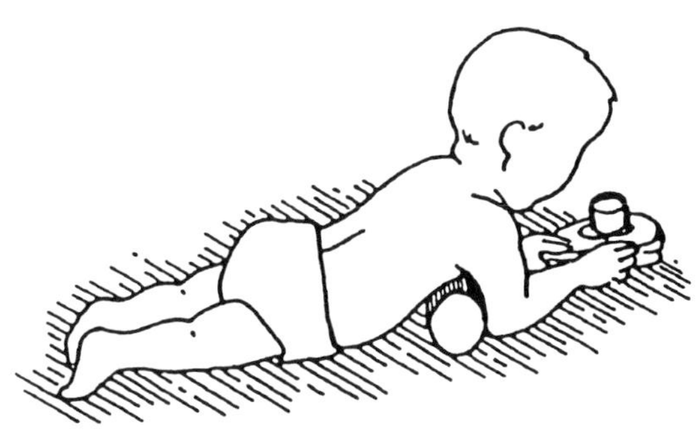

Fine Motor

Some of the fine motor problems encountered in the drug-exposed toddler include:

- Immature grasp patterns
- Poor midline control
- Poor bilateral hand use, either for reciprocal movements or for stabilization with one hand and movement with the other
- Difficulty with in-hand manipulation
- Poor tool use and pencil and scissor skills
- Tremors, especially when arms are off supporting surfaces (such as to stack blocks for a tower)
- Decreased hand strength

Treatment Strategies

TO IMPROVE SHOULDER GIRTH STABILITY

1. Weight bearing on scapulae in supine
2. Upper-extremity weight bearing, in prone (on elbows or extended arms), side sitting, with or without support
3. Horizontal weight bearing against a surface: Pulling vinyl-cling forms off a mirror, playing with foam on a mirror
4. Reaching up to put rings on a stick held by the therapist
5. Pushing a toy shopping cart while walking (Cart can be weighted with cans for more resistance and stability.)

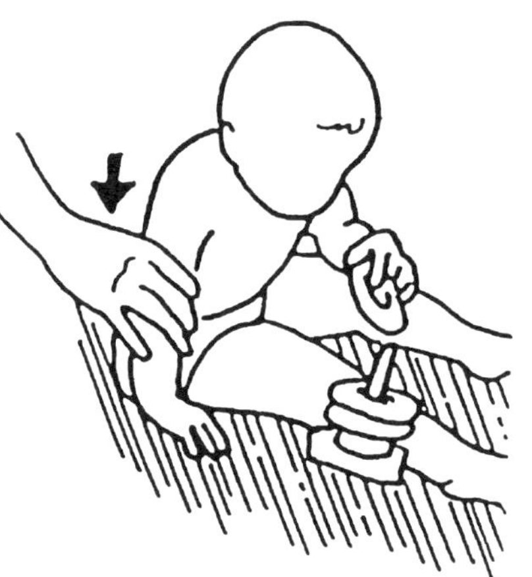

6. Pushing down to activate a toy (Some large toys with levers or buttons to be pushed require two hands. Usually, something spins when the button is pushed.)
7. Helping the child roll and catch large therapy balls (This is a good activity for involving siblings or the caregiver.)

TO IMPROVE BILATERAL HAND USE AND MIDLINE ORIENTATION

1. Encourage the child to hold a toy with one hand and activate it with the other. Start with your hands over the child's hands.
2. Present two-handed activities–pop beads, large wooden beads strung on thin plastic tubing (from an aquarium store), straws, or pipe cleaner; magnetic wands and chips; pulling apart therapy putty or clay to find hidden plastic figures.
3. Encourage side-sitting with weight on one arm, with activities positioned so the child's opposite hand will be at midline or across midline.

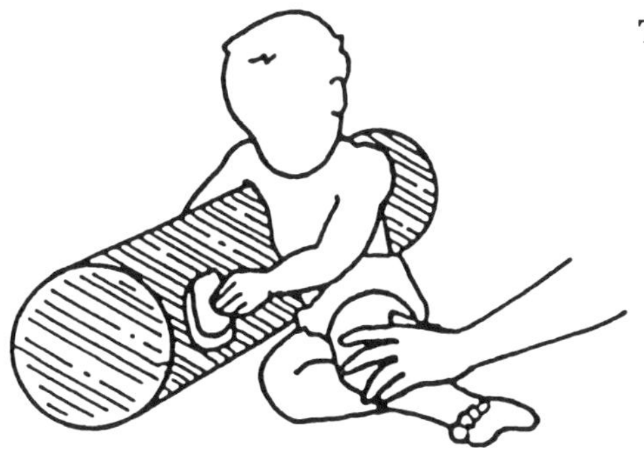

TO IMPROVE FINE MOTOR SKILLS

1. Put pegs in pegboards, then take them out.
2. Put pellets in small bottles.
3. Put coins or poker chips in slots.
4. Play with poke-toys with dials.
5. Put cereal pieces in small bottles.
6. Poke pieces of foam or sponge through holes in margarine-container lids.
7. Put small plastic figures into empty toilet paper rolls.
8. Put blocks in coffee cans. (Cut various-sized holes in lids; kids like the sound they make as they drop.)
9. Push buttons on electronic toys and pianos.
10. Squeeze squirt toys or triggers on squirt bottles during water play. Look for two-handed squirt toys, where one hand is needed to stabilize the toy while the other activates it.

TO IMPROVE PENCIL GRASP

1. Crayons and markers. Some marker sets have “magic” marking pens that change the color or erase what was colored.
2. Crayon rubbings. Place an object under paper, and rub hard with a crayon to make a design. Tape the design and paper to a wall, and encourage horizontal upper-extremity weight bearing.
3. Work on an easel or slant board for a variation.
4. Break crayons into smaller pieces to prevent holding too high on the shaft.
5. Glue sticks and scraps of paper to make a collage.

TO IMPROVE SCISSOR SKILLS

1. Rip paper. Encourage opposing movements of both hands (one hand forward, one hand back) rather than pulling the paper apart.
2. Rip strips of holes from edges of computer paper. Stabilize the paper with one hand; rip with the other.
3. Use plastic knives to cut clay or putty.
4. Use scissors to cut putty snakes into pieces.
5. Use tweezers or tongs to pick up small pieces of sponge and put them into a container.

Hints

Keep in mind the behavioral components of drug-exposed children. They are easily distracted visually and auditorily, and they may have short attention spans. Low frustration tolerance and limited problem-solving capabilities also impede their ability to cope. These are important characteristics to share with the mother so she can learn to better help her child.

When coordinating several therapies, it may be helpful to have physical therapy before occupational therapy or speech. Initial work on trunk control can assist in the child's ability to sit and to use the hands for fine motor activities, or the mouth for feeding or speech. Sometimes a child may need sensory input before tolerating handling in physical therapy, so it may be helpful to have occupational therapy first. It may be necessary to juggle therapies if the child's attention drifts in the last therapy due to fatigue. Coordination of services can be a very important aspect of treatment for these children.

References

Ayres, A. J. 1979. *Sensory integration and the child.* Los Angeles: Western Psychological Services.

Coling, M. C. 1991. *Developing integrated programs: A transdisciplinary approach for early intervention.* Tucson, AZ: Therapy Skill Builders.

Some Commonly Used Evaluation Tools

Bayley, N. 1992 *Bayley scales of infant development–R.* San Antonio, TX: The Psychological Corporation.

Beery, K. 1989. *Developmental test of visual motor integration.* Cleveland: Modern Curriculum Press.

DeGangi, G. A., and R. A. Berk. 1983. *DeGangi-Berk test of sensory integration.* Los Angeles: Western Psychological Services.

De Gangi, G. A., and S. I. Greenspan. 1989. *Test of sensory function in infants (TSFI).* Los Angeles: Western Psychological Services.

Early learning accomplishment profile for developmentally young children (E-LAP). 1978. Winston-Salem, NC: Kaplan Press.

Erhardt, R. 1982. *Developmental hand dysfunction: Theory, assessment, and treatment.* Tucson, AZ: Therapy Skill Builders.

Gardner, M. 1986. *Test of visual motor skills (TVMS).* Burlingame, CA: Psychological and Educational Publishers, Inc.

Miller, L. J. 1982. *Miller assessment for preschoolers (MAP).* San Antonio, TX: The Psychological Corporation.

Morris, S. E., and M. D. Klein. 1987. *Pre-feeding skills: A comprehensive resource for feeding development.* Tucson, AZ: Communication Skill Builders.

Peabody developmental motor scales. 1983. Allen, TX: DLM.

Rogers, S., and D'Eugenio, D. 1981. *Early intervention developmental profile.* Ann Arbor: University of Michigan Press.

Vineland Social Maturity Scale. 1984. Circle Pines, MN: American Guidance Service.

Readings

Ayres, A. J. 1979. *Sensory integration and the child.* Los Angeles: Western Psychological Services.

Boehme, R. 1988. *Improving upper body control: An approach to assessment and treatment of tonal dysfunction.* Tucson, AZ: Therapy Skill Builders.

_____. 1990. *Approach to treatment of the baby* Revised. Tucson, AZ: Therapy Skill Builders

Click, M., and J. Davis. 1982. *Moving right along: Developing goals for physically disabled children.* Phoenix, AZ: Educational Corporation.

Johnson-Martin, N., K. Jena, S. Attermeier, and B. Hacker. 1991. *The Carolina curriculum for handicapped infants and toddlers with special needs* 2d ed. Baltimore: Brooks Publishing Co.

Moore, C. 1990. *A reader's guide for parents of children with mental, physical, or emotional disabilities.* Rockville, MD: Woodbine Press.

Siegling, L., and M. Click. 1984. *At arm's length: Goals for arm and hand function.* Phoenix, AZ: Educational Corp.

Chapter 12

Physical Therapy with Substance-Exposed Infants and Toddlers

Kathleen Harp, M.H.S., PT, PCS, and
Andrea Santman Wiener, PT, PCS

In recent years, there has been an increase in illicit drug use by pregnant women. This phenomenon transcends socioeconomic groups. It is often associated with lack of prenatal care, poor nutrition, polydrug use, lack of education, poor preparation for motherhood, and a paucity of family and community support. All of these factors combine to put the unborn child at risk.

Children born to these women often have neuromotor, musculoskeletal, cognitive, and social-emotional problems. There has been a plethora of research that attributes these problems to substance abuse; however, it remains unclear whether these developmental problems are solely the result of substance abuse or of other risk factors. Regardless of the cause, developmental problems exist in many of these children. Often these children are seen by a variety of developmental specialists including physicians, psychologists, speech-language pathologists, occupational therapists, educators, social workers, and physical therapists. These professionals work as a team with the family to promote an optimal outcome for the child.

The purpose of this chapter is to explain the role of physical therapy in the treatment of children, from birth to two years, who were exposed to environmental toxins. First, the role of the physical therapist will be discussed. This will be followed by a description of the common neuromotor problems these children exhibit. Finally, an explanation of the evaluation, treatment planning, and intervention strategies used with this population will be reviewed.

The Physical Therapist

A physical therapist is a professional who has been trained to address problems in motor development. Problems with motor development can include muscle tightness, muscle weakness, tremors, joint contractures, bony deformity, and delayed attainment of developmental milestones. Physical therapists use both objective and subjective evaluation tools to identify problems and plan individualized treatment programs for their patients. They take into account other factors which may accentuate the motor problems, such as the child's neurobehavioral state or extrinsic environmental factors.

The role of the physical therapist who works with children who have been exposed to environmental toxins is to address these children's motor development needs. This process involves assessment, treatment planning, and intervention. However, this process does not occur in isolation. The physical therapist is just one member of a team of which the most important members are the family (Abel 1991).

Assessment

Physical therapy for the child begins with an assessment. Initially, the physical therapist consults the family and other team members to determine their concerns relative to the child's motor development. This is followed by clinical observations made by the therapist. A formal standardized assessment may or may not be performed.

It may take careful questioning and prodding for the physical therapist to ascertain the family's concerns regarding the development of their child. After explaining the physical therapist's role to the family, the therapist may ask an open-ended question. This may be difficult for the family to answer. Specific questions (such as, "Does your baby spend more time sleeping than you think he should?" or "Does your baby feel stiff when you hold her?") may be more helpful in identifying the family's concerns. After the family has articulated their concerns–or if they are unable to articulate concerns–it may be helpful to explain to the family the motor development concerns that other team members have expressed.

Ideally, the therapist begins to make clinical observations about the child during the interview process. If the child is not in the room, the observations will begin after the initial interview. There may be times when the therapist performs clinical observations and formal assessments before meeting with the family. However, it is preferable to meet with the family first and have them present for the assessment process so they can learn more about their child.

Clinical observations are made of the musculoskeletal system, the neuromotor system, and the neurobehavioral system. Observations of the musculoskeletal system include range of motion, postural alignment, and strength. Evaluation of the neuromotor system involves observations of muscle tone and quality of movement. In terms of the neurobehavioral system, the therapist is looking at the infant's ability to maintain a quiet alert state for optimal interaction (Russell and Free 1991). The therapist takes the information gathered from these observations and uses it to identify problem areas and develop a treatment plan.

Formal assessment provides the therapist with an objective measurement of the infant's developmental level. Commonly used assessment tools include the *Bayley Scales of Infant Development* (Bayley 1969, 1992) and the *Peabody Developmental Motor Scales: Gross and Fine Motor* (Folio and Fewell 1983). Although these tools provide objective measurements and are well standardized, there are drawbacks to using these tests as well. For example, in one study the Bayley was not found to be sufficiently sensitive in identifying clinically observable motor dysfunction in these infants (Resnick et al. 1977).

Treatment Planning and Intervention

Treatment planning and intervention begin with using the information gathered in the assessment to formulate a list of the child's strengths and needs. There are a multitude of developmental problems commonly found in infants exposed to environmental toxins. To best relay this information to the reader in a useful way, the more common problems and ideas for intervention will be discussed.

In their first two years, children exposed to environmental toxins display various problems that affect their motor development. The actual mechanism or cause for many of these problems is not clearly understood. Some children have intrauterine growth retardation, interventricular hemorrhage, or cerebrovascular accidents, any of which can assuredly lead to delays in motor development. These problems are generally in conjunction with prematurity, and substance abuse cannot be proven as the isolated cause of these conditions. However, some full-term, otherwise healthy infants born to mothers who abused cocaine during their pregnancies demonstrate neuromotor delays. These infants typically display difficulty moving against gravity, show poor quality of movement as evidenced by jerky, stiff movements, and tend to exhibit excessive extensor posturing (Schneider 1990).

The common areas in which neuromotor problems are identified during physical therapy assessment of these children will be discussed. A brief description of prenatal neuromotor responses will be provided. This will be followed by a review of problem areas during the postnatal period. Finally, treatment planning and intervention for specific neuromotor problems in these areas will be covered.

The Prenatal Period

Although the physical therapist is not involved in the care of these children prenatally, it is interesting to note the motor behavior of the fetus exposed to environmental toxins. Hume et al. (1989) performed a study looking at the prenatal behavioral state of 20 infants of mothers who had used cocaine during their pregnancies. Using ultrasonography, the behaviors studied included fetal heart rate variability, breathing motion, body tone and movements, and chin, mouth, and eye movements.

The researchers found abnormal behavioral states in 13 of the 20 infants. The abnormalities observed included increased fetal motion, increased eye and sucking movements, excessive flexion of the infant, irritability, and increased heart rate. In addition, the authors found that six of the fetuses displayed growth retardation . They also reported the neonatal outcome of these infants. They found that the 13 infants displaying abnormal behavioral state prenatally demonstrated this postnatally as well. In the neonatal period, these infants demonstrated tremors in their extremities, hyperresponsiveness, fast breathing, and difficulty with arousal.

The Postnatal Period

It is difficult to ascertain the effects of one type of substance abuse from another (Sztuman et al. 1990). In addition, it is difficult to determine the effects of environmental toxins versus other risk factors such as poor prenatal care and poor nutrition. However, there are several common areas in which children exposed to environmental toxins display difficulties.

One of the most frequently encountered problems with these infants is a poor ability to self-regulate their neurobehavioral state. This is not specifically a problem of motor development, but it is something that can significantly affect the acquisition of developmental milestones. The normal infant displays several states of arousal, from deep sleep to a quiet alert state to a state of crying (Randall et al. 1991; Russell and Free 1991). The healthy infant spends time in each of the phases. As the child grows, there is proportionately more time spent in the quiet alert state. The quiet alert state is optimum for interaction with the environment and for learning (Brazelton 1973).

Infants exposed to environmental toxins have difficulty achieving and maintaining a quiet alert state. According to Griffith (1988) and Schneider (1990), there are four behavioral responses common to cocaine-exposed infants. The first response is that infants will withdraw into a deep sleep in response to stimulation. They will not arouse with handling, making interaction with the environment difficult.

The second response is one of agitated sleep. The infant remains asleep in response to environmental stimuli but exhibits signs of stress such as color changes. Again, this makes interaction with the environment difficult.

In the third response, these infants tend to oscillate between deep sleep and agitated crying. When in a deep sleep, they are difficult to arouse; and when they are in a state of agitated crying, they are quite difficult to console. This sets up a situation that is frustrating for caregivers as well as detrimental to the developmental progress of the child.

The fourth behavioral response is one in which the child is able to achieve a quiet alert state. However, this is only for short periods of time, and the child often requires the assistance of the caregiver to maintain the state. This has been termed a panicked awake state (Griffith 1988; Schneider 1990).

The many problems such an infant displays with controlling and maintaining the neurobehavioral state significantly impacts the motor system. Due to the brief period these infants spend in the quiet alert state, it is difficult for them to interact with their environment through motor acts such as controlled batting at nearby objects, reaching, or rolling the body. In addition, when the child is inconsolable or remains in a deep sleep, muscle tone abnormalities (which will be discussed later) will be compounded.

Poor development of antigravity flexion control is a problem common to many infants exposed to environmental toxins (Chasnoff 1989; Schneider 1990). Antigravity flexion refers to the infants' ability to move their limbs toward the body against gravity. Problems with antigravity flexion can cause a paucity of movement and decreased quality of movement. Commonly, with the substance-exposed population, tremors and poor coordination of movement are noted (Randall et al. 1991; Russell and Free 1991). This is most easily illustrated by considering an infant lying on its back. Typical infants easily reach for things placed above their bodies. They kick their legs, bringing their buttocks off the floor, clasp their hands in midline, and bring their feet to their mouths. Infants displaying problems with antigravity flexion have difficulty performing all of these activities. These are not only important motor skills, but they provide children with a means to explore and learn about their bodies and the environment. Difficulty with these activities, coupled with other risk factors such as poor parenting skills, places these children at great risk for cognitive delays as well as motor delays.

Problems with antigravity flexion continue to affect motor development in terms of independent mobility and upright postures as well. These children demonstrate difficulty with rolling, sitting, quadruped, crawling, standing, and walking. Often they will find an atypical way to move which may be inefficient and place abnormal biomechanical stresses on their bodies. Abnormal biomechanical stresses over a long period of time can result in secondary problems such as joint contracture and bony deformity, which can further affect their motor functioning.

Atypical muscle tone is a third area in which these infants often display difficulty (Schneider 1990; Schneider and Chasnoff 1987). These infants often feel very stiff or very floppy. The term *hypotonic* may be used to describe infants with low tone, while *hypertonic* is a commonly used term to describe infants displaying stiffness. In addition, infants with hypertonia commonly exhibit tremulousness of the extremities. Family members may relate that their stiff infants are very strong. However, most often, the infant's extensor musculature (the muscles on the back side of the body) is active, while the flexor musculature is relatively inactive. This relates to the difficulty with antigravity flexion described above. The stiffness in these infants makes them difficult to hold and cuddle and may make interaction with the infant difficult. In addition, the stiffness makes it more difficult for the infant to move. Often these infants will display only a limited variety of movement patterns.

Floppy infants have difficulty activating their extensor as well as their flexor musculature. These infants often exhibit poor head control, decreased initiation of movement, decreased responses to their environment, and a poor ability to move against gravity. As one would expect, these characteristics place the infant at risk for delayed development in all areas.

Finally, there is a low incidence of congenital anomalies found in this population (Farrar and Kearns 1989). A detailed discussion of the various congenital anomalies found in this population is beyond the scope of this chapter. However, anomalies of the musculoskeletal and cardiac systems certainly impact motor development.

In summary, there are four common areas in which infants exposed to environmental toxins exhibit difficulties that can affect their motor development. The first, self-regulation of neurobehavioral state, although not a problem of the motor system, can directly affect motor development. The second problem, concerning control of antigravity flexion, is a problem of the neuromotor system and can significantly affect motor development throughout the first two years of life. Third, atypical muscle tone is common in these infants. It is often classified as stiff (hypertonic) or floppy (hypotonic). Atypical muscle tone can affect motor development throughout the first two years of life. Finally, there is a low incidence of various congenital anomalies which can impact the motor system of the developing infant.

Physical Therapy Intervention

An integral part of physical therapy is teaching movement. It is through movement that children learn motor skills and explore their environment. Children born exposed to environmental toxins, displaying problems in one or more of the four areas previously described, are at risk for motor development delays. The physical therapist will focus treatment on addressing the neuromotor needs of the child in a functional manner which promotes motor-skill learning and exploration of the environment.

Typically, the physical therapy session may last from 30 minutes to one hour and will address the problems identified during the assessment process. Before beginning a session, the physical therapist will speak to the family and other caregivers such as nurses, and will read the medical chart if it is available. During treatment, the child is provided opportunities for independent, spontaneous, and assisted movement. Practice, introduction of new motor skills, and education are the important components of intervention.

Practice is necessary to learn new motor skills. Therapy is essentially a time to practice new motor skills. For instance, the physical therapist may be working on an infant learning to bring the hands to midline. The therapist would assist the child as needed to bring the hands together to hold the edges of a blanket. The child would be encouraged to do this in several different positions such as supine, sidelying, and supported sitting. This would provide an opportunity for the child to practice the skill in a functional manner in different positions.

Because infants exposed to environmental toxins often have difficulty controlling and maintaining their behavioral states, it is necessary to practice skills slowly. It may be helpful to reduce the effects of other stimuli in the room. For example, a quiet environment with soft lighting may assist the infant in maintaining a quiet alert state during practice of motor skills. Finally, the infant may tolerate only a brief amount of practice of a single skill. The therapist respects this and terminates the session if the child becomes overstimulated.

Introduction of new skills is also emphasized during intervention. A new skill can be a small movement, such as a weight shift in prone on elbows to allow the infant to reach, or a larger movement, such as rolling supine to prone. It is important when practicing new skills to keep the infant's frustration to a minimum. Excessive frustration may cause the infant to move into a state of agitated crying or deep sleep. In either case, the infant does not benefit from the intervention.

Education of the family occurs throughout the session. The therapist describes what is being observed and how the activities being used are addressing the child's neuromotor needs. If it is not possible for the family to be present during a session, keeping a chart with illustrations is helpful. Videotaping may be an option if the family has a VCR. Polaroid pictures are helpful and can be placed in the charts with descriptions.

Finally, the physical therapist will need to continually reassess the child's strengths and needs. Changes in environment, such as hospital to home and caregiver changes, can profoundly affect the infant's neuromotor functioning. The therapist also will maintain communication with personnel in other disciplines involved with the child and family.

The following discussion will center on treatment strategies which the physical therapist commonly uses when treating infants exposed to environmental toxins. First, positioning will be reviewed. Therapeutic positions and the problems they address will be discussed. Second, treatment techniques to assist children in controlling their neurobehavioral states will be provided. Third, treatment strategies for problems of antigravity flexion and atypical muscle tone will be reviewed. The problems that will be addressed include poor head control, poor hand-to-foot play, rolling, and poor reaching and midline skills. Treatment strategies for various congenital anomalies are beyond the scope of this chapter.

Positioning

Positioning is an essential component of treatment. It is easy for the family and other caregivers to implement positioning techniques. Proper positioning improves muscle tone, promotes good postural alignment, facilitates developmental skills, and provides the child with different views of the environment.

Therapeutic positions frequently used include sidelying, prone, supine, and sitting. Sidelying promotes midline skills, facilitates good muscle tone, and encourages reaching and good shoulder alignment. Deficiencies in midline skills, reaching, and shoulder alignment are all problems related to poor antigravity flexion. In sidelying, gravity is eliminated, making the practice of these skills easier. A child placed in sidelying should be well supported. Blanket rolls should be placed behind the child to maintain the position. A roll also can be placed between the legs to promote neutral hip alignment and limit pressure between the legs. The infant may be provided something to hold onto to promote good shoulder positioning and midline skill development.

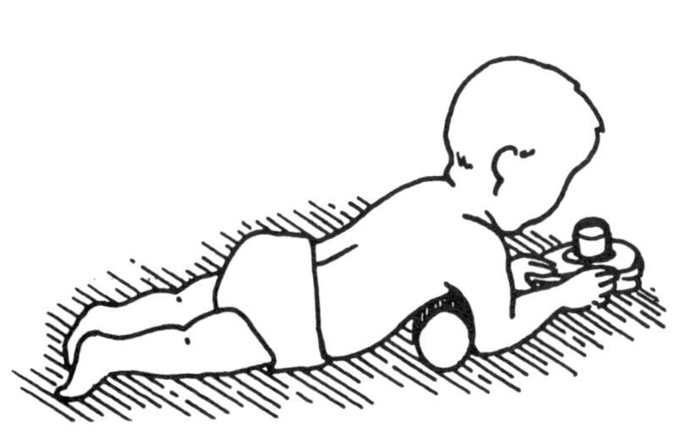

Prone

The figures on pages 89-90 are reprinted from *Developing Integrated Programs: A Transdisciplinary Approach for Early Intervention* by Marcia Cain Coling. © 1991 by Therapy Skill Builders, a division of Communication Skill Builders, Inc., P.O. Box 42050, Tucson, AZ 85733. Reprinted by permission.

The infant also may be swaddled and placed in sidelying. Swaddling assists the infant in increasing periods of alertness and interaction, prevents excessive extensor posturing, and decreases irritability and tremors. Schneider (1990) points out that although swaddling may be needed initially, it is necessary to begin to withdraw this so that the infant learns to control the neurobehavioral state independently.

Sitting

The prone position, in which the infant is placed on the stomach, is good for promoting good muscle tone, especially flexion. It also facilitates good head control and controlled extension throughout the body. The child can be placed and maintained in prone with rolled blankets along the sides of the body and under the chest. In a very young infant, a rolled blanket can be placed under the hips as well.

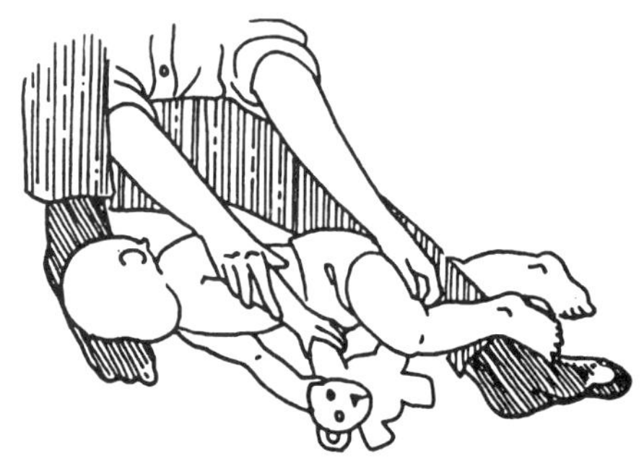

Sidelying

Supine, in which the infant is placed on the back, is not generally a position of choice from a therapeutic standpoint. This is because supine encourages extension and makes flexion difficult. Infants exposed to environmental toxins typically have difficulty with excessive extensor muscle tone and inadequate flexor muscle tone. This atypical muscle tone and insufficient flexor activity cause poor shoulder girdle alignment and difficulty with reaching and kicking. Poor shoulder girdle alignment involves increased shoulder elevation and retraction with neck hyperextension. The arms are abducted (drawn away from the body) and flexed out to the side in a "surrender" position.

Supine in flexion

However, for all the drawbacks of the supine position, it remains the easiest position in which to interact with the child. It is a good position, albeit difficult, for the child to learn antigravity skills such as reaching and kicking. Therefore, when the supine position is indicated, it is important to position the child properly to minimize the effects of atypical muscle tone and to maximize the child's functional abilities in this position. When placed in supine, the infant should be supported with blanket rolls placed underneath the shoulders and along the trunk to reduce shoulder retraction and promote midline positioning of the hands. If the child cannot maintain the head in midline, place a rolled blanket around the child's head. Place a blanket roll under the knees to further promote flexion.

A swim ring is an alternative to blanket rolls for small infants. The infant can be placed in the swim ring in supine. The swim ring promotes flexion by flexing the hips and neck. Blanket rolls may be needed to fill in the gap between the shoulders and the head in order to reduce stress on the neck and support the upper extremities in flexion.

Supported sitting or reclined sitting are important positions for the developing child. Sitting allows the child to view the world from a vertical perspective and to use the hands freely to interact with the environment. A reclined sitting position assists the development of antigravity flexion by partially limiting the effects of gravity. Therefore, some skills, such as midline positioning of the arms and reaching, may be practiced in this position before they are practiced in supine, which is more difficult.

Infant seats provide a good way to position infants in a supported, reclined sitting position. Infant seats usually have a certain amount of adjustability in terms of the tilt in space. While in the infant seat, blanket rolls should be placed to encourage a symmetrical posture, bring the shoulders forward, maintain neutral alignment of the head, and flex the hips.

Treatment Strategies for Problems with Neurobehavioral State

Infants exposed to environmental toxins display problems with self-regulation of neurobehavioral state (Cohen et al. 1989; Randall et al. 1991; Russell and Free 1991). This was described in detail in the section on problems of the postnatal period. Briefly, these infants have difficulty achieving and maintaining a quiet alert state which is optimal for interaction and learning. They tend to oscillate between extreme states of deep sleep and agitated crying. They are often irritable and difficult to console. Therapists must be able to assist these infants in learning to control their neurobehavioral states if they are going to be successful in facilitating the infants' motor development.

Vestibular input can be helpful in addressing the neurobehavior problems of these infants. Vestibular input refers to movement, such as rocking and swinging, that stimulates the vestibular system in the inner ear. Gentle movements in the vertical direction while being held can be calming to an irritable infant. More brisk movement in the horizontal direction can be arousing to a less alert infant. Vestibular input can be provided through swings and other means as well as by the caregivers.

Swaddling also is helpful in assisting these infants to control their neurobehavioral states. Firm swaddling helps the infant maintain a flexed position with the shoulders forward and hands in midline. Swaddling can be combined with vestibular input. The heat from the blanket appears to decrease excessive movement (Umphred and McCormick 1985; Randall et al. 1991; Russell and Free 1991).

Treatment Strategies for Problems of Antigravity Flexion and Atypical Muscle Tone

Head Control

Head control is essential for maintaining the head in upright. In order for good head control to develop, the infant must gain control of both the extensor muscles and the flexor muscles. Infants exposed to environmental toxins typically have difficulty with control of the flexor muscles. In supine, these infants' shoulders are retracted and elevated with the neck held in hyperextension. The lack of flexion control coupled with the resultant malalignment makes it extremely difficult for the infant to lift the head when pulled to sit. While in prone, these infants demonstrate difficulty lifting their heads as well. In prone, they are unable to sufficiently press into the supporting surface with their arms so that they have a stable base from which to lift their heads.

Treatment strategies to address poor head control are aimed, therefore, at increasing control of the anterior neck and trunk flexors. First, it is necessary to correct the malalignment of the shoulder girdle and neck. This can be done with the infant in supine on the therapist's lap or on the floor. The shoulders are brought gently down and forward. The infant's head can be placed in slight flexion using a rolled blanket. The therapist then can encourage chin tucking by placing an interesting toy on the abdomen or gently but firmly tapping the chest muscles. As chin tucking becomes more adept, the child can be brought slowly to the upright position. During the transition, the infant should be given sufficient time to respond with activation of the neck flexors. Careful observation is necessary to ensure that the infant does not substitute shoulder elevation with retraction or protraction and excessive hyperextension of the neck for activation of the neck flexors. Perform all movements slowly, and pay close attention to the child's neurobehavioral state. If necessary, the child may be swaddled while working on this activity in supine.

Hand-to-Foot Play

The lack of flexor musculature development makes hand-to-foot play difficult for infants exposed to environmental toxins. Supine or semireclined are good positions for working on hand-to-foot play. The child may be positioned in supine in a swim ring as described on page 91. The baby then is better able to see the feet, and this may motivate the child to attempt to reach for them. Socks with bells can be placed on the child's feet to encourage reaching for the feet. (However, this should be done with care, because an irritable infant may be extremely sensitive to sound.) It may be helpful to assist the infant by lifting the pelvis slightly to bring the feet closer to the child's hands. The swim ring helps to maintain flexion passively while the therapist attempts to elicit active movement into flexion. The semireclined position allows gravity to assist the body into flexion. This may be a good starting point for an infant who displays a great amount of extension.

Rolling

Rolling is an activity requiring activation of the flexor musculature. It is an important skill for mobility and exploring the environment. Rolling can be facilitated on the infant's bed or floor. The movement can be initiated at the pelvis or the shoulder girdle. It is often easier to start at the pelvis by flexing the infant's leg and bringing it across the body. The infant should be given time to attempt to bring the arm and head over independently. If unable to accomplish this, the infant may be assisted at the shoulder girdle as well. Good chin tucking should be encouraged throughout the roll. Another way of assisting is to place the infant on a small incline such as a wedge or slightly elevated bed. Gravity then can assist the infant in using flexor musculature. A toy or the therapist's voice can be used to motivate the child.

Reaching and Midline Skills

Reaching and bringing the hands together in midline are very complex motor tasks that require good control of flexion. Reaching is important for exploring and interacting with the environment. The development of midline skills is important in developing the ability to use the two sides of the body together. Due to problems with control of flexion, the development of reaching and midline skills can be impaired. The malalignment of the shoulder girdle and neck described on page 92 also inhibits reaching and midline skills. Neck alignment can be improved by assisting the infant to tuck the chin and gently bringing the shoulders down and forward. This should be the first area to be addressed. Midline skills can be facilitated by assisting the infant to clasp the hands or by providing a toy that is easy to hold with two hands. This activity may be initiated in sidelying first, because it eliminates gravity and may make it easier for the infant to see the hands or the toy. The activity also may be practiced in supine or in a semireclined position, but the infant may need more assistance in maintaining an optimal alignment. Reaching skills can be worked on in these positions. Play gyms are a good way to encourage reaching activities and swiping at reachable objects with the hands. It is best to hang only a few simple toys from the play gym so that the infant does not become overstimulated and lose control of the neurobehavioral state.

Summary of Therapeutic Intervention

We have presented some ideas for appropriate therapeutic intervention for infants exposed to environmental toxins. Although these infants may display a myriad of motor problems, this information should provide a general basis for early intervention. Positioning techniques were reviewed. This was followed by treatment strategies for regulation of neurobehavioral state and problems of atypical muscle tone and flexion control. All techniques should be tailored to the individual needs of the infants and their families. Further, for the most effective intervention, good communication should be maintained among all members of the team working with the family.

References

Abel, E. L. 1991. The future of cocaine babies: Primary care and early intervention. *Journal of Pediatric Health Care* 5(6):321-23.

Bayley, N. 1992. *Bayley Scales of Infant Development-R.* San Antonio, TX: The Psychological Corporation.

Brazelton, T. B. 1973. Neonatal behavioral assessment scale. *Clinics in Developmental Medicine 50.* Philadelphia: J. B. Lippincott.

Chasnoff, I. J. 1989. Cocaine, pregnancy, and the neonate. *Women and Health* 15(3):23-25.

Cohen, M. E., E. K. Anday, D. S. Leitner, and N. E. Kelley. 1989. Effects of in utero cocaine exposure on startle and its modification. *Developmental Pharmacology Therapy* 12(3):137-145.

Farrar, H. C., and G. L. Kearns. 1989. Cocaine: Clinical pharmacology and toxicology. *Journal of Pediatrics* 115(5):665-75.

Folio, M. R., and R. R. Fewell. 1983. *The Peabody developmental motor scales and activity cards.* Allen, TX: DLM Teaching Resources.

Griffith, D. R. 1988. The effects of perinatal exposure on infants' neurobehavioral and early maternal infant interactions. In *Drugs, alcohol, pregnancy and parenting,* edited by I. J. Chasnoff. Lancaster, UK: Kluwer Publishing.

Hume, R. F., K. J. O'Donnell, C. L. Strange, A. P. Killam, and J. L. Gingras. 1989. In utero cocaine exposure: Observations of fetal behavior state may predict neonatal outcome. *American Journal of Obstetrics and Gynecology* 161(3):685-90.

Randall, V. F., D. R. Cook, C. Mandelson, and T. E. Finch. 1991. A demonstration project on military installations: Child care for infants and toddlers with special needs, including those with HIV infection. *Infants and Young Children* 3(3):25-36.

Resnick, R. B., R. S. Kestenbaum, and I. K. Schwartz. 1977. Acute systematic effects of cocaine in man: A controlled study of intranasal and intravenous routes. *Science* 195:696-97.

Russell, F. F., and T. A. Free. 1991. Early intervention for infants and toddlers with prenatal drug exposure. *Infants and Young Children* 3(4):78-89.

Schneider, J. W. 1990. Infants exposed to cocaine in utero: Role of the pediatric physical therapist. In *Touch: Topics in Pediatrics,* Lesson 6. Arlington, VA: APTA.

Schneider, J. W., and I. J. Chasnoff. 1987. Cocaine abuse during pregnancy: Its effects on infant motor development—A clinical perspective. *Topics in Acute Care Trauma Rehabilitation* 2(1):59-69.

Sztuman, L., J. J. Ducey, and M. L. Tancer. 1990. Intrapartum, intranasal cocaine use and acute fetal distress: A case report. *Journal of Reproductive Medicine* 35(10):917-18.

Umphred, D. A., and G. L. McCormick. 1985. Classification of common facilitory and inhibitory treatment techniques. In *Neurological Rehabilitation,* edited by D. A. Umphred. St. Louis: C. V. Mosby.

Readings

Appel, C. 1991. Perinatal cocaine, mothers and infants. *Journal of Obstetrics and Gynecology* 15(3): 10-12.

Bateman, D. A., and M. C. Heagarty. 1989. Passive freebase cocaine (crack) inhalation by infants and toddlers. *American Journal of Diseases of Children* 143:25-27.

Bingol, N., M. Fuchs, V. Diaz, R. K. Stone, and D. S. Gromish. 1987. Teratogenicity of cocaine in humans. *Journal of Pediatrics* 110:93-96.

Braude, M. C., H. H. Szeto, C. M. Kuhn, L. Bero, D. Ignar, E. Field, S. Lurie, I. J. Chasnoff, J. H. Mendelsohn, B. Zuckerman, H. Amaro, K. Kyei-Aboage, and J. Howard. 1987. Perinatal effects of drug abuse. *Federation Proceedings* 46(7):2446-53.

Brazelton, T. B. 1984. *Neonatal behavioral assessment scale* 2d ed. Philadelphia: J. B. Lippincott.

Chandler, L. S., M. S. Andrews, and M. W. Swanson. 1980. *Movement assessment in infants: A manual.* Infant Movement Research, P.O. Box 4631, Rolling Bay, WA 98061.

Chasnoff, I. J. 1988. Drug use in pregnancy. *The Pediatric Clinics of North America* 35(6):403-12.

Chasnoff, I. J., K. A. Burns, W. J. Burns, and S. H. Schnoll. 1986. Prenatal drug exposure: Effects on neonatal and infant growth development. *Neurobehavioral and Teratology* 8:357-62.

Chasnoff, I. J., W. J. Burns, S. H. Schnoll, and K. A. Burns. 1985. Cocaine use in pregnancy. *New England Journal of Medicine* 313:666-69.

Chasnoff, I. J., M. E. Bussey, R. Savich, and G. Stack. 1986. Perinatal cerebral infarction and maternal cocaine use. *Journal of Pediatrics* 111:571-78.

Chasnoff, I. J., and D. R. Griffith. 1989. Cocaine: Clinical studies of pregnancy and the newborn. In *Cocaine, pregnancy and the newborn.* Annals, New York Academy of Sciences 260-66.

Chasnoff, I. J., D. R. Griffith, C. Freier, and J. Murray. 1992. Cocaine/polydrug use in pregnancy: Two-year follow-up. *Pediatrics* 89(2):284-89.

Chasnoff, I. J., D. R. Griffith, S. MacGregor, K. Dirkes, and K. A. Burns. 1989. Temporal patterns of cocaine use in pregnancy: Perinatal outcome. *Journal of the American Medical Association* 261(12):1741-44.

Chasnoff, I. J., H. J. Landress, and M. E. Barrett. 1990. The prevalence of illicit drug or alcohol use during pregnancy and discrepancies in mandatory reporting in Pinellas County, Florida. *New England Journal of Medicine* 322:1202-06.

Chasnoff, I. J., D. E. Lewis, D. R. Griffith, and S. Willey. 1989. Cocaine and pregnancy: Clinical and toxicological implications for the neonate. *Clinical Chemistry* 35(7):1276-78.

Coles, C. D., K. A. Platzman, I. Smith, M. E. James, and A. Falek. 1992. Effects of cocaine and alcohol use in pregnancy on neonatal growth and neurobehavioral status. *Neurotoxicology and Teratology* 14(1):23-33.

DeGangi, G. A., and S. I. Greenspan. 1989. *Test of sensory function in infants* (TSFI). Los Angeles. Western Psychological Services.

DeStefano-Lewis, K., B. Bennett, and N. Hellenger Schmeder. 1989. The care of infants menaced by cocaine abuse. *Maternal Child Nursing* 14:324-29.

Dixon, S. D., and R. Bejar. 1988. Brain lesions in cocaine and methamphetamine exposed neonates. Abstract. *Pediatric Research* 23:405A.

______. 1989. Echoencephalogram findings in neonates associated with maternal cocaine and methamphetamine use: Incidence and clinical correlates. *Journal of Pediatrics* 5(1):770-78.

Fulroth, R., B. Phillips, and D. J. Durand. 1989. Perinatal outcome of infants exposed to cocaine and/or heroin in utero. *American Journal of Diseases of Children* 143:905-10.

Hadeed, A. J., and S. R. Siegel. 1989. Maternal cocaine use during pregnancy: Effect on the newborn infant. *Pediatrics* 84(2):205-10.

Hannig, V. L., and J. A. Phillips. 1991. Maternal cocaine abuse and fetal anomalies: Evidence for teratogenic effects of cocaine. *Southern Medical Journal* 84(4):498-99.

Howard, J., L. Beckwith, C. Rodnig, and V. Kropenske. 1989. The development of young children of substance-abusing parents: Insights from seven years of intervention and research. *Zero to Three* 9(5):8-12.

Hoyme, H. E., K. L. Jones, S. D. Dixon, T. Jewett, J. W. Hanson, L. K. Robinson, M. E. Msall, and J. E. Allanson. 1990. Prenatal cocaine exposure and fetal vascular disruption. *Pediatrics* 85(5):743-47.

Ioffe, S., and V. Chernick. 1988. Development of the EEG between the 30 and 40 weeks gestation in normal and alcohol-exposed infants. *Developmental Medicine and Child Neurology* 30(6): 797-807.

Keith, L. G., S. MacGregor, S. Friedell, M. Rosner, I. J. Chasnoff, and J. J. Sciarra. 1989. Substance abuse in pregnant women: Recent experience at the perinatal center for chemical dependence of Northwestern Memorial Hospital. *Obstetrics and Gynecology* 73(5):715-20.

Lifschitz, M. H., G. S. Wilson, E. O'Brien-Smith, and M. M. Desmond. 1985. Factors affecting head growth and intellectual functioning in children of drug addicts. *Pediatrics* 75(2):269-74.

Litle, R. E., K. W. Anderson, C. H. Ervin, B. Worthington-Roberts, and S. K. Clarren. 1989. *New England Journal of Medicine* 321:425-30.

Livesay, S., S. Ehrlich, and L. P. Finnegan. 1987. Cocaine and pregnancy: Maternal and infant outcome. *Pediatric Research* 21:238-A.

MacGregor, S. N., L. G. Keith, J. A. Bachicha, and I. J. Chasnoff. 1989. Cocaine abuse during pregnancy: A correlation between prenatal care and perinatal outcome. *Obstetrics and Gynecology* 74(6):882-85.

MacGregor, S. N., L. G. Keith, I. J. Chasnoff, M. A. Rosner, G. M. Chisum, P. Shaw, and J. P. Monogue. 1987. Cocaine use during pregnancy: Adverse perinatal outcome. *American Journal of Obstetrics and Gynecology* 157:686-90.

McCalla, S., H. L. Minkoff, J. Feldman, I. Delke, M. Salwin, G. Valencia, and L. Glass. 1991. The biologic and social consequences of perinatal cocaine use in an inner city population: Results of an anonymous cross sectional study. *American Journal of Obstetrics and Gynecology* 625-30.

Milani-Comparetti, A., and E. A. Gidoni. 1967. Pattern analysis of motor development and its disorders. *Developmental Medicine and Child Neurology* 9(5):625-30.

Newald, J. 1986. Cocaine infants: A new arrival at hospital steps? *Hospitals* 60(7):96.

Oro, A. S., and S. D. Dixon. 1988. Waterbed care of narcotic exposed neonates. *American Journal of Diseases of Children* 142:186-88.

Perlow, J. H., D. L. Schlossberg, and H. T. Strassner. 1990. Intrapartum cocaine use: A case report. *Journal of Reproductive Medicine* 35(10):978-80.

Peters, H., and C. J. Theorell. 1991. Fetal and neonatal effects of maternal cocaine use. *Journal of Gynecological Nursing* 20(2):121-26.

Petitti, D. B., and C. Coleman. 1990. Cocaine and the risk of low birthweight. *American Journal of Public Health* 80(1):25-28.

Schmitt, B., J. Seeger, W. Kreuz, S. Enenkel, and G. Jacobi. 1991. Central nervous system involvement of children with HIV infection. *Developmental Medicine and Child Neurology* 33(6):535-40.

Schneider, J. W., and I. J. Chasnoff. 1992. Motor assessment of cocaine/polydrug exposed infants at 4 months. *Neurotoxicology Teratology* 14(2):97-101.

Schneider, J. W., D. R. Griffith, and I. J. Chasnoff. 1989. Infants exposed to cocaine in utero: Implications for developmental assessment and intervention. *Infants and Young Children* 2(1): 25-36.

Sobrian, S. K., N. L. Robinson, L. E. Burton, H. James, D. L. Stokes, L. M. Turner, and W. H. Ashe. 1990. Neurobehavioral effects of prenatal cocaine exposure in rats. *Pharmacology, Biochemistry, and Behavior* 35(3):617-629.

Spear, L. P., C. L. Kirstein, and N. A. Frambes. 1989. Cocaine effects on the developing central nervous system: Behavioral, psychopharmacological, and neurochemical studies. *Annals of the New York Academy of Science* 290-307.

Tong, S., and A. J. McMichael. 1992. Maternal smoking and neuropsychological development in childhood: A review of the evidence. *Developmental Medicine and Child Neurology* 34(3)191-97.

van de Bor, M., F. J. Walther, and M. E. Sims. 1990. Increased cerebral blood flow velocity in infants of mothers who abused cocaine. *Pediatrics* 85(5):733-36.

Villarreal, S. F., L. E. McKinney, and M. H. Quackenbush. 1992. *Handle with care: Helping children prenatally exposed to drugs and alcohol.* Santa Cruz, CA: ETR Associates.

Walpole, I., S. Zubrick, J. Pontre, and C. Lawrence. 1991. Low to moderate alcohol use before and during pregnancy, and neurobehavioral outcome in the newborn infant. *Developmental Medicine and Child Neurology* 33(10):875-83.

Zuckerman, B. 1992. Crack kids: Not broken. In *Pediatrics.* Boston: American Academy of Pediatrics. (Reprints from B. Zuckerman, Boston City Hospital, Talbot 214, 818 Harrison Avenue, Boston, MA 02118.)

Zuckerman, B., and K. Bresnahan. 1991. Developmental and behavioral consequences of prenatal drug and alcohol exposure. *Pediatric Clinics of North America* 38(6):1387-1406.

Zuckerman, B., D. A. Frank, R. Hingson, H. Amaro, S. M. Levenson, H. Kayne, S. Parker, R. Vinci, K. Aboagye, L. E. Fried, H. Cabral, R. Timperi, and H. Bauchner. 1989. Effects of maternal marijuana and cocaine use on fetal growth. *New England Journal of medicine* 320(12):762-68.

Chapter 13

Speech-Language and Oral Motor Feeding Considerations

Anne Reynolds, M.S., CCC-SLP

The material in this chapter is based on the author's work with a small sample of substance-exposed infants and toddlers from three to 36 months, seen over a 24-month period. The patterns observed in this sample are generally consistent with other small-scale samples, suggesting that the types of treatment outlined in this chapter could be effective generally. Due to the paucity of published material on this topic, the extent to which these observations can be generalized is unclear.

A substance-exposed infant or toddler referred to a speech-language pathologist should receive a complete speech-language evaluation, including assessment of receptive and expressive language skills, cognition and play skills, pragmatics, and oral motor and feeding skills.

The following developmental scales are useful in assessing the receptive and expressive language skills in infants and toddlers: *Infant Scale of Communicative Intent* (comprehension and expression sections) (Sachs and Young 1982); *Hawaii Early Learning Profile* (expressive language) (Furuno et al. 1985); *Early Intervention Developmental Profile* (receptive and expressive language) (D'Eugenio and Rogers 1975); and *The Carolina Curriculum for Infants and Toddlers with Special Needs* (Johnson-Martin et al. 1991). "Assigning Structural Stage" (in Miller 1981) is informative when analyzing structural development.

In general, receptive and expressive language development is not a weakness in the substance-exposed infant and toddler population. However, if a delay in these areas is evident, typical treatment strategies are recommended.

Cognitive skills may be assessed using *The Hawaii Early Learning Profile, The Early Intervention Developmental Profile,* and *The Carolina Curriculum for Infants and Toddlers with Special Needs.* Play skills may be evaluated using *The Westby Symbolic Play Scale* (Westby 1980) and "The Fewell Play Assessment Scale" (in Fewell and Vadasy 1983). One chapter in *The Carolina Curriculum for Infants and Toddlers with Special Needs* assesses functional use of objects and symbolic play.

Assessment of oral motor and feeding skills is based upon experience, information gathered from several workshops, and from *The Normal Acquisition of Oral Feeding Skills: Implications for Assessment and Treatment* (Morris 1988) and *Pre-Feeding Skills* (Morris and Klein 1987).

Based upon this author's small-scale sample, areas of difficulty for this population appear to be development of oral motor and feeding skills, cognition and play skills, and auditory attention. Each of these areas will be examined below.

Oral Motor and Feeding Skills

The primary goal of oral motor treatment is the development of the appropriate use of the mouth, respiratory and phonatory systems in exploration, sound play, and oral feeding (Morris 1988). Some prenatally substance-exposed infants and toddlers show abnormal or aversive responses to sensory information in the mouth or to food. These abnormal or aversive reactions may be due to, but are not limited to, poor integration of sensory information, overresponsiveness to sensory stimulation, and reduced tolerance to novel input.

Substance-exposed infants show a general disorganization of movement to a variety of sensory stimuli. This may be in response to touch on the tongue and to a lighter touch on the face and the body. Touch to the body, extremities, and face may cause involuntary movement, rapid shifts of attention, and a general disorganization that can influence the coordination of the mouth (Morris 1988).

Alterations in the child's sensory thresholds can influence a child's response to oral input and to feeding (Morris 1988). In treatment, begin by reducing the amount of multisensory information that the child must deal with in the feeding environment. Reduce visual and auditory distractions, and create a positive and supportive environment. Use music to help the child organize and integrate sensory reactions in the nervous system. Baroque music with a slow tempo of 60 beats per minute has been found to be helpful (Morris 1988).

When there is sensory defensiveness, oral exploration may be avoided. It is necessary to encourage discriminative exploration of the infant's own body and a wide variety of toys of different textures. Encourage hand-to-mouth activities. A child who initiates touch in the mouth usually is better able to accept it than when others introduce it, perhaps in a more intrusive way. A child can be exposed to a variety of smells and tastes when food is placed on the child's fingers and brought to the mouth. Encourage the child to use the lips, cheeks, and tongue to explore a variety of fabrics, textures, and shapes. The development of greater discriminative oral skills has been shown to improve sensorimotor organization and articulatory skills in children (Morris 1988).

Use activities that introduce slow vestibular stimulation. This type of input to the sensory nervous system helps the child to integrate multiple sensory information. It is particularly effective in integrating tactile information (Morris 1988). The following activities completed before or during the mealtime have been found to be very helpful:

- Rocking in a rocking chair while holding the child
- Gently bouncing the child on a large therapy ball
- Swinging the child slowly on a swing or in a hammock

Consult an occupational therapist regarding the use of these movements.

Explore different ways of touching the infant or child. Firm touch with deep pressure is usually more easily accepted and integrated. When touch is provided to the least sensitive areas of the body first (arms, legs) and is directed slowly to the more sensitive parts (oral-facial) it can be more easily accepted. The following oral-facial stimulation exercises are recommended to be completed before a mealtime:

1. With firm pressure, rub from the child's ears forward to the mouth. Repeat three to five times.
2. Using your thumbs, rub down along both sides of the child's nose. Repeat three to five times.
3. Using your index finger, rub below the child's nose to the upper lip. Repeat three to five times.
4. Using your index finger, rapidly stroke the lower jaw below the child's chin. Repeat three to five times.
5. Place thumb and index finger together at the center of the child's upper lip; then separate finger and thumb, rubbing to corners. Repeat on the bottom lip three to five times.

Normalize the child's response to sensory stimulation by stimulating the oral area. (Caution: Use universal precautions when going into the mouth.) Use the initial toothbrush in the NUK™ toothbrush trainer set, your finger wrapped in gauze or a washcloth, or the Infa-Dent™ finger toothbrush (available through New Visions catalog, Route 1, Box 175, Farber, VA 22938; 804-361-2285). Stimulate each of the four quadrants of the mouth by vibrating the brush or finger in each cheek pocket. Rub the biting surfaces and the inside surfaces of the teeth or gums. The toothbrushes may be dipped in water or apple juice to add flavor. With either toothbrush or the index finger, "walk" on the tongue from front to back.

An electric toothbrush can be used if the child likes and accepts it. Some children enjoy oral vibration. A number of small vibrators are commercially available; the Egg™ (from New Visions catalog) is well liked by infants and toddlers.

Self-Feeding

By 6½ months, typical children can feed themselves a cracker independently; and by nine months, typical babies have perfected finger-feeding skills (Morris and Klein 1987). The child needs to be well supported in sitting to allow the hands to be free for self-feeding. Avoid tiny pieces of food because these can "get lost" in the child's hand and are difficult to place in the mouth. Strips of food, cookie, soft bread strips, and soft steamed vegetables such as carrot strips or green beans are easy to hold (Morris and Klein 1987).

Substance-exposed infants and toddlers have been known to show lack of initiative in self-feeding and to require more assistance, prompting, and breaking down of sequences into smaller steps to achieve these skills.

Spoon Feeding

By 12 to 14 months, typical children will bring a filled spoon to the mouth, turning the spoon over enroute. (They don't yet have the coordination to rotate the wrist efficiently.) By 15 to 18 months, children will scoop food and bring the spoon to the mouth, spilling some (Morris and Klein 1987). Recommended first spoon foods (which will adhere to the spoon, thus reducing this spillage) include pudding, oatmeal, cream of wheat, yogurt, and foods that stick together such as rice, macaroni and cheese, and "wet" scrambled eggs.

By 24 months, typical children will bring a spoon to the mouth with hand palm-up. By 31 to 32 months, they can feed themselves with little spilling; and between 30 to 36 months, they will use a fork to stab food (Morris and Klein 1987).

For the child who is just beginning to use a fork, foods cut up into small chunks can be easier to "stab." Examples include chunks of fruit, cheese cut into small pieces, and soft cooked vegetables such as sweet potato.

Some substance-exposed infants appear to be sensitive to the texture of early foods fed to them by spoon. Begin with a pureed food that is accepted by the child (for example, pears) and simultaneously a thin cereal such as oatmeal or cream of wheat.

Alter the texture of the accepted food by very gradually thickening it. For example, a thin oatmeal can be gradually thickened over several days. A pureed fruit or vegetable can be gradually thickened with the accepted cereal, and again should be done very minimally each time and over several days.

Small changes in textures are much easier for the infant with oral sensitivities to accept. In *Pre-Feeding Skills,* Morris and Klein (1987) provide excellent progressions in increasing food textures.

Tremors of the tongue have been observed in substance-exposed infants. Reduction of this can be facilitated by a variety of oral input including:

- Mouthing of toys. Intermittently hold onto the toy while it is being mouthed, and firmly depress the tongue. (A variety of small "mouth" toys are available through the New Visions catalog.)
- Use the NUK™ toothbrush to "walk" on the tongue from front to back, providing firm input.
- When feeding with a spoon, use the bowl of the spoon to place firm, intermittent pressure on the tongue. (Maroon™ Spoons have flat bowls which provide good input. Maroon Spoons are available from Therapy Skill Builders, P.O. Box 42050, Tucson, AZ 85733; 602-323-7500/FAX 602-325-0306.)

These techniques, provided at different stages of development, will all help to reduce tongue tremors.

Positions for Therapy

When working with infants and small children, create a semicircle or oval shape with your body and legs. Have the child lie in supine in this space with the head supported on your feet or a small pillow. This position allows face-to-face contact with the child for communication and monitoring of the child's reactions to input, and it reduces confusing sensory input from gravity and movement that could occur if the child were sitting or standing. Use speech and eye contact only when you sense that these can be integrated (Morris and Klein 1987).

With infants, use a large, partially inflated beach ball. Create a well, and cover it with a towel or piece of lamb's wool. Lay the infant in the well. Provide gentle rocking back and forth to help the infant integrate information.

Play

Substance-exposed infants and toddlers display major deficits in the area of unstructured or free play. As a group, their play may be characterized by generalized banging of toys, throwing and scattering of toys, and repeated picking up and putting down of toys. The more typical advanced play skills of purposeful exploration, combining two toys in play, appropriate use of common objects and toys, and symbolic and representational play tend to be absent. Further, when a play scheme has been taught in therapy, it does not often appear to spontaneously generalize to other materials. For example, if a substance-exposed child of nine to 12 months is taught that objects exist when not seen and can find a ball hidden under a box and a car under a can, it does not follow that, for this child, the skill will generalize to finding a block hidden under a cup.

In general, play themes (such as feeding a baby doll, stirring pretend items in a pot, or visiting a doctor's office) are restricted and lack variety. Sand and water play often remain at the dump-and-fill stage without much experimentation. The play is often poorly organized and is not sustained over an appropriate length of time. Of most importance, these children often lack *play initiative.* When left to themselves, the play is stilted and uncreative.

Utilizing the "Westby Symbolic Play Scale" (in Westby 1980) as a guideline, the following suggestions are made for improving the quality of play in the substance-exposed population.

Stage I–9 to 12 Months

When teaching object permanence (the awareness that objects exist when not seen), do so with a wide variety of materials and in a variety of settings which will encourage generalization of this skill. Hide objects under boxes, inside pots with lids, and behind doors. When you are looking for something (even if you know where it is), ask the child to help you look for it. This reinforces remembering where objects were last seen (Johnson-Martin et al. 1991).

Encourage the appropriate use of some toys and the awareness that toys do not need to be only mouthed and banged. For example, a car can be pushed, a ball rolled, one can drink from a cup, eat with a spoon, look at pictures in a book, and brush hair with a hairbrush.

General goals for the speech-language pathologist at this stage are to expand receptive vocabulary (looking at books and magazines, pointing to pictures, and naming what is seen). Point and ask, "Where is the _____?" or say, "Show me the _____." Elicit imitation of speech and nonspeech sounds through vocal turn-taking games. Present a sound you have heard the child produce; and after the child imitates it, introduce a new one. Include coughs, raspberries, and tongue clicks as well as speech sounds. Encourage the labeling of familiar objects. Ask questions such as "What's that?" to help the child in naming objects in the environment.

Stage II–12 to 18 Months

In this important stage, the child is learning how to purposefully explore toys, using trial-and-error patterns to discover how a toy works. Use a variety of toys which will encourage the child to attempt a variety of motoric schemas, such as pull toys, a drum and a stick, a xylophone that can be pulled as a pull toy or hit to make music, cups, spoons, dolls, and a pound-a-peg and hammer (Johnson-Martin et al. 1991). Encourage the child to follow simple commands and requests, expand receptive vocabulary skills, facilitate use of jargon and inflection, and develop expressive vocabulary of single words.

Stage III–18 to 20 Months

Autosymbolic play (pretend play involving the child) is the highlight of this stage. Pretend activities, such as going to sleep, eating from a spoon, or drinking from a cup, can be played out with a variety of materials (different cups, spoons, bowls, pillows, blankets) and in different sequences and locations.

At this stage, the child is finding toys invisibly hidden (a ball goes in one hole and comes out another).

The idea of "tool use," or using a stick to reach a toy, can be elaborated to include other tasks such as pulling a string to get a toy and using a scoop to retrieve floating water toys.

Stage IV–20 to 24 Months

Here, the symbolic play extends beyond the child's self. The child plays with dolls—brushes the doll's hair, gives the doll a bottle, feeds the doll with a spoon, covers the doll with a blanket, requires the doll to follow a number of motoric acts such as sitting, running, and sleeping.

The child performs pretend activities on more than one person or object. A child might feed the doll, a significant person, or perhaps another child. (Again, this emphasizes the weak areas of initiation and generalization often seen in substance-exposed children. These play schemas can be played with an adult as a model of both motoric acts and developing language skills.) The child will combine two toys in pretend play, perhaps putting a spoon in a pan, pouring from a pot into a cup, or placing a baby doll in a car.

Stage V–24 Months

This is the beginning of representational play, when the child plays about daily experiences. The child plays house and pretends to be a number of different people (mommy, daddy, baby). Encourage the child to use objects that are realistic and close to life-size. The events played out are short and isolated. Real sequencing of events occurs later in development.

Sand and water play are popular at this age. Provide a variety of toys which encourage the skills of filling, pouring, and dumping. From an earlier developmental level, encourage combining of two toys and some pretend play, such as stirring "food" in a pot or pouring "tea" into a cup.

Stage VI–24 to 30 Months

Parallel play predominates. Children play alongside one another with similar materials but with little or no personal interaction. At this stage, often children will play out impressive or traumatic events. Helping a child through modeling to expand on these themes and to sustain this play could be helpful to the child's emotional well-being.

At this age, children should respond appropriately to some Wh questions in context, including *what, who, whose, where,* and *what . . . do.* This play environment is useful to the speech-language pathologist in assessing a child's processing of these question types. For example, when playing house with dolls or stuffed animals, ask questions such as, "Who is at the table?"; "Where is the baby's blanket?"; "What is the dog eating?"; or "Whose show is this?"

Stage VII–36 Months

Associative play predominates in this stage. The children's play is loosely organized around a common activity, shared interests, and materials.

Substance-exposed children typically exhibit depressed interactive behavior early in life. In some, it may continue as the child matures and will affect the degree to which the child interacts with peers.

The play usually has a sequence where the child might, for example, make cookie batter, bake cookies, and serve them. For the substance-exposed population, these play themes are less varied and do not occur as spontaneously as one would expect. This may be due, in part, to the fact that children need to have repeated exposure to these real-life activities before they can play them.

Providing a wide variety of props (play furniture, clothing for dress-up) and materials (including clay, foam, rice in a bowl, water) will encourage imaginative and creative thinking and more readily allow for variations on a theme to occur.

In general, interventionists should expect to "play along with" the substance-exposed child to provide rich language stimulation and to model age-appropriate play skills. One cannot expect to provide the stimuli and expect the play to develop without adult modeling and support.

Auditory Processing

Substance-exposed infants and toddlers typically demonstrate poor auditory attending skills and are easily distracted both visually and auditorily.

The following guidelines are based on strategies designed to minimize the impact of such problems on a child's availability for learning.

In therapy, it is best to work in an area which has minimal auditory and visual stimulation. It should be free of clutter, with no items hanging on the walls or from the ceilings. It should be painted a soft color, such as light rose or peach, and be located away from noisy classrooms. Soft music with regular rhythm, slow tempo, and constant volume can create a calming auditory space (Morris 1988). Music containing the special sound combinations known as Hemi-Sync creates a more nearly equal balance of activity in both the right and left hemispheres of the brain, and has been effective in assisting in the focus of attention and the enhancement of learning (Morris 1988).

Children with even mild auditory attending problems function better if they can both look and listen. Therefore, in the classroom these children should be kept within close approximation of the teacher, where they can better utilize auditory and visual cues.

Always gain the child's attention (attain eye contact) before conversing, giving directions, or making requests. Give gentle cues to alert the child to focus on incoming information.

Check attending by asking the child to repeat or rephrase what you have requested.

Children with attending difficulties tire more readily than other children because it is with great effort that they pay attention and stay focused. It can be helpful to provide short breaks in therapy or classroom time in which the child can move around freely.

Help the child to focus and maintain attention by communicating with enthusiasm.

References

D'Eugenio, D. B., and S. J. Rogers. 1975. *Early intervention developmental profile.* Ann Arbor: University of Michigan Publications.

Fewell, R., and P. F. Vadasy. 1983. *Learning through play: A resource manual for teachers and parents–Birth to three years.* Allen, TX: DLM/Teaching Resources.

Furuno, S., K. O'Reilly, C. Hosaka, T. Inatsuka, T. Allman, and B. Zeisloft. 1985. *Hawaii early learning profile (HELP).* Palo Alto: VORT Corp.

Johnson-Martin, N., K. Jena, S. Attermeler, and B. Hacker. 1991. *The Carolina curriculum for infants and toddlers with special needs.* 2d edition. Baltimore: Paul H. Brooks.

Miller, J. F. 1981. *Assessing language production in children.* Baltimore: University Park Press.

Morris, S. E. 1988. *The normal acquisition of oral feeding skills: Implications for assessment and treatment.* Workshop manual.

Morris, S. E., and M. D. Klein. 1987. *Pre-feeding skills: A comprehensive resource for feeding development.* Tucson, AZ: Communication Skill Builders.

Sachs, G., and E. Young. 1982. *Infant scale of communicative intent.* Philadelphia: St. Christopher's Hospital for Children.

Westby, C. 1980. Assessment of cognitive and language abilities through play. *Language, Speech, and Hearing Services in the Schools* 11(3):154-168.

Chapter 14

Educational Interventions for Substance-Exposed Children Now in Preschool and Kindergarten

Diane E. Powell, Ph.D.

During the past few years, the media have been saturated with articles on the devastating effects that drugs are having on society. Specific attention has been placed on prenatal exposure to drugs in utero, and the dire consequences of the mothers' substance abuse on their unborn children. While much attention has been given to prenatally exposed infants, the implications for young school-age children are currently being examined in school systems across our country. Much of the response to the needs of these children has been triggered by the mass hysteria engendered by press who have labeled these children as "unlovable, unteachable, damned, and a biogenic underclass" (Goodman 1992).

Fortunately, longitudinal research studies conducted by the National Association for Perinatal Research and Education (NAPARE), and ongoing educational programs such as Project DAISY* and the Salvin Special Education School (a project of the Los Angeles County School District) have indicated that the prognosis with early intervention and sound educational planning is optimistic. In fact, the descriptive findings from Project DAISY suggest that these children do well in fully integrated environments with their nonexposed peers when given appropriate related service supports as well as environmental interventions. Further, it has been noted that the environmental modifications not only benefit the children who are prenatally exposed, but also have a positive impact on the social and emotional adjustment of nonexposed children who may be at risk due to other stressors in their environments.

---

*The District of Columbia Public School System's Project DAISY, for preschool and kindergarten children, is an early childhood intervention program serving 60 children–five substance-exposed and 10 nonexposed children in each of four classrooms across the District. The program uses an integrated, multi-age, multi-ability classroom model to provide opportunities for cross-age grouping across a broad developmental continuum. Project DAISY has been operational since the 1989-90 school year. Approximately 120 children have been served by Project DAISY since its inception. Children can remain in the project for two years prior to transitioning to first grade.

Psychosocial Stressors

Poulsen (1991) and Powell (1991) have identified similar psychosocial factors which may place young children at risk. These factors may impact on how children adapt to structured learning environments or other settings which place social demands on the child. It is important to note that these stressors similarly impact on children who have not been exposed prenatally to drugs.

These psychosocial stressors are:

- Early separation from maternal figure
- Parental abuse
- Parental neglect
- Poor nutrition
- Exposure to lead paint
- Chaotic home environment
- Multiple caregivers
- Homelessness
- Parental substance abuse
- Prolonged exposure to violence in the environment
- Problems with maternal bonding and attachment
- Emotionally labile parent
- Inadequate health care
- Exposure to secondary health risk factors (smoke)

School-Related Risk Factors

Multiple environmental stressors may impact on the child's ability to develop and exhibit coping skills to respond to the demands of a school environment. In addition, many behavioral and neurodevelopmental problems may manifest themselves in observable behaviors which impede the child's learning. In Project DAISY, approximately 50 behaviors were identified which placed the young school-age child at risk in the classroom. Some of the more frequently observed behaviors include:

- Low frustration tolerance
- Overaggressive thematic play
- Short attention span
- Receptive/expressive language delays
- Poor impulse control
- Destructiveness
- Problems with attachment and trust
- Problems with motor planning
- Problems with eye-hand coordination
- Difficulty accepting limits and structure
- Limited task persistence
- Hypersensitivity to environmental stimuli
- Poor social interaction skills with peers
- Noncompliance and willful resistance to adults
- Limited organizational skills
- Poor decision-making and problem-solving skills
- Problems with transitioning from activities

While these behaviors were noted in children who were prenatally substance exposed, they also were frequently observed in children for whom no risk factors had been identified. Consequently, it is important to note that many children exposed to substances in utero and environmentally will present characteristics that are similar to those of their same-age peers. According to Chasnoff (1992) and Project DAISY findings, many of these children are cognitively intact and are scoring within the normal range on standardized tests and developmental screening inventories. Others are performing well on structured tasks, but display problem behaviors which interfere with their generalization of skills across multiple settings.

The findings from Project DAISY clearly document that the majority of the identified prenatally exposed children were indistinguishable from their same-age peers when multiple observations in the educational setting were conducted over time by trained observers. What is apparent is that there is no consistent profile of these children. They are unique in their display of strengths and deficits. What is most important is that these children can and will learn in highly structured nurturing environments. In recognizing that some of these children will be medically fragile, it is understood that for some children, special education will be a viable placement alternative. The majority of these children can be educated within regular classrooms; however, they may require related service supports and must have skilled, sensitive, and nurturing teachers who understand these children's developmental needs as well as the needs of their families. Poulsen and Cole are quoted by *The New York Times* as saying, "Teachers should be trained to help children surmount specific problems like hyperactivity or speech impairments, rather than tag them with labels that will haunt them forever" (Chira 1990).

These sentiments have been reiterated by Linda Delapenha (1991), who directs an intensive teacher-training program in Hillsborough County, Florida, and by Maurice R. Sykes (1991), who is the Deputy Superintendent, Center for Systemic Educational Change, District of Columbia Public Schools, where the Project DAISY intervention project was established in 1989.

According to Ira J. Chasnoff, past president of the National Association for Perinatal Research and Education (NAPARE), "The school environment will be an additional challenge for children who began life at risk because of their mothers' use of cocaine and other drugs during pregnancy. Educators face the challenge of providing these children with the kind of teaching and school environment that will allow them to reach their potential" (Chasnoff 1992).

Educational Implications

In designing quality early childhood programs which will include children exposed to risk factors, a major point of focus must be on the learning environment. The recommendations reflected here are an outgrowth of the District of Columbia Public School System's Project DAISY, a multi-age program for preschool and kindergarten children.

In establishing a learning environment for children at risk, it is crucial that teachers and other practitioners reflect on the appropriateness of their educational practices. This is necessary in order to fully address the broad span of needs within the classroom. It is necessary for teachers to understand the developmental needs of their students and organize the classroom environment to support those needs. The teacher must examine each child individually, assess what the child brings into the learning environment, and provide opportunities for learning which are in context with a child's culture and prior experience. Children must be contributors in the learning environment and provided with multiple opportunities to expand their bases of knowledge and to engage in novel experiences. These experiences should encourage the child to explore and actively engage in the learning process. The teacher should become a facilitator of the experiences.

In designing learning environments for children who have been exposed to multiple risk factors, consider the following environmental recommendations.

Student-to-Teacher Ratio

The desired student-to-teacher ratio is 15 children to two adults in each classroom. When this is not possible, it is highly recommended that the National Association for the Education of Young Children (NAEYC) ratio of two adults to 20 children be used (Bredekamp 1986).

The teacher should be a certified early childhood practitioner who understands child development and has a strong commitment to working with at-risk children and their families.

The teacher must provide a developmentally appropriate learning environment which is child-centered and experientially based as articulated under the guidelines of the NAEYC (Bredekamp 1986).

The teacher should have training in strategies such as whole language/emergent literacy, facilitating play, and in accommodating children with differing abilities in early childhood settings.

- It is important that the ratio of pupils allows for flexibility in the learning environment. Maintenance of a low number of pupils maximizes the pupils' opportunities to benefit from small-group, whole-group, and individualized attention.
- By having both exposed and nonexposed children in the same classroom, children have opportunities to learn modeled behaviors in a natural setting. Children learn through play experiences which can be facilitated as opportunities to test out new skills and to learn through imitation.

Sensitive, Nurturing Teachers

Young children need to have teachers who create a nurturing verbal environment. What the teachers say, as well as how they support the children's learning, is important in developing children's sense of self-esteem.

- Teachers must understand child development and recognize that children who have developmental delays in a particular area must be given opportunities to develop at their own pace.
- Teachers must understand that children's developmental levels drive the way which they perceive and interact with thc world. Consequently, learning opportunities should be geared to each child's level of understanding and awareness.
- Children need to formulate rules that govern the social climate of their classroom. The teacher should serve as the model, guide, and facilitator of learning so that children begin to understand the logical consequences of their actions without fear or anxiety.
- Teachers must understand the benefits derived by having children of differing abilities fully participating in a classroom, and recognize how children learn from each other.

Table 14.1
Considerations in Working with Children at Risk

Teacher Attributes	Impact on Children
Shows respect for children	Children develop respect for themselves
Serves as a guide and facilitator	Children demonstrate independence
Positively reinforces learning	Children develop self-confidence
Provides opportunities for error-free learning	Children take increased risks
Interprets behaviors	Children receive feedback and learn to interpret environmental cues
Provides opportunities for children to share their experiences	Children develop confidence and increased self-esteem
Values the experiences of all learners as a group	Children develop a sense of community
Provides structure	Children develop control and feel secure
Provides opportunities for children to make choices	Children take responsibility for their actions
Provides multiple opportunities for children to present their work	Children show ownership for their classroom and their experiences
Understands child growth and development	Children learn to understand, accept, respect, and support children of differing abilities

A Safe Environment

- Children should feel free to explore their environments without fear or harm. Within a safe, nurturing classroom, children feel a sense of security. This security is derived from the knowledge that the environment is for the children. All children should be respected by adults who demonstrate respect for one another. Children in turn develop skills to demonstrate respect for each other and their classroom environment.
- Utilizing natural situations to teach care and safety in the environment will allow children to trust. Children should be given opportunities to discuss what is unsafe and safe and how it affects others and self, and to allow the group to have shared input into these discussions.
- Children should feel that adults will protect them and serve as mediators to help in problem solving within the learning environment.
- Teachers should be able to view all children from many places in the classroom. Proximity and touch control can be used to provide students with a sense of security.

Boundaries that divide the classroom learning centers should be well defined by low shelving and stable partitions made of sturdy material. All areas should have adequate space for individual or small-group exploration of materials in the area.

The lighting, color, space, and location of the classroom should be taken into consideration. Intrusions into the environment (such as excessive use of the school public address system and other interruptions which disrupt the flow of children's activities) should be taken into consideration in the environmental design.

A Nurturing Environment

Areas within the classroom should be designed to allow children to be held and nurtured by adults and peers during activities. Cozy beanbag and rocking chairs should be placed in the library corner and also used to console children who need support during group and circle time. Cozy pillows should be available so that children can sprawl across the floor as they engage in their work.

Mats and towels should be available to provide multiple textures and to provide children with a clearly defined work area, so that work can be left out and returned to at a later time. Mats and towels also can be used to provide children with their own space which can be transported from area to area in the classroom. Masking tape can be used to clearly delineate space for children on rugs, floors, and tables. Other types of space markers, such as footprints, can be left on floors as subtle cues to remind children to be respectful of individual spaces until children have internalized the routines of the classroom.

Teachers should understand that children self-regulate their behaviors and often find a sense of comfort in behaviors such as thumb sucking and hair twirling. This behavior should be viewed in the context of the child's experience and developmental level. Unless these behaviors become self-injurious, they should be allowed to persist. In most instances, the aforementioned behaviors will fade over time. The teacher must ultimately see the child as the center, and develop a relationship built on trust in which the teacher provides a sense of warmth, comfort, and security for the child.

Materials and Equipment

Materials and equipment should be appropriate for the developmental level of the child. Because many children may have problems in waiting to use a particular toy or material, it is important to have multiple sets of favorite materials. There should be enough materials in each choice center so that all children can be engaged. For example, if the water or sand table is a favorite area, it is wise to invest in two of them so that children do not have to experience the anxiety of not being able to choose to use these centers. The quality of the equipment is critical. Materials should allow for further extensions of learning. Children should be able to explore the properties and attributes of the materials and to use them imaginatively as well as for the function for which they were designed. Consequently, they must be durable and well constructed for extended and multiple use. It is important to find materials that have multiple uses and to introduce these materials through a process of guided discovery. Charney and Clayton (1990) have defined guided discovery as a teaching technique used to introduce materials, working areas, or learning processes into a classroom. Guided discovery helps children to learn to make a variety of choices, to use materials in many ways with successful outcomes, to explore the multiple uses and functions of a material, and to take care of the classroom environment. Guided discovery can be done with a whole group, with individual children, or with small groups.

In addition to containing purchased materials, the environment should reflect things that are normally encountered in a child's environment. For example, the child might find containers in the sociodramatic play area which represent products found at the local grocery store. Also, products which are culturally congruent for the group of children who make up the composition of the classroom should be available.

Materials should be accessible to children, stored in low cabinets or shelves so that children can engage with them independently. It is important that the environment is user-friendly. New materials should be introduced and old materials should be removed periodically so that the environment remains dynamic. Children should be taught to care for the materials and given pictorial cues so that materials can be returned to their proper places. When new children enter the classroom, students who have knowledge of the classroom should be given the responsibility to introduce classroom materials and equipment and model proper use, care, and handling. When children are highly distractible, the number of materials available for choice should be limited. As children are able to make selections and persist in their engagement with materials, additional materials should be added to the environment.

While learning centers will vary in all classrooms, the essential elements of a developmentally appropriate classroom are the same (Bredekamp 1986).

Some of the centers that should be found in classrooms to support the children's interests include these:

- Language Center and Library
- Math Center
- Science and Discovery Center
- Art Center
- Music and Listening Center
- Sociodramatic Play Center
- Manipulatives Center
- Blocks and Construction Center
- Sand and Water Exploration Center
- Computer/Technology Center

In arranging the centers, it is critical to understand the implication of the design and configuration of the classroom on learning outcomes. Minimize visual and auditory distractors. Plan the centers that are highly interactive and constructive (such as the Block Center or Sociodramatic Play Center) to be located a distance from the Language Center and Library.

The lighting in the room, the size of the furniture, and the accessibility of the materials and supplies are all critical elements in establishing a successfully orchestrated classroom environment.

Resources and Support

When children need related service support, such as speech-language intervention and play therapy, these services should be integrated into the child's activities within the classroom.

Service providers can engage children through their play and selection of materials and can provide support in the context of the child's work. Related service providers can model strategies which can be integrated into the curriculum and provide ongoing consultation to teachers. Consultation should reflect ways in which related supports can be integrated into the daily plan or thematic unit. Children should perceive related service providers as a part of, not apart from, their experiences in the classroom. The provision of services within the classroom promotes collaboration and further enhances the learning opportunities for the child. See Table 14.2 for some of the areas in which service providers might be integrated into the classroom.

Table 14.2
Implications for Integrating Related Services into the Classroom

Service Provider	Activities	Developmental Implications
Speech pathologist	Morning meeting Blocks Center Library; Music and Listening Center Math Center; Manipulatives Center Sociodramatic Play Center—Whole-language activities	Expressive language Auditory processing Receptive language Expansion of contextual vocabulary
Psychologist	Sociodramatic Play Center Art Center Quiet Area Science and Discovery Center Morning meeting	Alternative play skills Increase social interactions Develop trusting relationships Learn alternative responses to stressors Acceptance of the child's reality Opportunities to talk about concerns in a safe setting
Social Worker	Sociodramatic Play Center Art Center Quiet Area	Alternative play skills Realistic home expectations Improve social skills
Movement Specialist	Music Center; Blocks and Construction Center Sand and Water Center Woodwork Gross motor time Creative Arts Center Morning meeting	Improved/normalized muscle tone Improved sensory skills Planned movement Perceptual motor integration
Nutritionist	Housekeeping area Science and Discovery Center Morning meeting	Develop awareness of health and nutritional needs
Suzuki violin	Music Center	Fine motor skills Improved task persistence Pre-writing skills Body awareness Self-control Internalization of routines

All adults providing services to the children must schedule regular times to meet and discuss the child's needs and ongoing progress. Strategies should be identified, developed by the team, implemented, and evaluated as a part of the ongoing process within the classroom. Strategies should be shared with parents so they can become involved in their children's educational programs and understand the implications of the teams' recommendations on their children's development. Parents and primary caregivers should be included in the development of strategies by sharing with the team what works best for them, since they are their children's first teachers. Collaboration by team members will help all practitioners to understand the broad range of a child's developmental strengths and weaknesses and to support these developmental needs through integrated programming.

Developmentally Appropriate Curriculum

The curriculum should be designed so that children are actively involved within the classroom environment. The classroom should encourage children to explore and interact with peers. Trial-and-error experimentation should be encouraged so that children develop a perspective of the world through a sense of natural and logical consequences. Play, which is the basis of the work of young children, should be encouraged, not inhibited. The classroom should be structured. Structure is reflected in the teacher's organization of the environment, selection of materials, and introduction of materials into the social environment. Multiple opportunities should be available throughout the day for children to engage in both real and structured choice. There should be a balance of child-initiated and teacher-guided activities. Children should have the opportunity to remain with the same teacher longer than one year so that they can develop a sense of comfort and move from dependence to autonomy within the classroom environment. Children should be given multiple options as to how they represent their work, and they should be given time to share their representations with their peers. A portfolio of the child's work should be maintained as evidence of progress throughout the course of the year. The curriculum should be representative of multiple cultures and minimize gender bias. The developmentally appropriate classroom will support children across the continuum of needs and incorporate principles of behavior management which includes:

- Flexibility
- Support from routine
- Reduction of frustration through error-free experiences
- High teacher mobility and proximity
- Modeling of desired behaviors
- Planned ignoring of inappropriate behaviors
- Continued affective support
- Opportunities to use planned movement
- Engagement through the introduction of novel tasks
- Support in transition

Other models and activities which are being successfully implemented in Project DAISY classrooms are:

- Guided discovery
- The morning meeting
- An adapted Montessori curriculum
- Collaborative reading and writing
- Integrated movement activities
- Math "your way"
- Choice time
- Suzuki violin

Within the developmentally appropriate classroom setting, specific strategies are used to respond to the needs of individual children. These strategies are incorporated into the classroom and reflected in various facets of the educational milieu such as the design of the environment and selection of materials, as well as in specific techniques used to support children. Specific strategies are linked to observable behaviors and used to increase, decrease, and/or extinguish behaviors which may adversely impact the child's educational or social progress over time and lead to identification for special education.

See Table 14.3 for a few examples of successful strategies from Project DAISY 1992.

Table 14.3
Intervention Strategies that Work

OBSERVABLE BEHAVIOR	INTERVENTION STRATEGIES
Overly Aggressive Thematic Play	➡ Refocus play to more constructive learning. ➡ Use puppets to role play. ➡ Provide an outlet such as a plastic punching doll. ➡ Encourage storytelling and picture drawing to express feelings. ➡ Provide opportunities for creative sociodramatic play that reflects themes. ➡ Decode behaviors so that they have meaning in context with the child's actions. ➡ Engage in the play scheme and model an alternative response, but do not change the content of the child's play. ➡ Use touch or proximity control as a prompt or cue. ➡ Remove child from play area; reintroduce play area through guided discovery.
Poor Impulse Control	➡ Identify specific situations that cause loss of control. ➡ Reinforce the behavior when you observe a child exhibiting self-control. ➡ Teach child to self-monitor by pointing out times when the child is in control. ➡ Identify what happens before and immediately following loss of control. ➡ Use peers to help child self-monitor behavior. ➡ Model self-control, and refer to peers' modeling ("I like the way Roberto is sitting"). ➡ Plan movement into the curriculum, and provide many opportunities to move which are appropriate. ➡ Reinforce successive approximations of self-control behaviors. ➡ Reinforce increased control by allowing child to engage in a favorite activity when control is maintained.

(continued)

Table 14.3
Intervention Strategies that Work (continued)

Limited Vocabulary	➠ Provide a good language model. ➠ Provide hands-on activities to help the child see how words are related to objects. ➠ Use body language, pictures, and gestures to facilitate comprehension and the use of language. ➠ Provide actual words and phrases for nonverbal behaviors. ➠ Elaborate and expand the child's words and phrases. ➠ Provide a wide variety of new experiences as a strong base for vocabulary development. ➠ Use multiple modalities to teach words and their uses (for example, visual kinesthetic-integrated tactile learning experiences). ➠ Model appropriate labeling of objects in the environment. ➠ Use books and writing to promote language-literacy development. ➠ Provide models of literacy activities through whole-language experiences.
Short Attention Span; Distractibility	➠ Be aware of attention as it relates to child development. ➠ Observe the child to determine the actual length of the attention span across multiple tasks. ➠ Design the instructional program to be highly engaging. ➠ Plan to deliver the instructional activity in short instructional bursts. ➠ Provide reasonable accommodations for the student's learning style—small-group, large-group, one-to-one, and peer-mediated activities. ➠ Identify a stimulus-free space for learning tasks. ➠ Use external cues to set limits (bell tone, timer, verbal warnings, flicking of lights, taped music between activities). ➠ Provide consistent positive reinforcement for on-task behaviors. ➠ Reinforce successive approximations of the desired behavior each time it is observed. ➠ Remove overstimulating objects. ➠ Provide short bursts of engagement time. ➠ Plan and use highly structured transitional activities. ➠ Gradually increase the length of activities as the child demonstrates an increased capacity for attending. ➠ Redirect attention by calling the child's name. ➠ Observe and time the child in a favorite activity. ➠ Physically redirect the child when necessary. ➠ Conduct continuous observations of the child in multiple activities over time.

Discussion of Strategies (Table 14.3)

Intervening through Play

These descriptors relate to Overly Aggressive Thematic Play.

When intervening with children through the use of sociodramatic play, it is important for adults to decode behaviors so that they have an understanding of the intentionality of the child's play. Decoding is a process of nonjudgmental observation that takes into account both verbal and nonverbal behaviors. When using this process during a play-based intervention, it is important that the intervention occurs in the context of the child's play and not in the thematic content of the play. The adult will need to observe the events and take on a role that is in the context of the child's imaginative play. Once the adult takes on a role, the intervention should become a part of the play scenario. Using a technique defined by Scarlett (1986) as "co-play," the adult's intervention becomes a part of the child's play. For example, if a child is beating her pretend baby, the teacher might hold a doll and say, in the context of a role, "Oh, sometimes my baby makes me angry, too. When my baby makes me upset, I talk with her." The teacher then models a conversation with the doll, adding, "If my baby doesn't listen, I will have to give her time out," and again models.

It is important to be aware that many children who exhibit poor impulse control in play settings have not developed the social skills needed to control their behaviors. The misbehavior is resulting from limited opportunities to interact within the context of a social group, and control must be learned through modeling and opportunities for practice and rehearsal.

There also are children who may have an organic inability to inhibit responses to overwhelming internal and external stimuli. As a result, it is important to design the environment to provide external support and consistency in the play-based interactions. This can be achieved through small-group play, which teachers can structure externally by providing multiple props in the classroom for the sociodramatic play. Teachers who engage in co-play can provide consistency through their interaction in a role as well as provide external organizers by providing support through proximity control, cuing, redirecting; and they can allow children to regain their composure by giving wait time when needed. It is important to recognize that children develop differently. Many behaviors observed in children are appropriate for the individual child's developmental age. Consequently, many of the problems perceived as belonging to the child are not child-centered but linked to a lack of understanding the child's developmental needs and how these experiences can be appropriately integrated into the curriculum.

Play and Language Development

It is important to understand that children learn more elaborative language within the context of their play (Similansky and Shefatya 1990). Specifically through the use of sociodramatic play, children learn to take on a role and to act out that role using both constructive and nonconstructive materials as props. When play is symbolized using the children's past experiences, their language becomes extremely rich and descriptive. Because of the social nature of sociodramatic play and the opportunities which are provided to teachers to engage in co-play, children are able to hear multiple models of language. Through the context of a role, the teacher as a co-player can help to enrich the child's vocabulary through engagement with children in imaginative play. Not only can play be used as a strategy for language development, but guided discovery can be used when materials are introduced and discovery occurs through both language and the play experience. The language can be enriched by placing the appropriate constructive and nonconstructive props in the classroom. Props which support the play should be in the context of the theme of the play experience. For example, if the play is centered around going to visit a doctor, then the props might be a doctor's kit, a nurse's hat, a note pad and pencil, an empty bottle for prescriptions, a telephone. and a baby doll.

It is important that the props are appropriate to the experience and familiar to the children so that they can be incorporated spontaneously into the sociodramatic play scenario. Similansky and Shefatya (1990) suggest the importance of not overrelying on props, and encouraging children to use nonconstructive, unrelated materials so that they can imaginatively engage in the use of language.

Language-Based Interventions

These descriptors relate to Limited Vocabulary.

In order to expand and enrich children's language, it is recommended that the intervention occur in the context of a social group in which there are peers who can provide appropriate language models.*

When in a small group, children can be taken through the guided discovery process so that they can learn about materials, give input by naming the materials, and share how they would use a material. As part of the language-based intervention, children should be encouraged to elaborate on their authentic experiences and share thoughts and feelings and ideas with their classmates. Through this process, the adult can ask questions and help the child by modeling expanded responses as well as asking the child to "tell me more" or asking, "What else can you tell me about?"

Often, limited language is equal to limited experiences. Consequently, field trips should be viewed as wonderful opportunities to expand children's vocabulary. These activities can be used as a teaching tool so that children can be encouraged to talk about what they did, what they saw, and how it made them feel. As children become more confident and have varied shared experiences, the quantity and the quality of their language will improve. Children also should be given models of incidental language and literacy experiences. Adults can label common objects such as *door* and *chair,* and can introduce the word associated to the print as the child's interest emerges. Language experiences should be a part of the daily classroom routines and rituals. For example, in morning meeting, children should be encouraged to share experiences and ask for questions and comments. Children should engage in activities that require language involvement (for example,

*In order for children to develop language, they need to hear it used in a natural setting in the context of their work–which is "play."

singing and chanting). Children should be encouraged to take books home and to read books in class to their classmates (pretend reading). Through the process of collaborative reading and writing, children will read to each other; draw a story about what they have read; initially describe the story while the adult writes the descriptors; and later caption their own work as they begin to invent their own spelling. They should be encouraged to share with classmates what they wrote and given time to respond to questions about their work.

Managing Classroom Behavior

These descriptors relate to Poor Impulse Control.

It is important to note that impulsivity is a characteristic of normal development. All children can become excited and exhibit a loss of self-control. Further, no research suggests that all children who have been prenatally substance-exposed will be impulsive. What is important to note is that children display different behaviors under different circumstances, many of which are driven by the external cues received from the child's environment. Consequently, it is more important for teachers to look at the behavior and determine what is triggering the behavior and the environmental response to the behavior versus the etiology of the child's problems. Teachers need to understand the simple ABCs of behavior analysis. They must understand that for all behavior there is an antecedent or precipitating event. That event is followed by a behavior, and the response to the behavior is the consequence. If the child considers the consequence to be reinforcing in a positive sense, the behaviors will continue. If the reinforcer is removed or the behavior is redirected, then the behavior will diminish and ultimately stop. Children also need to be given cognitive cues to *stop, think, and then do,* in order to help them understand the logical consequences of their behaviors.

One common problem is that classroom rules and routines are not a daily ritual and children do not have a sense of predictable consistent structure. As a result, behaviors emerge which may be viewed as nonproductive and which interfere with the child's ability to function effectively. This sense of external disorganization may cause the child to feel internally out of control, and the disorganization may be manifested in observable behaviors which are labeled as impulsive.

It is critical to understand that there is no checklist of behaviors which characterizes children exposed to risk factors. Each child is different; some may appear to be very disorganized while others are not. Some may display situational impulsivity which can be extinguished when teachers have a clearly structured, well-organized program with routines, rituals, classroom limits, and high expectations for the children.

The establishment of rules minimizes unnecessary disruptions and transitions. Children usually need about eight weeks to settle into the classroom routine and to clearly understand how the classroom is orchestrated as well as to develop a clear sense of ownership for the environment. Creating a sense of balance, classroom community, and common ownership in the environment helps children to organize their experiences. Consistency, clear directions, and simple rules which are developed and owned by children as a part of the classroom management system can help to reduce uncertainties that can be unsettling for children.

Teachers need to have a consistent repertoire of strategies and interventions. By identifying the strategies in advance of the problem, teachers are able to engage in a process of preventive planning. To reduce impulsive behaviors and to redirect children, some techniques have been effectively implemented in Project DAISY. They include:

- Proximity control. The adult is positioned close to the children. The physical presence of the adult signals that the adult will take care of the children and the classroom is a safe place to be.
- Verbal reminders to refocus. Gentle verbal reminders are used to refocus students (for example, "Put your brakes on").
- Physical prompting. A gentle touch cues students to refocus to task.
- Signaling. Calling the child by name ("Diane . . ."), or asking, "Who can remind me of the rule for. . ." cues the child to get back on task.
- Task analysis. Breaking tasks into small component parts allows the children to have manageable bits of information to master, rather than attempting to complete a task entirely without assistance.
- Planned movement. Tasks are identified that involve movement, and children are permitted to engage in them as a transition from activity to activity.
- Structured choice. Children are provided with two choice options, versus allowing open-ended choice.
- Activities designed to be presented in short instructional bursts to maximize the child's limited span of engagement.

Providers must understand that many behaviors that children exhibit are beyond their control. In order to accommodate these children, the environment must be evaluated and a continuum of protective factors must be put into place.

Family-Based Intervention

The involvement of the child's family is critical to the implementation of intervention strategies both at home and at school. Strategies which are developed by the team members must be shared with the home. These strategies should be modified so that they are user-friendly to the family for home implementation. For example, a member of the classroom team or a specific related service provider might work with the family on play skills, self-help, or language-based interventions. A member of the team might work with the family to address an area which, while indirectly related to the child, may have a significant impact on the family's ability to be involved in the child's school program (for example, lack of day care for siblings, application for Supplementary Security Income benefits, loss of Public Assistance or food stamps).

Going into the home to work with the family to address areas of concern imparts a clear message of the importance of the family's role in the child's education. This support also encourages families to become actively involved and to take ownership of and become involved in problem resolution rather than assuming a passive dependent role. This level of empowerment provides families with a sense of control and gives them a vested interest in their children's educational and therapeutic intervention plan. Ultimately, this level of support and involvement will maximize the degree to which early intervention may positively impact on the child's acquisition of skills within the educational milieu.

The composition of the home-based intervention team may shift, depending upon the particular needs of the child and the family. Through the parent-education group, family members identify areas of interest and topics of discussion centered around their children. These sharing sessions may involve the parent coming into the class to watch the child at work to see how the child is using the classroom environment and to discuss areas of interest that may be reinforced at home. There also is sharing around areas in which the child needs early intervention and how the parent can be a part of the intervention team.

For example, a child might have some specific delays in language. In this instance, the speech-language pathologist would become the significant member of the team in conjunction with the teacher, working with the family on activities that could be implemented in the home. The speech-language pathologist would be involved in sharing and modeling strategies within the context of the child's home environment. This type of intervention would involve an identified family member working collaboratively with the team to implement and develop family-based activities in which language could be encouraged and stimulated as a part of the family's normal routine.

Teachers often play the most important role in the intervention process. They work in collaboration with the interdisciplinary team in the implementation of strategies, documentation of learning outcomes, and modification of intervention strategies. The team maintains documentation which can be shared with the family so that progress can be charted over time for each child in the classroom, thus creating a student profile. This student profile should reflect the impact of supports from both the home and school. This process serves to create an interactive dialogue between the home and the school which allows families to view school personnel as both partners and advocates for the child who is at risk. It also allows teachers to view parents as experts as it relates to their knowledge of their children and the primary concerns and needs they have identified for their children.

It is evident that the role of the school in support of young children prenatally exposed to multiple risk factors has shifted dramatically. In models such as Project DAISY, schools become proactive versus reactive. Emphasis is placed on the implementation of best practices in regular education with the inclusion of related services without labeling or identifying children. This shift in thinking provides multiple challenges to educators which can be addressed with awareness, systematic training, and the implementation of multiple strategies that address the developmental needs of young children. We do not know the long-term impact that drugs and alcohol will have on children. What we do know is that early intervention works, and that developmentally appropriate learning experiences foster growth in all children. Further, we know that with support and appropriate accommodations and adaptations to the learning environment, children exposed to risk factors look more like, than unlike, their same-age peers.

Finally, the majority of these children can and will be served in the regular education environment. Research suggests that both alcohol and nicotine present major risk factors to the developing fetus, and that we must not narrow our perspective of substance abuse to only illicit substance use.

As educators we must recognize that *all children* in today's society are at risk. Consequently, our teaching methods must shift to support the needs of *all children.* By placing children first, and focusing on their needs, appropriate interventions can be implemented to support their learning irrespective of early exposure to risk factors.

References

Bredekamp, S. 1986. *Developmentally appropriate practices.* Washington DC: National Association for the Education of Young Children.

Charney, R., and M. Clayton. 1990. *Guided discovery.* Handout: North East Foundation for Children, 71 Montague City Road, Greenfield, MA 01301.

Chasnoff, I. 1992. Hope for a lost generation. *School Safety Journal* Winter:4-6.

Chira, S. 1990. Crack babies turn 5 and schools brace. *The New York Times,* May 25.

Delapenha, L. 1992. New challenges for changing times. *School Safety Journal* Winter:11-13.

______. July, 1991. Educational implications of children prenatally exposed to drugs. Presentation to House Narcotics Committee, Washington, DC.

Dodge, D. T., and L. J. Elken. 1992. The creative curriculum for early childhood. In *Teaching strategies* 3d ed. Hillsboro, FL: Educational Partnership Foundation.

Goodman, E. 1992. *The myth that became a media hit.* Boston: The Boston Globe Newspaper Company, *Washington Post* Writers Group.

Jackson, S. A. 1992. *Report and resource compendium: Educating young children prenatally exposed to drugs and at risk.* Comprehensive School Health Education Program, Office of Education, Research, and Improvement. Washington, DC: U.S. Department of Education.

Neuman, S. B., and K. Roskos. 1990. Play, print, and purpose: Enriching play environments for literacy development. *The Reading Teacher* 44(44):3.

Poulsen, M. 1991. Schools meet the challenge: Education needs of children at risk due to substance exposure. *Resources in Special Education.* Sacramento, CA: Children's Resource Institute.

Powell, D. May, 1991. *Senate Select Committee: Exemplary programs serving young children prenatally exposed to drugs.* Washington, DC: Senate Select Committee: Government Printing Office.

Scarlett, G. 1986. Co-playing: Teachers as models for friendship. In *Connecting: Friendship in the lives of young children and their teachers,* edited by D. Wolfe. Buffalo, NY: Exchange Public Division Press.

Similansky, S., and L. Shefatya. 1990. *Facilitating play: A medium for promoting cognitive, socio-emotional, and academic development in young children.* Gaithersburg, MD: Psychosocial and Educational Publications.

Sutter, C. 1992. Crack: Healing the children. In "Kappan Special Report," *Phi Delta Kappan* (November):1-12.

Sykes, M. 1991. *Early learning years collaborative.* Washington, DC: Deputy Superintendent, Center for Educational Systemic Change, District of Columbia Public Schools.

Vincent, L., M. Poulsen, C. Cole, G. Woodruff, and D. Griffith. 1991. *Born substance exposed, educationally vulnerable.* Reston, VA: The Council for Exceptional Children.

Chapter 15

Reaching the Child through the Family

Nika St. Claire, M.S., and Gale Berkowitz, Dr.P.H.

While all families may have occasional problems or need professional attention, drug- and alcohol-exposed children and their families have ongoing special needs that warrant a unique response. Interventions that target the family have the ability to make an impact 24 hours a day, seven days a week, and represent the greatest hope for success.

Service providers may be reluctant to provide services to families when substance abuse is involved for many reasons. Yet, interventions aimed at supporting the caretaker have an enormous impact on the child. Substance-using women may not have the information or experience necessary to more adequately read their infants' cues and form the appropriate attachments that are so important to ultimate developmental outcomes. Clearly, all families affected by the parents' use of substances will need recovery-oriented treatment and support, while some also may need more intensive services, including case management and help with parenting skills.

While moving to a family focus is relatively new for many who have worked with children, it is now clearly seen as vital to our understanding of how children develop. Substance-exposed children may have more constitutional vulnerability that demands focusing on the broader context of that child's environment–the family.

Family-centered approaches are now recognized as the most effective modality for children with special needs (Dunst et al. 1988; Johnson et al. 1989; McGonigel and Garland 1988; Shelton et al. 1987). Some would argue that early intervention services have been successful not so much for what happens in the half-day of programming but for empowering and encouraging families. Sameroff and Chandler (1975) and Sameroff and Fiese (1990) emphasize the importance of continuous and progressive interactions between the child and the environment. Their transactional model suggests that children born with a biological insult, such as drug exposure in utero, will develop optimally in a supportive rather than poor caretaking environment. While this is true for all children, the more vulnerable the child, the more important the caretaking becomes in determining developmental outcomes. Caretakers themselves are the most critical element in any child's environment, and as such should be the primary recipients of interventions.

Despite the increased challenges of working with families, no single agency or service modality can match the potential of a family. How does one design and implement a program that is responsive to the needs of these children and families?

The Center of CARE (Chemical Addiction Recovery Efforts) at Children's Hospital, Oakland, California, represents one model for working with children who have been drug- and/or alcohol-exposed in utero and their chemically dependent mothers. Although the entire extended family is engaged in some cases, the model is designed as a parent-infant program serving three clients: the woman, the child, and the relationship between them.

Background

Chemical dependency exists among all socioeconomic and racial groups. However, most of the mothers identified and referred to the Center of CARE program subsist on inadequate income. They may live in subsidized housing projects which do little to enhance self-respect or support a person's efforts to remain clean and sober. When there is no other affordable housing, they often feel helpless to improve their situations.

Society often rejects chemically dependent women, especially when they are mothers, and the chemically dependent woman finds herself under public scrutiny. Many mothers either temporarily lose or are threatened with loss of custody of their children when their use of illicit drugs is discovered. Medical staff may exhibit a special disdain and disrespect for pregnant and parenting chemically dependent women and may blame them for their disease. This attitude can foster feelings of inadequacy and failure for these women even before motherhood has begun. For many women, parenthood is one of the few socially acceptable means of self-esteem available (Rosenbaum 1981). If parenting is denied, there may be very little left.

A network of adequate social support is rarely found for these women. Families may be more a source of distress than of support. Women's own mothers and fathers often abused substances themselves, and relationships continue to be conflicted. Their mothers may be critical, angry, withholding, enhancing the women's feelings of failure; and the fathers are often absent. Many chemically dependent women are victims of childhood sexual abuse. The women's partners are either abusive or no longer involved with the child. Family relations in general are often characterized by abuse and neglect, and often reflect an intergenerational pattern.

There are very few resources for pregnant or newly delivered chemically dependent women. Neither health services nor drug treatment programs are sufficiently sensitive to issues of chemical dependency in women and their needs as mothers. The myriad of problem areas requires a comprehensive, coordinated, continuous, and concerted case-management effort. The program may need to integrate developmental interventions with psychotherapy, treatment and recovery, issues of parenting, and the very real and pressing demands of daily life. Some children will need a therapeutic nursery or preschool with a more rigorous developmental and social-emotional content.

Family Factors and Child Health

Children are dependent on their families and their communities not only for food and shelter, but also for their sense of self-worth and their values. A healthy social and emotional environment is necessary for healthy development. Genetic material and family environment shape who a child will become.

Health and well-being are shaped by early social and family experiences. Among these experiences, those directly related to the family are perhaps the strongest and have the greatest potential for intervention. Family health is instrumental to normal child development and future well-being. Thus, the target of early interventions should be the "emotional and cognitive climate of the family and the degree to which youngsters can draw on the internal environment of the family for their security, sense of self, and future expectations and aspirations" (Mechanic 1989, 4). That effective family functioning and family support are imperative to future well-being has been repeatedly shown.

The experience of having one person who cares is an important characteristic of the children who are resilient in spite of biological vulnerability. Several longitudinal studies of children at risk have shown that affectional ties with those who provide support are essential ingredients of resiliency (Garmezy 1976; Parker et al. 1988; Rutter 1987; Werner and Smith 1982). These studies consistently show that a good relationship with at least one caretaker is necessary to provide the protection needed for most children to stay healthy.

Attachment to mothers or significant others is important to future development and self-esteem (Rutter 1987). Several evaluations of early intervention programs for children showed that early interventions were enhanced by the involvement of at least one parent (Lally et al. 1988; Woodhead 1985). Lack of such involvement has been linked to psychiatric disorder, antisocial behavior, and developmental problems among children (Rutter 1972).

Maternal characteristics, such as mental health, attitudes toward pregnancy and parenting, and social class, have been shown to significantly influence child development (Sameroff 1974). There is strong evidence demonstrating the potential lasting effects of family factors in promoting child health and development. For example, children of depressed mothers are more likely to be developmentally delayed than children whose mothers are not depressed (Rutter 1979; Wadsworth 1988).

In a study of low-income, black, single-parent families, it was found that the greatest buffer of stress was the family and its own internal resources (Lindblad-Goldberg et al. 1988). Conversely, family disruption has been shown to affect children negatively in terms of lowered self-esteem and school performance, increasing feelings of helplessness, and lack of permanency (Dubowitz et al. 1988).

Program Philosophy

The philosophy at the Center of CARE is based on the recognition that the child's environment may prove far more influential than prenatal factors in determining the potential of that child. The development of the infant may best be served by promoting the mother's positive investment in the child (Fraiberg 1980). This investment may be hampered by both individual psychological and severe environmental obstacles. The needs of the child and mother are evaluated both through direct reports from the mother and clinical observation of mother-infant interactions. Developmental guidance, infant-parent psychotherapy, social support, and practical assistance are used as needed to support the relationship.

Promoting the woman's participation in her recovery from an addictive disease is the critical foundation upon which the Center of CARE intervention model depends. If she continues to use alcohol and other drugs, the intervention has limited value. Recovery is critical because a woman who is actively using may not participate in center-based visits or home visits. She may shift her attention from her parenting responsibilities to maintaining her addiction. Even if she is physically present, she may be less able to fully experience her feelings, and thus will be less available for therapeutic work.

Many addicts and alcoholics were raised in alcoholic or otherwise dysfunctional families themselves. Psychotherapy may help heal childhood wounds that have laid a foundation for the mother's initial use of drugs and alcohol.

Both the parent and the infant may bring obstacles to the relationship. Because of their drug exposure, the children may be organically compromised, medically fragile, and at risk of developmental delay. The Center of CARE acknowledges that the woman's needs for recovery and parenting support and the infant's ongoing medical and developmental needs must be addressed simultaneously and in the context of promoting a healthy relationship between mother and child. These tasks are addressed through a combination of center-based and home-based services.

The needs of both the women and their children demand incorporating the following set of services:

- Recovery services–Chemical dependency education and relapse prevention groups, home visits with one-to-one counseling, on-site 12-Step meetings and field trips to outside meetings, and referrals to residential treatment when appropriate
- Parenting support–Developmental guidance, education and information, parenting groups, infant-parent psychotherapy
- Attendance to concrete needs–Case management, emergency food, advocacy with bureaucratic systems, referrals, diapers, formula, and so on
- Services to the child–Pediatric care, developmental assessments, early intervention home guidance, therapeutic nursery

Center-based recovery support and education groups are an essential element in promoting a woman's recovery from her addictive disease. Chemical dependency is a chronic, progressive, relapsing disease that is characterized by compulsion, loss of control, and continued use despite adverse consequences.

While many women referred to the program come into treatment in denial of a drug problem, the program stresses the importance of the groups for support until the mother recognizes her need for recovery and while she is confronting various issues. As addicts and alcoholics abstain from their drugs of choice, they face powerful feelings that previously they may not have dealt with successfully. Pregnant and parenting women in the program frequently need the support of other recovered women to help them learn to deal with these feelings more appropriately. They learn from each other's experiences and feel accepted and understood in a unique way.

Infant-parent psychotherapy is a primary approach of the Center of CARE as a relationship intervention. As described by Fraiberg et al. (1975), infant-parent psychotherapy focuses on the infant and the parent's unconscious conflict with the infant. This modality may be particularly relevant when the infant represents figures from the mother's past, including the mother herself when she was an infant. This is accomplished through a clinical exploration of the mother's and infant's experiences in the context of their actual interaction, as it unfolds in the home sessions. The infant-parent psychotherapist works to expand the mother's empathy with the child through techniques designed to alleviate psychological conflict. The mother's own experiences of emotional neglect as a child and her anger and ambivalence toward her infant are explored in the therapeutic process. Insight gained in this way helps the parent to avoid reenacting her own conflicts from childhood. As Fraiberg and associates indicated, "With the reexperiencing of childhood suffering along with the memories, each of these young mothers was able to say, 'I would never want that to happen to my child' " (Fraiberg et al. 1975).

Description of Outreach and Referral at the Center of CARE

Social workers at high-risk obstetrical programs and at local hospitals following labor and delivery are a primary referral source. The social worker may interview the woman, inform her of resources in the community, and make a referral to the program. Few of the referrals to the Center of CARE are because of court mandates. A case manager is assigned by CARE. By letter or telephone, that professional makes an appointment for an initial visit. The visit can be held at the hospital, the woman's home, or at the Center.

At that first visit, the woman is oriented fully to the components of the program. There is a strong attempt to establish trust and rapport, perhaps by complimenting her on her baby and acknowledging the positive steps she has already taken toward her own recovery and her child's well-being. The family is given a schedule, invited to groups, made a pediatric appointment if appropriate, and observed for motivation and ability to comply. The staff continues to be friendly while rescheduling and trying to engage her into treatment—or at least to the parts of the program she agrees might be helpful. After at least three unsuccessful attempts to engage her, the Center may refer her elsewhere and alert Child Protective Service. We receive approximately seven referrals for every family that actually enters the program.

The most common reason for noncompliance is the woman's denial of the extent of the problem and her unwillingness to address her need for recovery.

Interventions

The program is designed as a three-year intervention. Throughout the first year, most women continue to be in some stage of denial about their addiction and alcoholism. Despite the perniciousness of crack cocaine addiction, we actually have had a fair success in getting women to stop their use of cocaine, although many are unwilling to eliminate their use of alcohol. We continue to provide education about addictive diseases, continue to provide support, promote self-esteem in the woman, and continue to treat and monitor the child's health and development. Our persistence and consistency in not giving up on the woman and providing intensive case management and concrete assistance, appear to keep families intact until the mother is fully engaged. In sum, we are aggressive and persistent in our efforts to engage the women in the program. Client retention is significant, because it takes many mothers up to two years before they can remain abstinent and active in recovery.

Case Study

Linda, a 29-year-old Hispanic/African-American woman, was referred to the Center of CARE two months postpartum from the jail liaison program. She had used heroin and smoked cigarettes daily and had used crack cocaine several times per month during the first two trimesters of her pregnancy until jailed on a petty-theft charge and placed on methadone maintenance.

While incarcerated, Linda delivered a six-pound term infant whom she named Sierra. The child was placed with another family until the mother's release from jail and admission to our program. The father, David, had only limited contact with the family. Linda had two other dependent children—a four-year-old female living with the paternal grandmother, and a two-year-old son in foster care but to be returned to the father shortly. Mother and child were residing in a hotel and receiving assistance from the jail liaison program to find more suitable housing. Linda had an eight-year history of narcotic abuse and had several unsuccessful detox attempts.

Linda was the first of two daughters born to Rosa and Ron. Rosa was a practicing addict, and Ron was a practicing alcoholic who was frequently abusive both to Rosa and the two girls. Linda was sexually abused at the age of nine by her mother's boyfriend. Linda was placed in foster care at the age of 12, where she remained until she was emancipated at 17.

Upon admission, Linda presented herself as highly motivated to maintain custody of her daughter Sierra, and she voiced tremendous guilt and shame over losing custody of her two older children. She appeared to be very bright but quite guarded with the therapist because of difficulty trusting an outsider to help her.

Linda agreed to bring Sierra to our pediatric clinic and to attend weekly support groups, but she was reluctant to receive regular home visits. We agreed to the following goals of treatment: support of Linda's participation in recovery, promotion of Sierra's health and development, and support of Linda's ability to maintain custody of Sierra.

Linda completed a 21-day outpatient detox program, but admitted that she had used heroin on several occasions while in treatment. She attended groups at the Center of CARE, although not weekly, and she was counseled about environmental triggers and letting go of drug-using associations. She was given education about addictive disease and relapse and was encouraged to attend Narcotics Anonymous meetings. We also worked closely with the jail liaison program to move her into her own apartment. She also attended dependency hearings for Sierra's two siblings. She showed signs of depression when she was not awarded custody, and we linked that with her desire to continue to use drugs.

As Linda's ability to trust increased and concerns regarding Sierra's development emerged, the family was referred to our most intense infant-parent program. Linda continued to use drugs intermittently, met a new recovered boyfriend, and they moved with Sierra into a studio apartment. She continued to be counseled about her inability to quit using drugs despite the threat of violating probation, returning to jail, and losing custody of Sierra.

Linda then became abstinent of heroin, began attending NA meetings with the father of her three children, and hoped for a reconciliation. The boyfriend became abusive when she attempted to break up with him, and Linda was given support for a restraining order and ways to stay safe. At that time, she accepted emergency infant formula and diapers and referrals to WIC, and she began acupuncture therapy to help with drug cravings. Linda also began to attend support groups weekly. She could both ask for support and give it to other group members.

Linda's recurrent drug use jeopardized her freedom from the criminal justice system. Consequently, the program was enlisted in treatment planning both by probation and Child Protective Services. There were no available beds in residential treatment, and Linda resisted referrals for waiting lists. She began to share her fears that she was repeating the pattern of her own mother, and we began to explore childhood memories.

Linda also began regular visits with both older children, and was counseled regarding talking about her feelings of anger rather than acting on them. The program continued to provide developmental guidance regarding Sierra in the clinic and group settings and sought Linda's acceptance of weekly home visitation. After eight months of participation in aspects of the program and five of our attempts in a four-week period, Linda relented and allowed our first home visit. Upon being confronted with her avoidance behavior, Linda admitted to using heroin more regularly now, but she was willing to enter residential treatment at the insistence of her probation officer.

The therapist engaged in intensive case-management activities, helping to coordinate Sierra's treatment and Linda's treatment with Child Protective Services, probation, the case manager for the Regional Center's high-risk infants, and the intake worker, counselor, and case manager for the residential-treatment facility. Linda was encouraged to enter another 21-day detox to prepare for residential care and to establish sobriety until she was admitted. Linda's unwillingness to refrain from associating with her family led to repeated relapses. (Both Linda's mother and sister were actively using drugs and refused treatment.) Linda's inability to protect herself from her family's influence was linked with painful memories from childhood when she was placed in foster care and felt rejected by her mother. The therapist continued to explore Linda's unconscious recreation of her childhood, in that continued drug use by her would result in Sierra being placed in foster care.

Linda began to use the weekly developmental nursery at CARE for Sierra, although with reluctance. Initial developmental assessments of Sierra indicated mild to moderate delays in speech and in the fine motor cognitive area with a generalized delay of about 1½ months. Although Linda was concerned with her child's emerging developmental delays, she had difficulty separating from Sierra. For several sessions, we explored the meanings of this insecure attachment. Linda also began another detox treatment, and began to follow through with suggestions made to promote Sierra's developmental progress. Sierra learned to walk and talk, and she seemed to gain new skills each visit. Both mother and therapist delighted in this catch-up phase.

During this time, Linda had an irregular pap smear, and we provided support by accompanying her for a follow-up visit. She was relieved to hear she did not have cancer, but admitted to increased drug use around her fears. She committed again to getting clean. Linda still had not followed through with requirements to enter residential treatment, and referrals again were pursued.

Linda again recognized how her continued drug use combined with uneven use of the program affected her ability to follow through with goals for herself and Sierra. At this point, Linda allowed the therapist to drive her to an intake appointment for residential care. She agreed to attend daily outpatient treatment until admitted, and this time she was able to follow through.

The therapist worked closely with Linda regarding her use of corporal punishment as discipline, especially with the older siblings. The therapist noted that Linda had expectations of behavior that were not age-appropriate. Linda was encouraged to attend crisis couples' counseling sessions with her boyfriend, because they were having difficulty in the relationship. We encouraged the development of a trusting relationship between them because the boyfriend appeared to be a stabilizing force in her life and in Sierra's. The therapist also continued to discuss Linda's fears and ambivalence about treatment.

Nearly 14 months after beginning treatment at the Center of CARE, Linda entered a residential treatment program where she could bring Sierra with her. Linda was concerned about the effect on the two older siblings, and we revisited her own sense of abandonment from her mother as a child. Linda was very protective of her mother, Rosa, and she continued to express her forgiveness while appearing to be unable to tolerate feelings of rage with her mother. At Linda's request, the therapist met with the two older children and the father to help explain what Linda needed to do.

We continued to meet with Linda weekly. During this time, Linda again explored her feelings of ambivalence between her boyfriend and the children's father. She needed encouragement to remain in treatment. With each incident where she became angry with staff or peers, she threatened to leave. She was further encouraged to talk about her parallel ambivalent commitment to treatment.

After 30 days clean while in treatment, Linda said she was ready to talk more about her childhood history of abuse. While the therapist was cautious about going too fast, it did appear as if Linda needed to experience the feelings again to concretize her recovery. At the next home visit, Linda raged against her mother, ventilated anger at being placed in foster care, and relived the horror of the molestation experience and her mother's inability to protect her. Linda expressed fervently how she wanted it different for her children.

Linda subsequently used a nonprescribed drug while in treatment, and she became angry about being terminated from treatment. She could not see how perhaps she had set herself up to be discharged as a way of dealing with her ambivalence. Two days later, mother and daughter left treatment. After two weeks, Linda telephoned the therapist to relate her whereabouts–in an apartment with her boyfriend. She was unavailable for home visits for the next three months, did keep one pediatric appointment during that time, and was unable to explore how she felt she needed to stay away from therapy for a while as a means to protect herself from the powerful feelings related to the molestation.

The next home visit further revealed that Linda was still clean, but three months pregnant. We informed her that we could suspend home visits for a while, because it appeared that she was requesting that. Linda appeared relieved. She was encouraged to continue her prenatal care and ask for more support if she feared relapse so this baby could be born drug-free. During the next several months, Linda and Sierra participated only with clinic visits; but as delivery loomed closer, Linda again requested monthly home visits, ostensibly to help with toilet training Sierra. Developmental assessments conducted at six-month intervals revealed that Sierra was continuing a mild delay, according to the *Bayley Scales of Infant Development* (Bayley 1969), but her scores on the Mental Development Index (MDI) indicating cognitive functioning had improved from 81 to 102.

One month later, Linda gave birth to Lamont, the first drug-free child she had delivered. Linda is still reluctant to attend groups, yet brings Sierra to the weekly developmental nursery and is receptive to monthly home visits. Significantly, the family has remained in treatment for more than 2½ years. Sierra and Lamont are developing within normal limits on standardized testing, and they are fully immunized. Linda, her boyfriend, and three of her children reside together in a spacious two-bedroom apartment away from the drug-using area. Linda has been clean of all substances for more than one year. Even Linda's mother and sister are now in recovery.

Implementation Issues and Challenges

The case study suggests many of the challenges inherent in working with families. The lifestyle of the chemically dependent woman poses serious health and social management challenges to providers. Some of the issues that need to be addressed include history of abuse and neglect as children, effects of poverty and racial inequality, family history of substance abuse, effects that the drugs themselves exert, waiting lists for ancillary services, timing of introduction of healing from the molestation without precipitating a relapse, history of incarceration, inadequate educational levels and limited job skills, domestic violence, effects of being a single parent with continuous child-care responsibilities, issues related to maintaining custody, inadequate housing, poor health, and nutritional status. Since the average woman in treatment at the Center of CARE has more than two children, lack of transportation and child care become formidable obstacles. To overcome some of these barriers, the Center of CARE has incorporated bus tickets, cab vouchers, a healthful lunch, and child care during all activities to assist the families in their ability to make use of the services.

Engaging women in treatment proves very difficult for many reasons. Women may be in denial about their drug dependency; they refuse services because they do not see their substance use as a problem. Mothers may be afraid to let a visitor in the home for fear of having their children removed from their custody, or they may be unwilling to attend groups. Lack of trust in the health-care "system" is pervasive. Many women will be experiencing trust and compassion for the first time, and may have difficulty being able to accept and utilize social support.

Promoting the well-being of staff is equally important. Staff may have their own set of special needs. Because it may take a very long time to establish a therapeutic alliance, this can be frustrating to staff. It is critical, however, that despite rebukes and slow progress, the therapist remains consistent, persistent, and nonjudgmental. Until a relationship is established, clients may be noncompliant in attendance and availability. Therapists who are working independently may begin to question their sense of competence. Staff need a rich menu of support to continue the work, including individual clinical supervision, group case presentations, didactic training, peer support, and administrative recognition of these ongoing needs. Support in the way of salary incentives to continue in this demanding line of work may provide more program continuity and prevent staff burnout.

Families affected by drug and alcohol use often present a complex set of needs best met by the coordinated effort of a multidisciplinary team. The Center of CARE team consists of a director, pediatrician, psychiatric consultant, clinical social worker, infant development specialist, nurse, drug and alcohol counselor, psychologist, and occupational therapist. Each family is assigned a primary interventionist and utilizes other team members' expertise as needed in consultation. Individuals working with these families may choose to develop their own network of other disciplines, for both clinical input and support.

Program Effectiveness

To assess the effectiveness of this model, a longitudinal tracking system was developed that monitors health and social outcomes of mothers and children. We are systematically tracking mothers and children every six months beginning at intake, assessing infant physical health and development, maternal substance use, and treatment compliance.

In spite of the gravity of the social and behavioral risk characteristics of our families, the program is proving to be effective. Among CARE clients, all mothers are substance users (most used cocaine), all children have been exposed to drugs in utero, and mothers and children live in stressed family relationships in substance-using environments and tend to be socially isolated. The mothers are unemployed single parents who live in poverty. Often they have come from substance-using families, and more than half experienced abuse or neglect as children. Many are depressed and have difficulties in social relationships and relationships with their children.

The primary service needs are for drug and alcohol treatment, support groups and counseling, and child-development guidance. The predominant case-management activity is counseling to support the mother's recovery and her relationship with her children.

To date, we have followed more than 75 families for one or more years. At intake, 60% of the children were rated by the pediatrician as having excellent or good health; 100% were rated this favorably after 12 months of participation. Similar results were observed for growth, as measured by height for age and sex.

Immunizations were up to date for almost all children after six months' participation in the program—an extremely positive outcome for a population where immunization compliance tends to lag far behind the recommended periodicity. To put this in perspective, less than half of the children in California are properly immunized, and this rate is worse for minority and poor children.

Favorable results are being found for participation in drug treatment. At intake, very few of the mothers were in any drug treatment program; after 12 months of participation in this program, almost half were consistently involved in drug treatment and another 13% were involved at least on some basis.

A preliminary review of developmental assessments of 49 children using the *Bayley Scales of Infant Development* (Bayley 1969, 1992) shows that on average, scores were well within the normal range for these drug-exposed infants. In fact, a significant number of them scored above average; 49% were above average on both motor and psychomotor subscales. Considering that many of these assessments are conducted within three months of admission and considered baseline, it might be misleading to attribute these stellar findings to the program. However, preliminary review of 16 six-month follow-up assessments showed improvement among all children, though the average Mental Developmental Index score fell from 101 to 95, and the average Psychomotor Developmental Index fell from 101 to 100. Considering that the mean standard score is 100, these differences are not significant. However, the current version of the Bayley does not give information on attention deficits or hyperactivity, which appear to be more adversely affected by drug exposure. Given the widely held perception that drug-exposed infants in general have serious developmental problems, these findings are extremely encouraging, especially when acknowledging that nearly one-third of the infants had the additional risk factor of prematurity.

These findings are compelling, given the families' status when they enter the program. The first six months of the program is intense and often difficult emotionally for families; it is a time when they are expected to be honest about their problems that bring them to the program, and they are dealing with many severe and long-standing problems. It is not uncommon for children to not look as well during this period of adjustment to treatment. By the first anniversary of participation, most families are on the road to recovery, and the children not only look well but *are* well and on a positive health trajectory.

Summary and Implications

With implementation of Public Law 99-457, Part H, early intervention programs will increasingly focus on the service needs of parents and children rather than individual children. Programs such as the Center of CARE have proven to be effective using just this kind of family-based intervention. Our experience with families has enriched our own experience and convinced us that it is not enough to focus on just the child; but rather, focus must be on the entire family. The greatest hope for intervening on the intergenerational cycle of addiction will involve treatment for the family.

While it is still not clear for whom this approach is most effective, all of our families have benefitted in some way. In our future efforts, we will be interested in determining what factors affect our ability to engage families into all or parts of the treatment program, and in facilitating positive change in their lives and those of their children.

References

Bayley, N. 1969, 1992. *Bayley scales of infant development-R.* San Antonio, TX: The Psychological Corporation.

Dubowitz, H., C. M. Newberger, L. H. Melnicoe, and E. H. Newberger. 1988. The changing American family. *Pediatric Clinics of North America* 35(6):1291-1311.

Dunst, C. F., C. M. Trivette, and A. Deal. 1988. *Enabling and empowering families: Principles and guidelines for practice.* Cambridge, MA: Brookline Books.

Fraiberg, S. 1980. *Clinical studies in infant mental health: The first year of life.* New York: Basic Books.

Fraiberg, S., E. Adelson, and V. Shapiro. 1975. Ghosts in the nursery: A psychoanalytic approach to the problems of impaired infant-mother relationships. *Journal of the American Academy of Child Psychiatry* 14:387-421.

Garmezy, N. 1976. Vulnerable and invulnerable children: Theory, research, and intervention. *Catalogue of Selected Documents in Psychology* 6(4):1-22.

Johnson, B. J., M. J. McGonigel, and R. K. Kaufman. 1989. *Guidelines and recommended practices for the Individualized Family Service Plan.* Washington, DC: Association for the Care of Children's Health.

Lally, J. R., P. L. Manione, A. S. Honig, and D. S. Wittner. 1988. More pride, less delinquency: Findings from the ten-year follow-up study of the Syracuse University Family Development Research Program. *Zero to Three: Bulletin of the National Center for Clinical Infant Programs* 8(4): 13-18.

Lindblad-Goldberg, M., J. L. Dukes, and J. H. Lasley. 1988. Stress in black, low-income, single-parent families: Normative and dysfunctional patterns. *American Journal of Orthopsychiatry* 58(1):104-19.

McGonigel, M., and C. Garland. 1988. The Individualized Family Service Plan and the early intervention team: Team and family issues and recommended practices. *Infants and Young Children* 1:10-21.

Mechanic, D. 1989. Chapter 2: Socioeconomic status and health: An examination of underlying processes. In *Pathways to Health: The Role of Social Factors,* edited by J. Bunker, D. S. Gomby, and B. H. Kehrer. Menlo Park, CA: Kaiser Family Foundation.

Parker, S., S. Greer, and B. Zuckerman. 1988. Double jeopardy: The impact of poverty on early child development. *Pediatric Clinics of North America* 35(6):1227-40.

Rosenbaum, M. 1981. *Women on heroin.* New Brunswick, NJ: Rutgers University Press.

Rutter, M. 1972. *Maternal deprivation reassessed.* Harmondsworth, England: Penguin Books.

______. 1979. Protective factors in children's response to stress and disadvantage. In *Primary preventions of psychopathology vol. III: Social competencies in children,* edited by M. W. Kent and J. E. Rolf. Hanover, NH: University Press of New England.

______. 1987. Psychosocial resilience and protective mechanisms. *American Journal of Orthopsychiatry* 57(3).

Sameroff, A. J. 1974. *Infant risk factors in developmental deviancy.* Paper presented at the meeting of the International Association for Child Psychiatry and Allied Professions, Philadelphia.

Sameroff, A., and M. Chandler. 1975. Reproductive risk and the continuum of caretaking casualty. In *Review of child development research* 4, edited by F. D. Horowitz, M. Hetherington, S. Scarr-Salapatek, and G. Siegel, 187-244. Chicago: University of Chicago Press.

Sameroff, A., and B. Fiese. 1990. Transactional regulation and early intervention. In *Handbook of early childhood intervention,* edited by S. J. Meisels and J. Shankoff. New York: Cambridge University Press.

Shelton, T., E. Jeppson, and B. Johnson. 1987. *Family-centered care for children with special health care needs.* Washington, DC: Association for the Care of Children's Health.

Wadsworth, M. E. J. 1988. *The influence of childhood on later life: Some evidence from a national cohort study.* Hugh Greenwood Lecture presented at the University of Exeter.

Werner, E. E., and R. S. Smith. 1982. *Vulnerable but invincible: A longitudinal study of resilient children and youth.* New York: McGraw-Hill.

Woodhead, M. 1985. Preschool education has long-term effects: But can they be generalized? *Oxford Review of Education* 2(2):133-155.

Chapter 16

Boarder Babies

Davene M. White, RN, NNP

A "boarder baby" is defined as any pediatric patient who remains hospitalized without medical problems to justify the prolonged stay. These "hard-to-place," "born-to-lose," "children in limbo" were simply left in hospital nurseries in escalating numbers during the 1980s (Fomufod and Street 1990). Partly as a result of some new programs developed in a few states and localities, the numbers have improved during the 1990s; at the very least, the situation is getting worse at a slower rate.

Magnitude of the Problem

In August, 1993, the United States Department of Health and Human Services (HHS) reported that in 1991, 10,000 "boarder babies" were deserted in 851 hospitals nationwide. About 75% of these infants tested positive for drugs (Van Biema 1994). Primary reasons cited for this large number are alcohol, drug abuse, previous involvement with child protective agency, homelessness, family breakup, teen pregnancy, poverty, and lack of federal and state program funds. About 75% of the boarder babies in this study were African-American, 12% were white, and 8% were Hispanic.

In 573 of the hospitals studied in the 1991 survey by HHS, there were a total of 303 boarder babies on any given day during the year. Nearly a quarter (24%) of these infants stayed in the hospital from three weeks to three months after medical discharge. Ultimately, two-thirds of all boarder babies go to foster homes from the hospital, and 19% go to relatives' homes (McGurk 1994).

Boarder babies present the hospital with a myriad of problems–medical, ethical, legal, staffing, and financial. Overcrowding in the nursery brings with it an increased potential for nosocomial infections and upper respiratory (RSV and adenoviruses) infections. The nursing staff can become strained trying to provide well-child care in addition to acute and chronic care. Inability to discharge the infants to an appropriate setting causes phenomenal financial losses to the hospitals; and the blocking of admission of those who need hospital care levies a burden on the community.

The infants pay a heavy toll. They are denied the benefit of a home-like environment, and often denied the opportunity to participate in normal childhood activities such as outside play or crawling about on the floor.

Boarder Babies at Howard University Hospital, Washington, D.C.

The problem of abandoned infants at Howard University Hospital was addressed in force early in 1989. The presence of "long-stay" infants was not new; however, by 1988 the increasing number of infants remaining after being declared medically stable and ready for discharge had created an occupancy rate of well over 100%. There were many occasions in which 10 to 15 infants occupied the nursery in addition to the stated maximum of 35. In December 1988, the occupancy rate was 132.6% of capacity (Fomufod and White 1989).

In February 1989, the Division of Neonatology at Howard University Hospital called a multidisciplinary meeting inviting nursing and social services staff to discuss methods to ease the congestion. At that time, there were nine infants in the nursery whose stays ranged from six weeks to seven months. The decision was made to transfer these infants to the pediatric unit, causing congestion there. Hospital administration was made aware that the District of Columbia Department of Social Services was having difficulty in obtaining legal custody of these children.

During the subsequent 11 months of 1989, 35 women abandoned their infants. Some averages and numbers yield at least a sketchy profile of the mothers. (See Table 16.1.)

Analysis of the infants (all born alive) of this same group of 35 women revealed 17 cases (50%) of premature delivery and 23 cases (68%) of low birth weight. Eleven children (31%) were small for gestational age. Ten children (29%) were

Table 16.1
Characteristics of 35 Women Abandoning Infants at Howard University Hospital, 2/5/89 - 12/31/89

	Averages
Average age	25.7 (range 15 to 40)
Average gravidity	3.5 (range 1 to 7)
Average parity	3 (range 0 to 4)
Length of substance use	5 years
Substance of choice	Crack cocaine (79%)
Marital status	Single (100%)
	Numbers
HIV-Positive	4
No prenatal care	25
Self-pay or no pay	23
Known to Protective Services prior to infant's birth	8
Incarcerated after delivery	3
Premature delivery	17

diagnosed with respiratory distress syndrome requiring mechanical ventilatory support, and five children later developed bronchopulmonary dysplasia (Dahl-Regis and Oyefara 1990).

A high number of these infants had been exposed to substances in utero. As noted above, 27 children (79%) were exposed to cocaine, 17 (50%) were exposed to alcohol, four (11%) were exposed to heroin, and six (17%) were exposed to PCP. Further, 23 infants (68%) were exposed to nicotine, and five (14%) were exposed to maternal use of intravenous heroin and cocaine ("speedball"). Throughout the neonatal and well-child pediatric stay, these children exhibited the irritability, poor feeding patterns, and irregular sleep patterns of drug-affected newborns. Their responses to interactive stimuli were initially depressed; yet with consistent nurturing, this condition improved.

Lost Inch: A Model Program

"Lost Inch" (Long-Stay Infants and Children), the boarder baby program, was established at Howard University Hospital in 1989 to provide these boarder babies with a homelike environment while awaiting linkage into the system of foster care, kinship care, and adoptive placement. Community donations and involvement created a physical environment that includes furnishings, equipment, clothing, and supplies. People volunteering their time provide the all-important human environment–someone to provide smiles, cuddles, a goal to crawl toward, a grownup to respond to cries of hunger, discomfort, or loneliness.

The program was given an initial boost in April of 1989, when the hospital director, Mr. Haynes Rice, Fellow of the American College of Hospital Executives, testified before the Select Committee on Children, Youth, and Families of the United States House of Representatives. Media interest was sparked. As more news coverage was given to the phenomenon of beautiful, healthy children growing up in hospitals, the public began to respond. Requests for volunteering and donations of clothing, toys, supplies, and money poured into the hospital. Service, social, and religious organizations responded with fund raisers and "baby showers." Soon the boarder infants were the best-dressed and best-equipped children on the block!

Within two months, 100 volunteers had been trained, and after 15 months those numbers had swelled to over 300. The volunteers are an important element in the socialization of these infants. Each volunteer comes at a different time, and each baby has more than one volunteer who is assigned to the child for the entire hospital stay. During the volunteer's two-hour minimum visit, all the volunteer's attention is concentrated on the assigned infant.

Program Format

In the Lost Inch nursery, daily care of long-stay infants and children is carried out as though the child were at home. Daily baths with a mild soap are comforting and approximate home-care routines. Formula type, volume, and frequency are prescribed as commonly done. Solids are introduced as appropriate for age.

The Lost Inch rooms are colorful and equipped as infants' bedrooms. Home-style cribs are used, with colorful crib sheets, mobiles, and bumper guards. Infants are kept in the cribs for sleep times only. Other equipment is supplied, such as strollers with seat belts. (Twin strollers are especially fun and appropriate.) Jumpers with adjustable height and mobile-like fixtures provide an alternative to the cribs for active, alert periods. Large, thick floor mats are covered with linen to provide for creeping and crawling. A floor safety mirror is placed in the area to encourage face recognition. Bolsters, inclines, and padded shapes are used to support the infant in assisted walking, sitting, and turning. Infants are constantly monitored during floor play.

Each infant has an assigned home-style dresser with padded top. The dresser is supplied with a child's lamp. Stored on the dresser are the infant's supplies—shampoo, comb and brush, lotion, wipes, and any special needs such as medication. The padded tops are used after the child's bath, for dressing, and for diaper changing. Each infant is given a baby bathtub, soap, cloth washcloths, and towels.

Currently the infants' clothes are laundered by the nurses or volunteers in a washer and dryer which were donated to the babies and is located on the unit. The hospital laundry continues to launder large items. Infant clothes are kept separate, with a laundry bag at each bed. When a child outgrows clothing, it is returned to the general stock. Commercial infant detergent, powdered non-chlorine bleach, and fragrance-free dryer sheets are used for the Lost Inchers.

Many people are needed to provide interactions to help the infants organize neurologically, learn social interaction, and benefit from handling and other sensory experiences. Occupational therapists and child-life therapists train the staff and volunteers to ensure that the children are benefitting from day-to-day interactions and that they are being positioned properly for normal development of crawling and walking skills. Strollers are available on the unit, and volunteers or staff take the child strolling around the halls and to the hospital patio. These activities are socially stimulating to the infants.

Immunizations and screenings such as PKU are done as appropriate for the age of the infant. DPT (0.5 ml IM), IPV (0.5 ml subcutaneously), HIB (0.5 ml IM), and HBV (0.5 ml IM) are given at two months, four months, and six months of age. Metabolic screening is done at three days and one month of age. Medical aspects of the child's care are managed as if the child were at home. The pediatrician and the nurse clinician review the infant's progress daily. As long as these children are not experiencing any acute illness, they are managed as normal, well children. Infants requiring specialty appointments (such as neurology, infectious disease, or surgery) are scheduled for visits by specialists. These infants also visit specialty clinics if available.

Physical exams by the pediatrician or pediatric specialist are comprehensive. The physician has the responsibility to determine medication dosages and frequency, and to order medications. The physician also reorders any equipment needed by the infant, such as an apnea monitor or humidification. Settings for apnea, bradycardia, and tachycardia, as appropriate for the child's age, are ordered by the physician. Requests for follow-up pneumograms are called in by the nurse clinician. Apnea monitoring is discontinued by the pediatrician when the sleep study results indicate the problem of sleep apnea is no longer noted.

Transfer Into the Lost Inch Program

To ensure quality transfer and discharge information, Howard University Hospital adopted a Transfer/Discharge Record. (See Table 16.2, pages 143-144.) The form was particularly helpful when Sibley Hospital in Washington, D.C., agreed to maintain two beds for boarder babies from Howard University Hospital. Utilizing this form has assured that the receiving pediatrician has a standardized basis of information on each child transferred.

Recordkeeping and Documentation

In the Lost Inch nursery, recordkeeping and documentation contain concise overviews of the infant's progress. Flow sheets are used to enhance legibility and accuracy of data such as feedings, excretions, and medication administration. Nurses and physicians record interventions on the flow sheets. Each infant has a baby book which is maintained by the volunteers. This book is given as a gift to the parent, family member, or foster or adoptive parent when the child is discharged. Progress notes are recorded at scheduled physical exams and in emergencies or at the time of an incident. The physician and nurse record subjective data, growth and development observations, an assessment of the infant's progress, and anticipated needs. Plans are presented to enhance the infant's social skills (for example, parties, visits from personalities, a "picnic" on the hospital grounds, or transport to the Special Well-Baby Reunion). Intervention with the parent or designated caretaker is documented. Training of caretakers is scheduled and monitored by the nurse clinician. Currently a visitors' log book is provided for parents or designated caretakers, to sign in and out whenever they visit. Nursing staff document visits and calls on a Family Communication Record which is kept on the infant's chart.

Parental involvement is extended when requested. Visits by the parents are monitored, because once a child has been referred to Protective Services for placement, the discharge permit must come from Protective Services. Monitoring is necessary to prevent parents from leaving the hospital with the child. The perinatal and pediatric social workers are the major liaison with the District of Columbia Child Protective Services. The social workers provide new information to the team so that plans for the child's discharge can be performed in a timely fashion. Some parents or designated caretakers really want to take the child home, yet need hours of hands-on training to prepare for the home care of a child with in utero exposure to substances.

Discharge

All Lost Inchers are given a two-week follow-up appointment to the Pediatric Continuity Care Office or to the Special Well-Baby Clinic, unless an alternate medical follow-up plan is known. At the time of discharge, it is important to provide the caretaker with an immunization record and a growth and development record for the child. Caretakers will need to know the child's feeding and sleep patterns and play activities. Special toys go home with the child. The children are discharged with their mobiles and the clothes in their dressers. Special "Going Home" bags are packed by volunteers, and each child receives one.

Conclusion

The Child Development Center at Howard University Hospital has begun to perform routine developmental assessments on these hospitalized well babies to identify developmental problems related to growing up in the hospital.

The Howard University School of Business has reviewed the hospital costs associated with these boarder babies and the time professional staff are required to provide this well-child care. The problem is being studied from a medical and administrative point of view.

In 1989 the American Civil Liberties Union filed, and in 1991 won, a suit against the District on behalf of children in foster care. The District hired 100 new social workers, and more adoptive and foster homes were found. Mencimer (1994), writing in *The Washington Post,* reported that thanks to an alliance between city bureaucrats and local institutions (including Howard University Hospital), the boarder baby problem is no longer just a tear-jerker; real progress has been made.

References

Boarder babies in selected hospitals in the United States: A survey. 1992. Child Welfare League of America. National Association of Public Hospitals.

Chasnoff, I. J., W. J. Burns, and S. H. Schnoll. 1984. *Perinatal addiction: The effects of maternal narcotic and non-narcotic substance abuse on the fetus and neonate.* National Institute of Drug Abuse.

Dahl-Regis, M., and B. Oyefara. 1990. Boarder babies: Children with special needs. *Journal of the National Medical Association* 82(7):474.

English, P. C. 1984. Pediatrics and the unwanted child in history: Founding homes, disease, and the origins of foster care in New York City, 1860 to 1920. *Journal of Pediatrics* 73(1):700.

Fomufod, A. K., and A. A. Street. 1990. Rearing children in hospital facilities (boarder babies). Letter in *Pediatrics* 85(1):137-38.

Fomufod, A. K., and D. M. White. 1989. Minutes of interdepartmental meeting, February 7. Department of Pediatrics and Child Health, Division of Neonatology, Howard University Hospital, Washington, D.C.

McGurk, M. 1994. California system avoids "boarder baby" problem. *Nurseweek* 7(1) January 3.

Melnick, V. L. 1992. *Boarder babies and drug-affected children in the District of Columbia* 1, Executive Summary. Center for Applied Research and Urban Policy, University of the District of Columbia, Building 48, Room 510, 4200 Connecticut Ave., N.W., Washington, DC 20008.

Mencimer, S. 1994. Nursing a miracle: A D.C. story. *The Washington Post* February 6, C1.

Mitchell-Wright, D. M., and V. M. Mitchell. 1990. Substance abuse affects everyone: Women are not immune. *Health Care.* Howard University, Washington, DC. Summer.

Reichelderfer, T. 1972. *Epidemiology of infants abandoned in hospitals.* Proceedings from Conference on Special Problems of Child Health in the Ghetto. Howard University Hospital, Department of Pediatrics and Child Health, Washington, DC.

Through the eyes of a child: Final report. 1992. The Child Welfare League of America, North American Commission on Chemical Dependency and Child Welfare.

Van Biema, D. 1994. Mother-and-child reunion. *Time* January 24, 143(4):58.

Table 16.2
Sample Transfer/Discharge Record*

Howard University Hospital
Division of Neonatology

High-Risk Infant Transfer/Discharge Summary

Infant's name______________________________

Parent's name ______________________________

Infant's date of birth ______________ Birth weight ______________

Gestation weeks __________ Sex ______ Current weight ______________

_____ AGA _____ SGA _____ LGA _____ NSVD _____ C/S

Diagnosis

_____ BPD ______________________________

_____ IVH ______________________________

_____ Seizures ______________________ Rx ______________

_____ In utero exposure to ______________________________

_____ Sleep apnea study ______________________________

_____ Other ______________________________

Neonatal History

_____ Mechanical ventilation ______________________________

_____ CPAP ______________________________

_____ Oxyhood ______________________________

_____ Hyperbilirubinemia Highest level __________ Rx ______________

_____ Sepsis ______________________ Rx ______________

_____ Cat Scan ______________________________

_____ Other ______________________________

Labs

Blood type __________ Coombs __________ Metabolic screen ______________

VDRL _______ Hepatitis _______ HIV _______ H/H ______________

(continued)

Table 16.2
Sample Transfer/Discharge Record (continued)

Current History

______ Formula ______________ Frequency __________ Amount _____________

______ Breast-feeding ______ Solids

Cereals __________________________________ Freq. _________ Amt. _________

Fruits __________________________________ Freq. _________ Amt. __________

Vegetables ______________________________ Freq. _________ Amt. __________

Juices __________________________________ Freq. _________ Amt. _________

Immunizations

DPT #________ Date _______ #_______ Date _______ #_______ Date ______

TOPV #________ Date _______ #_______ Date _______ #_______ Date ______

IPV #________ Date _______ #_______ Date _______ #_______ Date ______

HIB #________ Date _______ #_______ Date _______ #_______ Date ______

HBV #________ Date _______ #_______ Date _______ #_______ Date ______

Tine Date _____________ Results ______________________________________

Other ____

Supportive Services

______ Protective Services ____

______ WIC ____

______ VNA ____

______ Medicaid ____

______ Foster care ____

______ Adoption____

______ Kinship care____

______ Insurance carrier ____

______ Other home-care agency____

Comments ____

____

Signature ____

Date _____________________________ Time ______________________________

Chapter 17

Guidelines for Handling Infants

Ellen Aronson Kaplan, M.S., PT

Guidelines for Handling Infants was developed for the mothers and caregivers at Generations,* an outpatient treatment program for chemically dependent women and their infants. Biological, environmental, and observed risk factors associated with these children caused concern for the child-care workers at this program. The suggested methods of handling reflect interventions for behaviors exhibited by these children, from multirisk families, who were also exposed to substances in utero.

A significant responsibility for early intervention practitioners is defining and providing services that best meet the developmental needs of children from multirisk families. This area is made more complex because of the multiple environmental and biological risk factors affecting these children (Aylward 1990). An additional risk factor is the increased use of cocaine (along with other substances) by pregnant women. Frank et al. (1988) reported that 17% of 679 pregnant women enrolled for prenatal care used cocaine during pregnancy. These authors suggested comprehensive prenatal assessments to ascertain the number of infants exposed to cocaine in utero. Studies have indicated that these numbers may be increasing, with cocaine being the drug of choice in the 1990s.

Information about infants exposed to substances in utero, along with other high-risk factors, suggests that these infants will experience developmental difficulties. Oro and Dixon (1987) reported a study of 104 mothers and their infants who had tested positive for various substances. Group 1 consisted of mother-infant pairs who had tested positive for cocaine, group 2 consisted of mother-infant pairs who had tested positive for methamphetamine, and group 3 consisted of mother-infant pairs who had tested positive for cocaine combined with methamphetamine. All three groups of infants demonstrated altered neonatal behavioral patterns characterized by abnormal sleep, poor feeding, tremors, and hypertonia. Other risks for development associated with cocaine use in pregnancy include higher rates of premature birth, intrauterine growth retardation, and smaller head circumferences for the infants (Bignol et al. 1987; Oro and Dixon 1987; Zuckerman et al. 1989). A comparison of the cardiac status of 15 cocaine-exposed infants and 22 nonexposed infants found that infants exposed to cocaine in utero demonstrated decreased cardiac competency during the newborn period (van de Bor, Walther, and Ebrahimi 1990).

---

*Generations, located in Westchester County, New York, is a program of the Weekend Center, Inc., and is licensed by the New York State Office of Alcoholism and Substance Abuse Services. It is partially funded by Westchester County's War on Drugs and the Department of Social Services.

The degree of "jitteriness" (Parker et al. 1990) was investigated in 1,054 healthy and sick neonates. These findings were compared with those of infants who had been exposed to various substances in utero. This study found that neonatal jitteriness was significantly associated with maternal marijuana use and approached significance with maternal use of cocaine. In conclusion, the authors recommended continued research on the effects of maternal drug use in other neurobehavioral areas as the child matures. These reports demonstrate increased biological risk (as assessed in the neonate) associated with exposure to drugs in utero.

Schneider, Griffith, and Chasnoff (1989) compared normal infants and infants exposed to cocaine, using the *Neonatal Behavioral Assessment Scale* (Brazelton 1973) and the *Movement Assessment of Infants* (Chandler, Andrews, and Swanson 1980). Results demonstrated that infants exposed to cocaine exhibited difficulty in successfully regulating their behavioral states during the neonatal period. Assessment of movement demonstrated qualitative and quantitative motor deficits in the four-month-old infants who had been exposed to cocaine in utero. These authors also reported preliminary results of infants at age eight months which indicated that cocaine-exposed infants demonstrated motor abnormalities that were of concern. For example, these infants were slow in crawling and showed atypical patterns of stiff extension when placed in supported stance (Schneider, Griffith, and Chasnoff 1989).

Dixon, Bresnahan, and Zuckerman (1990) combined clinical experience and research evidence to establish guidelines for the pediatric management of infants exposed to drugs in utero. These authors reported that:

> In fact, neurobehavioral changes can be expected to persist during the first year, possibly longer. These are clinical impressions, based on considerable experience but not yet documented by systematic studies. (81-83)

They then concluded that:

> As these children develop, further neurobehavioral disturbances and developmental compromise may become evident, requiring ongoing monitoring and intervention. (92)

However, the effect of prenatal substance exposure along with other multirisk factors throughout the course of early childhood is still relatively unknown (Zuckerman and Brooks 1991). These studies reflect outcomes that are documented during the neonatal course of the infant exposed to substances in utero. The recommendations from these reports include specific concern for further investigation of infant and toddler development (Parker et al. 1990; Schneider, Griffith, and Chasnoff 1989). A recent report of children exposed to cocaine/polysubstances in utero demonstrated that:

> The incidence of Bayley PDI delays of a standard deviation or more from the established mean was significantly higher among the cocaine/polydrug-exposed infants than among the drug-free infants in 6, 12, and 24 months of age. (Chasnoff, Griffith, Freier, and Murray 1992, 286)

The population of families for whom *Guidelines for Handling Infants* was developed presented environmental risk factors that influence the developmental outcomes for their children. The environmental factors associated with the mothers included low socioeconomic status, limited educational background, involvement with child-protective agencies, involvement with the legal system, involvement with correctional systems, homelessness, and decreased access to health care for themselves and their children. In addition, the women had used cocaine or multiple substances during their pregnancies. The use of substances provided an additional biological risk factor that affected the developmental skills of their children.

The literature supports concerns for the developmental outcomes for these children. Preliminary work with 13 children from multirisk families at Generations was conducted by Kaplan in the summer of 1991. This pilot study provided descriptive data concerning movement skills, coping abilities, and general developmental abilities for this population of children. Results of this pilot study indicated that the residual effects of initial increased muscle tone are still evident as the children progress in the acquisition of motor milestone skills (Kaplan 1991). A second study assessing the movement components of 20 of the children (ranging in age from one month to 26 months) provided further support to the observations that these children demonstrated deviant components of gross motor development during the infant and toddler period of development (Kaplan 1992).

Early intervention efforts directed toward the infants, mothers, environmental factors, and support staff are recommended (Davidson and Short 1982) for children at risk. These efforts should include offering information that will enhance handling skills of parents and caregivers of these children and promote positive mother-child interactions. Early intervention directed at preventing and/or correcting problems, whether the problems are directly related to substances or a combination of maternal health and environment, should be included in programs addressing the issue of recovery from addiction.

These early intervention services could include:

- Teaching mothers various handling and caretaking methods as a segment of parenting classes
- Providing information to mothers concerning their children's development
- Assuring parents that gross motor skills will develop
- Training efforts directed toward caregivers in various day-care situations incorporating knowledge about appropriate handling for the children which facilitates the best behavioral states for the child.

Guidelines for Handling Infants attempts to address some of these issues.

Development of specific models for multirisk children and their families that integrate the components of care around specific problems is an area that requires further development and demonstration (Davidson and Short 1982; Greenspan 1987; Shelton, Jeppson, and Johnson 1987). Mandates from two federal laws reinforce this concept. P.L. 96-272 and P.L. 101-476 (1990) are based on the intent that the needs of the child are best served within the family. Each law promotes efforts to maintain the child within the family system. Therefore, services are required to make every attempt to preserve the family structure. Programs that serve substance-dependent women and provide for their infants represent services for a specific population of multirisk families encompassed by both of these laws.

Guidelines for Handling Infants was developed in order to provide information to mothers recovering from substance abuse, professionals dealing with mothers recovering from chemical dependence, and caregivers working with substance-exposed children from multirisk families.

Promoting Positive Mother-Child Interactions*

Ellen Aronson Kaplan, M.S., PT

Things to Remember—
Newborn through Three Months Old

Babies can adjust to their surroundings and the people who care for them. Infants who are withdrawing from substances have trouble adjusting to many activities that happen as part of their regular care. You will be able to help your baby adjust to these new situations.

Babies are very sensitive to stimulation–the sights, sounds, noises, smells, taste, and movement around them. You can control the surroundings so that your baby has a chance to adjust to any change. Introduce activities *one thing at a time.* First hold your baby, then look at your baby, and then talk softly to your baby. If the baby starts to cry or becomes stiff or jittery, slowly decrease the stimulation until the baby is comfortable. It is often helpful to "swaddle" the baby. Wrap a small blanket around your baby's body, arms, and legs. Tucking babies in by "swaddling" helps them adjust to the different stimulation around them.

If the baby starts to cry, gets stiff, or falls asleep quickly, there is too much stimulation for the baby to handle. A baby who is awake, active, and alert is ready to play quietly. Play games that allow the baby to spend time looking at you or at toys. Start by letting the baby look at your face and explore it. Next, find a favorite toy, and let the baby look and play with it until the baby loses interest in it.

*From *Generations—Guidelines for Handling Infants and Toddlers.*

Newborn to One Month

Typical Baby	Recovering Baby*	Handling Suggestions
The baby's movements are random and reflexive.**	Once in a while the baby shows tremors (shaking or trembling) of the lips or chin. Sometimes the baby's movements are jerky, or the baby may feel stiff.	Swaddling helps to quiet movements and makes your baby feel secure.
The baby's body can easily adjust to handling by an adult.	It takes a long time to find a comfortable position for the baby. The baby cries when held, and seems to resist attempts to cuddle.	Handle your baby *slowly.* Give the baby a chance to adjust to movements. Babies often prefer gentle up-and-down motion to rocking.
At the sound of a voice, the baby responds with some alertness. For example, the baby's eyes widen, or the baby quiets to the sound.	At the sound of a voice, the baby shows signs of stress. For example, the baby cries, stiffens, or hiccups when held and talked to at the same time. The baby "shuts down" by going into a deep sleep if there is too much noise in the room.	Wait until your baby has calmed down before you talk. You may need to do things one at a time. For example: 1. Swaddle the baby. 2. Hold the baby. 3. Talk in a soft voice. 4. Slowly look at the baby, face to face.
The baby stops sucking from a bottle to look at something and then continues to suck from the bottle.	Sometimes the baby falls asleep while drinking from a bottle, and may not get enough to eat. The baby may spit up frequently during a feeding. Your baby may require frequent bottle feedings.	*Bottle-feed your baby. Do not breast-feed.**** Feed your baby in a quiet area. Before you start feeding, be sure the baby is clean, dry, and comfortable. Hold the baby so the child feels secure. Swaddle the baby during bottle feedings.

*The babies for whom these guidelines apply are recovering from prenatal exposure to substances.

**Reflexive movements are actions that your baby always uses when reacting to a particular kind of stimulation. For example, stroking the bottom of the baby's foot causes the baby to pull back the foot.

***For discussion, see Chasnoff, I. J., E. L. Douglas, and L. Squires. 1986. Cocaine intoxication in a breast-fed infant. *Pediatrics* 80(6):836-838. This article is a case study of a two-week-old infant who developed irritability, vomiting, diarrhea, dilated pupils, loss of focusing, tremulousness, and other atypical neurological signs following breast-feeding from a mother who had used approximately 0.5 grams of cocaine prior to and during breast-feeding this infant. The authors concluded that education concerning the potential hazards of cocaine intoxication of infants should be provided to women who breast-feed their children.

One to Two Months

Typical Baby	Recovering Baby*	Handling Suggestions
When awake, your baby is active. For example, the baby kicks when lying on its back.	The baby's movements feel stiff and jerky. The baby is most stiff when placed on its back. The baby's arms or legs seldom move.	Move your baby slowly when you change the baby's position. Calm the baby by swaddling, and see if the baby will stay awake, alert, and quiet. When the baby is asleep, hold the baby, or place the baby on one side or on the belly. Avoid placing the baby on its back.
The baby starts to focus on a face. The baby may move its head in order to keep a face in view. The baby starts to smile when feeling comfortable.	The baby avoids too much stimulation. (For example, the baby's eyes close or the baby looks away from fast-moving objects, and cries or falls asleep if there is a lot of noise.) The baby is seldom quiet and alert, and is often fussy, asleep, or crying.	Swaddle and hold the baby facing you. Do not talk. Look at your baby, and wait for the baby to look at you. When the baby is quiet and looking at you, start to move your head and coo softly. Wait for the baby to respond by smiling or following the movement of your face and voice.
When sucking from a bottle, the baby may look at your face, stop drinking to look, then continue to drink.	The baby may be panicky before feedings. The baby may frequently spit up during and after a bottle. The baby may require frequent feedings.	Keep feeding time as quiet as possible. Use this time to encourage your baby to look at your face or toys. Talk softly with your baby.

*The babies for whom these guidelines apply are recovering from prenatal exposure to substances.

Two to Three Months

Typical Baby	Recovering Baby*	Handling Suggestions
The baby works to bring the head toward the middle when back-lying.	When placed on the back, the baby shows infrequent, stiff, uncoordinated movements. The baby feels stiff and may arch the back.	Use an infant seat instead of laying your baby on the back. This helps to support the baby in a comfortable position for resting and watching.
When you bring the baby toward a sitting position, the baby tries to help by tightening the muscles of the neck and trying to hold up the head. In a supported sitting position, the baby seems comfortable and does not resist.	The baby seems to resist going into a sitting position. It is difficult to get the baby to bend into a sitting position. The baby needs help to stay in this position.	Support your baby behind the shoulders and in front of the chest. This helps the baby to relax into a sitting position and become comfortable.
The baby will turn its head in the direction of a sound.	When hearing a noise, the baby often cries, startles, or becomes very fussy (for example, panic-cries), or the baby may fall asleep.	Be very patient and calm to get the child to settle down, and then introduce sound slowly and softly. Avoid loud and sudden sounds.
The baby likes to be watching and observing. The baby is able to watch a slowly moving toy.	It takes a long time for the child's eyes to open, and often the eyes close quickly when you look at the baby.	Swaddle and hold your baby facing you. Wait for the baby to start to look at your face. Change the position of your face as the baby watches you.
The baby cries with more rhythm and begins to laugh.	The baby makes few sounds other than crying. The baby does not play with sounds.	Talk softly with your baby. Imitate any sounds the baby makes. Be sure that you and your baby are looking at each other during this time.

*The babies for whom these guidelines apply are recovering from prenatal exposure to substances.

Three to Four Months

Typical Baby	Recovering Baby*	Handling Suggestions
The baby is getting better head control. When placed on the belly, the baby is able to lift up the head and rest on the elbows.	When placed on the belly, the arms are held back and the baby is unable to lift up the head to look around.	Place a small towel roll under your baby's chest. This will move the baby's arms in a position to provide support and enable the baby to hold up the head and look around. Encourage the baby to look at toys in this position.
There is less evidence of a Moro reflex** and startle reaction.***	Moro reflex and startle reaction are still evident.	Handle your baby slowly. Avoid sudden loud noises and quick movement. Give support around the back and chest when you change the baby's position.
The baby puts two hands together and plays with them. The baby holds toys that are placed in the hands. Babies may start to reach out for toys.	The baby's hands are held stiffly at the sides. The baby has trouble putting two hands together or bringing hands to mouth.	Cradle your baby in your arms, or position the baby comfortably in an infant seat. Hand the baby rattles, squeak toys, and other things to explore with both hands at the same time and put in the mouth.
The baby is beginning to make more sounds and sound combinations.	The baby makes few sounds between silence and crying.	Talk with your baby. Imitate any sounds the baby makes, and wait for the baby to repeat the sound.

*The babies for whom these guidelines apply are recovering from prenatal exposure to substances.

**When the baby's head is allowed to drop backward suddenly, the baby's arms and legs immediately move out to the sides of the body. This is called the Moro reflex.

***When the baby reacts to an unexpected noise, movement, or touch by suddenly jumping or crying, it is called a startle reaction.

Promoting Positive Mother-Child Interactions*

Ellen Aronson Kaplan, M.S., PT

Things to Remember—Four through Six Months Old

During this time, babies are becoming very visually alert, spending lots of time looking at things. When your baby is comfortable and alert, encourage the baby to look at your face or at toys. However, remain sensitive to the baby's ability to be alert and quiet or alert and active.

The baby will still need your help to adjust if there is too much stimulation. Be aware of signs of stress. For example, the baby might cry, stiffen, show tremors or jerkiness, or have difficulty settling down. Swaddle and hold the baby on your shoulder until the baby is calm and ready to play.

By this time, babies start to touch objects and explore toys and people that are in view. Encourage your baby to play with toys with both hands and to start holding the bottle independently. Gently touch and stroke the child's hands. Place toys in the baby's hands. The baby will touch and explore them. Soon the baby will begin to reach in the direction of the toys. Talk softly to your baby about the things that are happening. Wait for the baby to coo back, and then imitate the baby's sounds.

*From *Generations—Guidelines for Handling Infants and Toddlers.*

Four to Five Months

Typical Baby	Recovering Baby*	Handling Suggestions
When back-lying, the baby plays with both hands and feet together. The baby is able to reach up in order to get a toy.	The baby still has difficulty bringing hands and feet together. Often the baby's legs are stiff. The baby may have tremors (shaking or trembling) of the arms.	Place your baby in an infant seat. Avoid letting the baby spend lots of time lying on the back. Play games that allow the baby's hands to touch each other. Encourage the baby to reach toward the feet.
When placed on the belly, the baby can hold the head up and will try to reach for toys.	The baby has difficulty with lying on the belly. In this position, the baby's legs are stiff and the baby falls over while trying to reach for a toy.	Encourage playing in a belly-lying position. A small towel roll under the chest sometimes helps the baby to feel more secure.
When held in standing, the baby will bounce up and down on bent legs.	When held in standing, the baby will stand on stiff legs and has difficulty bending the legs. The baby usually stands on tiptoe.	Avoid holding the baby in a standing position. Encourage the baby to play while lying on its belly. *Do not use an infant walker or baby bouncer.***
The baby can hold a bottle independently.	The baby does not attempt to hold the bottle. Arms are down at the sides, and the baby seems to be fighting the bottle.	When the baby is held in a sitting position, the baby's arms and hands can hold the bottle more comfortably. Use a sit-up straw in the bottle. Sit-up straws are plastic drinking straws that can be pushed into the nipple of the baby's bottle. Then the liquid may be sucked up into the straw while the bottle is held upright. The baby can sit up and drink from a bottle even while the head is down. Sit-up straws are sold in the children's section of department stores.
The baby is beginning to watch and play with toys placed in each hand and change the toy from hand to hand. The baby likes to look in the mirror.	The baby makes few attempts to reach for toys. There are brief periods of looking, but the baby is often distracted by other things.	First have your baby look at a toy, then place a toy in the baby's hand. Let the baby play with one toy at a time.

*The babies for whom these guidelines apply are recovering from prenatal exposure to substances.

**For discussion, see Rieder, M.J., C. Schwartz, and J. Newman. 1986. Patterns of walker use and walker injury. *Pediatrics,* 78(3):448-493. This article is a study of the pattern of injuries related to infant walker use during the first year in 139 infants. The most severe injuries were related to falls down stairs (n=123). Injuries included skull fractures (n=19), forearm fractures (n=3), clavicular fractures (n=2), nasal fractures (n=1), closed head injury (n=93), burn (n=3), dental injury (n=7), laceration (n=6), abrasion (n=3), soft tissue injury (n=1), nasal injury, no fracture (n=1). The authors concluded that use of baby walkers represents a significant cause for injury in the infant population.

Five to Six Months

Typical Baby	Recovering Baby*	Handling Suggestions
When back-lying, the baby is able to bring hands and feet together. The baby tries to play by bringing the feet up to the mouth.	When placed on the back, the baby has difficulty lifting the legs or reaching toward the feet.	Hold the baby in a supported sitting position, and play games that encourage the baby to bring hands and feet together.
When placed in a sitting position, the baby tries to stay sitting.	It is difficult to get the baby to bend into a sitting position. The baby often pushes backward and falls. The baby's back is very stiff and straight, rather than curved.	Use your hands to support the child on both the front and back of the chest. Encourage your baby to play with both hands in front.
The baby is beginning to roll from belly to back.	The baby usually falls into a roll when moving from belly to back. The baby often stiffens and arches the back just before rolling over.	Help your baby to practice rolling. Place the baby on one side, put a toy within reach, and encourage the baby to roll over and get the toy.
The baby is able to reach for and play with a toy that is placed close by.	The baby needs encouragement to hold a toy and play with it.	Encourage hand play by using toys that require both hands.
The baby is able to look at things without becoming distracted.	The baby is easily distracted while looking at things.	Encourage your baby to look at toys during quiet times with little noise and few objects. Keep the baby's attention on one toy until the child shows signs of losing interest.

*The babies for whom these guidelines apply are recovering from prenatal exposure to substances.

Six to Seven Months

Typical Baby	Recovering Baby*	Handling Suggestions
The baby is working on sitting (with the hands placed in front for support). If falling, the baby usually falls forward.	The baby still requires your help and support in sitting. If falling, the baby falls backward. The baby's hands are usually down to the sides, rather than in front.	Support the baby in sitting. Place toys in front of your baby. Encourage the baby to place hands down and in front for support.
The baby is able to lift the head and upper body off the mat when playing on the belly. The baby is able to reach for a toy while lying on the belly.	The baby has difficulty staying on the belly or lifting up onto straight arms. Often, the baby extends too much and rolls onto the back.	A small towel roll placed under the baby's arms will help the baby to maintain a position on straight arms. This provides support so the child does not roll over unexpectedly. Encourage your baby to look down while playing.
The baby is able to sit and play with toys, transferring toys from hand to hand. The baby is able to reach for and grasp toys that are slightly out of reach.	The baby will not attempt to get toys that are out of reach or search for toys that roll away.	At first, place toys in your baby's hands, and then place the toy within reach. Encourage the baby to reach for the toy. Use toys the child can shake and bang.
The baby is beginning to imitate sounds.	The baby rarely makes sounds, but may appear interested in watching someone make sounds.	Imitate any sounds your baby makes. Make simple sounds, and see whether the baby enjoys hearing your sounds and words.

*The babies for whom these guidelines apply are recovering from prenatal exposure to substances.

Promoting Positive Mother-Child Interactions*

Ellen Aronson Kaplan, M.S., PT

Things to Remember—Seven through Nine Months Old

Babies use different types of play (grasping, shaking, and waving) to learn about things. This is important for learning. Allow your baby to touch and explore toys and people. Toys that the baby could use for exploring and learning include things that make noise (pots and pans). Babies also like to play with things placed in containers, such as blocks in a cup. This is a good time to start playing peek-a-boo and to hide toys for the baby to find. Encourage your baby to use both hands to play with balls, stuffed animals, and other toys.

By this time, your baby will begin to indicate some feelings and wants by making different sounds in cooing and fussing. This is a time when the child will spend a lot of time practicing sounds. Encourage your baby to make sounds by imitating the coos your baby makes. This shows your baby that you are interested.

Your baby is now on the move, so it is important to "childproof" areas where the baby is playing. The baby enjoys moving around but is not fully able to balance. Be careful! This is a time when frequent falls can happen.

*From *Generations—Guidelines for Handling Infants and Toddlers.*

Printed and published by Therapy Skill Builders, a division of Communication Skill Builders/602-323-7500

Seven to Eight Months

Typical Baby	Recovering Baby*	Handling Suggestions
The baby is starting to move out from a sitting position into crawling and is able to go from crawling back into sitting.	If beginning to crawl, the baby appears to go slowly (shows hesitancy) in going from sitting to crawling and back. Often it looks as if the baby gets stuck in the middle of doing this.	Play with your baby on the floor between your legs. Let the baby reach for toys on the other side of your legs.
The baby is beginning to try to pull up into standing by holding onto furniture.	The baby is able to pull up into standing, but then gets stuck and is unable to get down. When standing, the baby usually stands on tiptoe.	Encourage your baby to go from sitting to standing, so that the feet remain on the ground. Avoid placing or bouncing the baby in standing.
The baby can indicate pleasure, comfort, anger, and other things by using gestures (for example, kicking and waving). The baby is able to tell mother from other people by smiling and gestures, and indicates a desire to be with mother.	The baby cries when frustrated in not getting things desired. It is very difficult to calm the crying baby. The baby may get stiff and arch the body backward.	Pay close attention to your child in order to understand and interpret cues and avoid frustrating the baby.

*The babies for whom these guidelines apply are recovering from prenatal exposure to substances.

Eight to Nine Months

Typical Baby	Recovering Baby*	Handling Suggestions
The baby is able to go from sitting to crawling and back to sitting with ease. The baby enjoys moving and exploring, crawling very quickly.	The baby is hesitant to move into a crawl. The baby has difficulty going from crawling into sitting independently. Crawling is slow and seems to be hard to do.	Play with your baby on the floor or on a large surface. Encourage the baby to reach from side to side to get toys in sitting. This will help the baby to change positions from sitting.
When held in a standing position, the baby will rock and sway. The baby can bend down from standing to get a toy and return to standing with ease.	When held in standing, the baby's legs are stiff, and often the baby stands on tiptoe. The baby has trouble bending down to get a toy, and often falls from standing.	Encourage the baby to go from squatting to standing, so that the feet are flat on the floor. Do not put the baby on the floor feet first. Do not use a baby bouncer.
The baby is able to eat crackers or cookies independently. The baby can hold a bottle, and tries to help when drinking from a cup. The baby can pick up things between the thumb and fingers.	The baby shows little interest in self-feeding cookies, crackers, and other finger foods. If able to feed self, the baby may try to eat things other than food.	When feeding, give your baby something to hold that is also safe to put in the mouth.
The baby starts to understand words. The baby indicates wants and needs by changes of tone of voice and body language.	The baby may not show preference for one toy or another. The baby is either quiet or will cry.	Be sensitive to things your baby enjoys, and encourage smiles and happy sounds.

*The babies for whom these guidelines apply are recovering from prenatal exposure to substances.

Nine to Ten Months

Typical Baby	Recovering Baby*	Handling Suggestions
From sitting, the baby can go in any direction easily in crawling. Often the baby will crawl onto steps and other low objects.	The baby may get stuck in places and not be able to get out. For example, the baby may crawl under a piece of furniture and not be able to back up in order to get out.	Make an obstacle course for your baby with pillows. Encourage the baby to crawl over, under, around, and between the pillows in order to get a toy.
The baby may begin to walk while holding onto furniture or when you hold the baby's hands.	The baby pulls up to standing while holding onto furniture, but then may become stuck. The baby will not be able to get down into crawling. When standing, the baby is up on tiptoe.	Try to get the baby to stand with both feet flat on the floor. Rather than encouraging walking by holding the baby's hands, try to interest the baby in standing while you hold the baby's hips.
The baby will look for toys that are out of sight.	The baby will not show interest in finding a toy that is placed out of sight even after showing interest in that toy.	This is a good time to play hide-and-seek games with your baby. For example, hide the baby's bottle under a towel, or hide a toy under a blanket.
The baby will imitate what you do.	The baby appears more interested in watching than in doing.	This is a good time to play pat-a-cake and "so big" types of games.
The baby knows his or her name, is able to says single words, and will babble a string of sounds.	The baby does not say any words, and uses only simple sounds rather than a string of babbling.	Sing familiar songs, repeat nursery rhymes, and encourage your baby to try to join in with some of the sounds.

*The babies for whom these guidelines apply are recovering from prenatal exposure to substances.

Promoting Positive Mother-Child Interactions*

Ellen Aronson Kaplan, M.S., PT

Things to Remember—Ten through Twelve Months

By this age, babies are able to indicate their wants, and they can communicate those wants to people. Talk to your baby. Let the baby know you are trying to understand those wants. For example, you might say, "You want a bottle. I will get you your bottle." The baby enjoys playing turn-taking games, such as "Give me" and "Find the toy."

Ten- through twelve-month babies are able to move around quickly. They can go from sitting to crawling to standing, and they may try to walk. Be alert to what your baby is doing, and provide a safe place for the baby to explore. Have toys on hand that your baby can play with safely. Put away items that are dangerous, such as medications, cleaning supplies, and breakable objects.

*From *Generations—Guidelines for Handling Infants and Toddlers.*

Printed and published by Therapy Skill Builders, a division of Communication Skill Builders/602-323-7500

Ten through Eleven Months

Typical Baby	Recovering Baby*	Handling Suggestions
The baby is able to walk with one hand held. However, for speed, usually the baby will crawl. The baby has strong protective reactions. (For example, the baby will put hands out in front for protection in a fall.)	The baby is wobbly when starting to walk, still needs two hands held when walking, and usually walks on tiptoe. The baby tends to fall backward, or falls forward and hurts the head or face (possibly because of delayed or immature protective reactions).	Be very careful as your baby tries to walk. Frequent falls are common. Stay near your baby, and be ready to catch if the baby falls. Playing games like "wheelbarrow," with the baby's hands on the ground while you hold up the legs, will help to develop protective reactions.
The baby is able to follow a simple direction (for example, "Give me").	The baby does not respond to a simple command.	Play games that involve taking turns. When the baby is holding a toy, gesture with your palm up and say, "Give me." Praise any attempt the baby makes toward giving you the toy.
The baby shows interest in music and rhythm, and begins to move to music. The baby is able to imitate games. (For example, the baby will imitate your hand movements.)	If there is a lot of noise, or if music is too loud, the baby may "shut down" by crying or going into a deep sleep.	This is a good time to start singing simple songs and playing games that include hand movements (for example, "Open-shut-them" and "Itsy-bitsy-spider").

*The babies for whom these guidelines apply are recovering from prenatal exposure to substances.

Eleven through Twelve Months

Typical Baby	Recovering Baby*	Handling Suggestions
The baby may stand alone for a moment. When starting to walk, the baby stands with a wide base, feet flat on the floor, and holds hands up in the air.	The baby stands on tiptoe and may appear very stiff. If falling, the baby may not put arms out (protective reaction) and may injure the face or head.	When your baby is standing, provide support by standing in back of your baby and holding the baby's hips. Let the baby push things around the room (for example, a play shopping cart or a chair).
The baby is able to self-feed dry cereal, cookies, crackers, and other finger foods.	The baby does not show much interest in eating or assisting in eating. However, the baby may still put other things into the mouth besides food.	Meal time is still a slow process. When feeding, give your baby some food to hold. Take turns feeding the baby and showing the baby how to put some food into the mouth. Be careful to prevent the baby from putting things into the mouth that are not food.
The baby will make new sounds (for example, vroom, beep-beep).	The baby may coo or say familiar sounds, such as "da-da."	Play games that encourage the baby to use new sounds. For example, you might say, "The car goes vroom-vroom"; "The bell goes ding-dong"; "The dog says 'bow-wow.' "

*The babies for whom these guidelines apply are recovering from prenatal exposure to substances.

References and Notes

Aylward, G. P. 1990. Environmental influences on the developmental outcomes of children at risk. *Infants and Young Children* 2(4):1-9.

This article reviews various environmental and biological risk factors that influence child development. Environmental risks may be inherent in the mother-child dyad, the physical environment, availability of support systems, and/or they may be a reflection of family needs. These environmental risk factors have a strong influence on the cognitive development of the child. Biological risk factors are those which affect the child in utero, perinatally or during earliest childhood.

Conclusion: Multirisk families present several areas of concern to practitioners in the field of early intervention. Defining the type of service that will best meet the developmental needs of the child from a multirisk family is one area of concern. This area is made more complex because of multiple environmental and biological risk factors.

Bignol, N., M. Fuchs, V. Diaz, R. K. Stone, and D. S. Gromisch. 1987. Teratogenicity of cocaine in humans. *Journal of Pediatrics* 110:93-96.

A study of 50 women and their children who were exposed to cocaine, 110 woman and their children who were polydrug exposed, and 340 women and children who were drug free, describing outcomes for their newborn infants. The method of cocaine self-administration affected the consequences for the infant, with the highest rate of abnormalities noted with the groups of mothers who smoked or injected cocaine.

Conclusion: Cocaine abuse in humans significantly reduces the weight of the fetus, increases the stillbirth rate related to abruptio placentae, and is associated with a higher malformation rate.

Brazelton, T. B. 1973. Neonatal behavioral assessment scale. *Clinics in developmental medicine* 50. Philadelphia: J. B. Lippincott.

A standardized assessment of newborn behavior and neuromotor status, consisting of 28 behavioral items, 20 reflex and passive movement items, and nine additional items that include alertness, attention, persistence, irritability, endurance, regulatory capacity, state regulation, balance of motor tone, and reinforcement value of the infant's behavior. Observation of the states of arousal include deep sleep, light sleep, drowsy, alert, active alert, and fussing/crying.

______. 1984. *Neonatal behavioral assessment scale* 2d ed. Philadelphia: J. B. Lippincott.

Chandler, L. S., M. S. Andrews, M. W. Swanson. 1980. *Movement assessment of infants.* Infant Movement Research, P.O. Box 4631, Rolling Bay, WA 98061.

A standardized criterion-referenced assessment of the quality of motor skills for children ranging in age from 1.5 to 12.5 months. Components of movement which are assessed include: muscle tone, primitive reflexes, automatic reactions, and volitional movement.

Chasnoff, I. J., D. R. Griffith, C. Freier, and J. Murray. 1992. Cocaine/polydrug use in pregnancy: Two-year follow-up. *Pediatrics* 89(2):284-89.

A longitudinal study of three groups of infants who were followed from birth through age two years. Group 1 consisted of 106 infants exposed to cocaine and other substances (marijuana and alcohol), group 2 consisted of 45 infants exposed to marijuana and alcohol (without cocaine), and group 3 consisted of 81 infants who were not exposed to drugs prenatally.

Conclusion: Group 1 infants demonstrated decreased birth weight, length, and head circumference. They had caught up in length and weight by one year of age, yet were smaller than group 3 infants at age two years. Group 2 infants demonstrated smaller head size at birth. Head size in the two groups of exposed infants remained smaller than those of the control group. A significant number of the children who had been exposed to drugs scored more than one standard deviation below the mean on the Bayley Scales of Infant Development PDI at 6, 12, and 24 months of age. Head size was significantly correlated with developmental outcomes for each group of children.

Davidson, D. A., and M. A. Short. 1982. Developmental effects of perinatal heroin and methadone addiction. *Physical and Occupational Therapy in Pediatrics* 2(4):1-10.

A review of the history of narcotic use and the effects of heroin and methadone on both the adult and child. Findings from the various studies outlined indicate concerns for these children across multiple domains of behavior.

Conclusion: These authors advocate the use of an intervention philosophy that includes improving prenatal health care and providing educational efforts directed at teaching parents appropriate handling skills (meaningful stimulation), thus enhancing positive parent-child interactions.

Dixon, S. D., K. Bresnahan, and B. Zuckerman. 1990. Cocaine babies: Meeting the challenge of management. *Contemporary Pediatrics* 7(6):70-92.

An integration of clinical evidence and research findings concerning environmental and biological risks associated with substance exposure for the infant. This article offers guidelines for the general pediatric management of children exposed to substances.

Conclusion: Developmental issues are of concern for infants and children exposed to substances in utero. Continued research is needed to support the clinical impressions of this population of children. Assessment and intervention for the developmental and health needs of these children need to be addressed as the children mature.

Frank, D. A., B. Zuckerman, H. Amaro, K. Aboagye, H. Bauchner, H. Cabral, L. Fried, R. Hingson, H. Kayne, S. M. Levenson, S. Parker, H. Reece, and R.Vinci. 1988. Cocaine use during pregnancy: Prevalence and correlates. *Pediatrics* 82(6):888-895.

A study of 679 pregnant women who were being seen for prenatal care who were also evaluated for cocaine use by interviews and urine toxicology analysis.

Conclusion: Of the 679 pregnant women, 17% were found to use cocaine during pregnancy following urine assay. However, 24% of the women identified for cocaine use had denied it during interview alone. In addition to describing prevalence, this report suggests using both interview and urine assays of pregnant women in order to identify the numbers of infants at risk for in-uterine exposure to substances. Relationships between cocaine use and pregnancy outcome may be biased by inadequate identification of cocaine users and failure to control for confounding variables.

Greenspan, S. 1987. *Infants in multirisk families: Case studies in preventative intervention.* Clinical infant reports. Series of the National Center for Clinical Infant Programs. Number 3. Madison, CT: International University Press.

Various case studies are presented relating the flexible outreach design of this program toward multirisk families. A supportive and proactive approach is detailed along with a description of the various interventions provided to each of the families portrayed in the case studies.

Conclusion: Programs that meet the specific needs of the population they serve should be developed for multirisk families and their children.

Kaplan, E. A. 1991. Unpublished manuscript.

A descriptive study of 13 children exposed to substances in utero. Motor concerns as assessed on the *Movement assessment of infants* (Chandler, Andrews, and Swanson 1980) indicated risks during the infant period. However, the other screening instruments used did not indicate areas for developmental concerns.

Conclusion: Components of movement are of concern for infants from multirisk families who were exposed to substances in utero. Clinical evidence indicated that there were differences in the normal acquisition of motor skills for these children as they matured. Evaluation instruments need to be chosen carefully in order to obtain information that accurately reflects observed behaviors.

______. 1992. *Components of gross motor skills demonstrated by infants and toddlers from multirisk families who were also exposed to cocaine in utero.* Master's thesis. Ann Arbor, MI: University Microfilms Publication Number 1350572.

Motor skills of 20 infants exposed to substances were assessed using the *Movement assessment of infants* (Chandler, Andrews, and Swanson 1980) and the *Peabody gross motor development scales* (Folio and Fewell 1983).

Conclusion: Children from multirisk families who were also exposed to substances in utero demonstrated differing problems in the acquisition of gross motor skills as the children matured.

Oro, A. S., and S. D. Dixon. 1987. Perinatal cocaine and methamphetamine exposure: Maternal and neonatal correlates. *Journal of Pediatrics* 111:571-78.

Study of 104 mother-infant pairs divided into three groups. Group 1 tested positive for cocaine, group 2 was positive for methamphetamine, and group 3 combined cocaine with methamphetamine.

Conclusion: All three groups of infants had altered neonatal behavioral patterns characterized by abnormal sleep patterns, poor feeding, tremors, hypertonia, higher rates of prematurity, intrauterine growth retardation, and smaller head circumferences.

Parker, S., B. Zuckerman, H. Bauchner, D. Frank, R. Vinci, and H. Cabral. 1990. Jitteriness in full-term neonates: Prevalence and correlates. *Pediatrics* 85(1):17-23.

Compared "jitteriness" with a sample of 936 healthy full-term newborns and 118 "sick" newborns. This provided a sample size of 1,054 nondrug-exposed healthy and sick neonates. The study included 259 infants whose mothers reported marijuana use and 60 infants whose mothers were positive for postpartum marijuana use as determined by urine assay; 156 women who reported cocaine use during pregnancy; and 41 women who tested positive on postpartum urine assay for cocaine. Other substances evaluated in this study included cigarettes and alcohol.

Conclusion: Jitteriness in infants is associated with marijuana use. Infants exposed to cocaine were more "jittery" than infants who were not exposed to substances in utero. More studies on the effects of maternal drug use in other neurobehavioral areas are needed.

Schneider, J. W., D. R. Griffith, and I. J. Chasnoff. 1989. Infants exposed to cocaine in utero: Implications for developmental assessment and intervention. *Infants and Young Children* 2(1):25-36.

These authors evaluated infant behaviors at various ages (newborn, 4 months old, and 8 months old). They compared normal and cocaine exposed newborns using the *Neonatal behavioral assessment scale* (Brazelton 1973). *Movement assessment of infants* (Chandler, Andrews, and Swanson 1980) was used to evaluate the four-month-old and eight-month-old infants.

Conclusion: Newborn behavior demonstrated depressed interactive abilities and poor state control. Disorganized state control is described as a rapid change from one state to another including:

1. Deep sleep
2. Agitated sleep
3. Extremes of state, sleeping to crying
4. Panicked awake state

Frequent tremors of the arms and increased muscle tone of the legs also were noted. Four-month-old infants showed depressed interactive abilities and poor state control. Frequent tremors of the arms and increased muscle tone including the presence of primitive reflexes (that is, positive support reaction and increased extension) were reported. At age eight months, the motor abnormalities appeared to have decreased but the children moved slowly and stood on their toes with stiff extension in the legs. Information on handling these infants is provided.

Shelton, T., S. Jeppson, and B. Johnson. 1987. *Family-centered care for children with special health needs.* Washington, DC: Association for the Care of Children's Health.

This describes and defines a philosophy in which family strengths and individuality are assimilated into programs designed to serve a specific population.

Conclusion: Eight elements delineate this philosophy:

1. The family is central to the child's health and development.
2. Parent/professional collaboration is facilitated.
3. Information about the child is shared on a continuing basis.
4. Comprehensive programs that support the family are implemented.
5. The individuality of each family is recognized.
6. The developmental needs of the child within the care delivery system are appreciated.
7. Parent-to-parent networks are supported.
8. The health-care delivery system is accessible and responsive to the family's need.

van de Bor, M., F. J. Walther, and M. Ebrahimi. 1990. Decreased cardiac output in infants of mothers who abused cocaine. *Pediatrics* 85(1):30-32.

Reported on the comparison of 15 cocaine-exposed infants and 22 nonexposed infants in terms of cardiac status. Their findings indicate that infants exposed to cocaine in utero demonstrated decreased cardiac competency during the newborn period.

Conclusion: Infants exposed to cocaine in utero showed decreased cardiac output and stroke volume and increased mean arterial blood pressure in the newborn period.

Zuckerman, B., and C. Brooks. 1991. Women and Infants' Clinic: A model of one-stop shopping for the treatment of cocaine-using mothers and their infants. Boston City Hospital, Boston University School of Medicine.

This provided information on the Women and Infants' Clinic for the treatment of cocaine-abusing mothers and their children. The pilot program reported outcomes for 13 women and children following one year of involvement. The program provided twice-a-week intervention for the children and the mothers. Interventions were specific and responsive to the families' needs and met the developmental needs of the children.

Zuckerman, B., D. A. Frank, R. Hingson, H. Amaro, S. M. Levenson, H. Kayne, S. Parker, R. Vinci, K. Aboagye, L. E. Fried, H. Cabral, R. Timperi, and H. Bauchner. 1989. Effects of maternal marijuana and cocaine use on fetal growth. *New England Journal of Medicine* 320(12):762-68.

This study describes two methods of determining maternal marijuana and cocaine use along with their effects on fetal growth. Both interview and urine assay were used to determine substance use. Findings of studying 1,226 mothers and infants, using both interview and urine assay, revealed that 27% used marijuana and 18% used cocaine. Self-report/interview without urine assay indicated that 23% of these women used marijuana and 13% used cocaine.

Conclusion: Studies which have used interview and/or self-report alone may have underestimated the numbers of women who use substances during pregnancy and have thus limited the associations of particular prenatal substance exposure with problems of the infant. The use of marijuana or cocaine during pregnancy is associated with impaired fetal growth.

Readings

American Academy of Pediatrics, Committee on Community Health Services. 1988. Health needs of homeless children. *Pediatrics* 82(6):938-939.

Bailey, D., and M. Wolery. 1984. *Teaching infants and preschoolers with handicaps.* Columbus, OH: Charles E. Merrill.

Behrman, R. S., and C. S. Larson, eds. 1991. *The future of children* 1(1). Los Altos, CA: Center for the Future of Children, The David and Lucile Packard Foundation.

Bobath, B. 1971. *Abnormal postural reflex activity caused by brain lesions.* William Heinemann Medical Books Limited, England.

Brazelton, T. B. 1971. *Infants and mothers: Differences in development.* New York: Delacorte.

Caplan, F. 1974. *The first twelve months of life: Your baby's growth month by month.* New York: Grosset & Dunlap.

Chasnoff, I. J., E. L. Douglas, and L. Squires. 1986. Cocaine intoxication in a breast-fed infant. *Pediatrics* 80(6):836-838.

DeGangi, G. A. 1991. Assessment of sensory, emotional, and attentional problems in regulatory disordered infants: Part 1. *Infants and Young Children* 3(3).

DeGangi, G. A., P. Craft, and J. Castellan. 1991. Treatment of sensory, emotional, and attentional problems in regulatory disordered infants: Part 2. *Infants and Young Children* 3(3).

DeGangi, G. A., and S. I. Greenspan. 1989. The development of sensory functions in infants. In *Physical and Occupational Therapy in Pediatrics* 8(4). New York: The Haworth Press.

Fiorentino, M. R. 1972. *Normal and abnormal development: The influence of primitive reflexes on motor development.* Springfield, IL: Charles C. Thomas.

Folio, M. R., and R. R. Fewell. 1983. *The Peabody developmental motor scales and activity cards.* Allen TX: DLM Teaching Resources.

Jaeger, L. 1987. *Home program instruction sheets for infants and young children* (Rev.). Tucson, AZ: Therapy Skill Builders.

Linder, T. W. 1990. *Transdisciplinary play-based assessment: A functional approach to working with young children.* Baltimore: Brookes.

Morris, S. E., and M. D. Klein. 1987. *Pre-feeding skills: A comprehensive resource for feeding development.* Tucson, AZ: Communication Skill Builders.

New York City Department of Health. 1989. Maternal drug abuse: New York City. *City Health Information* 8(8).

Piaget, J. 1952. *The origins of intelligence in children.* New York: International University Press.

Russell, F. F., and T. A. Free. 1991. Early intervention for infants and toddlers with prenatal drug exposure. *Infants and Young Children* 3(4):78-89.

Sanger, S. 1991. *Baby talk/parent talk: Understanding your baby's body language.* New York: Doubleday.

Scherzer, A. L., and I. Tscharnuter. 1982. Early diagnosis and therapy in cerebral palsy: A primer on infant developmental problems. *Pediatric Habilitation* 3. New York: Marcel Dekker.

Task Force on Pediatric AIDS. 1988. Pediatric guidelines for infection control of human immunodeficiency virus (acquired immunodeficiency virus) in hospitals, medical offices, schools and other settings. *Pediatrics* 82(5):801-807.

Zelle, R. S., and A. B. Coyner. 1983. *Developmentally disabled infants and toddlers: Assessment and intervention.* Philadelphia: F. A. Davis.

Chapter 18

Future Directions

Antoine K. Fomufod, M.D., M.P.H., FAAP

Research Priorities

Individual and multicenter studies are needed in a variety of communities to identify the real numbers of infants exposed to drugs so as to design effective community-based intervention programs.

Further research is necessary to determine the factors contributing to low prevalence in some communities, so that the information can be used for the betterment of those with higher rates.

There is a need to advance the overall level of scientific and clinical knowledge in the management of drug addiction in pregnancy.

Treatment Interventions

Treatment programs need to be redesigned or enlarged to offer comprehensive medical, educational, and psychosocial interventions that also address the etiology of the problem and offer support that is very much needed for recovery. Essentials of such a program will be substance-abuse counseling; family planning and birth control; child development services; primary pediatric care for any growing infant; obstetric care of a current pregnancy; and education and counseling to assist the pregnant woman in making appropriate behavioral choices that are consistent with her best health and that of her developing child.

Addiction in a pregnant woman needs to be widely accepted as an illness that needs medical and psychosocial management rather than police, lawyers, and prisons. This approach is more likely to impact positively than that which seeks to punish mothers by bringing criminal prosecutions for "delivering drugs to the unborn." The latter measure impacts negatively on the willingness of women to obtain prenatal care and drug treatment. There is no evidence currently available to demonstrate that the threat of criminalization will deter addictive behavior.

Finally, since the pregnant woman is a part of her community, she and her family should not be viewed in an isolated way, but as an integral part of it. Behavior modification programs need to be conducted on a community-wide basis; churches and synagogues, schools, and the mass media need to convey similar messages. Education is very important, and when the same message is heard from all directions, adults and young people are likely to be strengthened in their resolve to resist negative peer pressure.

Appendixes

Early Intervention and Drug-Exposed Infants: A Case Study*

Ila Sherman, OTR

Early intervention combines a wide range of services provided for families with young children, from birth through three years of age, who are developmentally delayed or at risk for developing delays. This population includes those who are subject to environmental risks such as neglect or parental drug abuse (Tjossem 1976). An infant exposed to drugs in utero may have symptoms of drug withdrawal syndrome. These symptoms may include tremors, jitteriness, increased irritability, and difficulty being consoled. A mother who herself is addicted to drugs may not be able to properly care for her infant. This places the infant at risk for developmental delay and possible child abuse.

We first saw Brian in the neonatal intensive care unit of our hospital. He was delivered by Caesarean section for intrauterine growth retardation. His arrested growth was 28 weeks. The mother's pregnancy was complicated by maternal smoking (½ to 1 pack per day), maternal hypertension, and tachycardia. The mother reportedly had an upper-respiratory infection and treated herself with Sudafed. The obstetrician noted episodes of very agitated behavior during prenatal office visits. Brian was delivered at 36 weeks corrected gestational age. He weighed 1910 grams. His apgar scores were eight at one minute and nine at five minutes. The mother's and infant's urine were positive for cocaine.

Frame of Reference

An integration of two frames of reference was utilized for the best treatment approach:

1. The developmental approach. This is used with infants where there is evidence of a delay or interruption in the normal process of development. Using this approach, treatment is geared toward enhancing the appropriate sequential steps of a developing infant. Physical, sensory, perceptual, cognitive, social, and emotional aspects are connected and affect the developmental stage of the infant. Conditions of stress can cause the infant to regress to earlier levels of adaptation.

*Reprinted from *Occupational Therapy Forum*, Vol. V, No. 31, August 13, 1990. Reprinted by permission of the author and *Occupational Therapy Forum*.

2. The sensory integrative approach. Sensory integration is the neurological process of organizing and processing sensations for use. Awareness from action or feedback from somatosensory and vestibular systems provide organization for motor performance.

Problem Areas

Brian demonstrated decreased interactive skills, increased extensor tone in lower extremities, increased flexor tone in upper extremities, and decreased organizational skills. One of the difficulties with drug-exposed infants is that their states swing. They will arouse from a sleep state to an agitated one, with brief alert periods between.

Treatment

In the neonatal intensive care unit, treatment was geared toward increasing organizational skills, normalizing tone overall, and improving visual and auditory interactive skills. Initially, Brian was seen twice a day for range-of-motion exercises, general stimulation, and oral motor skills. As his feeding skills improved, he was seen once a day. In order to improve organizational skills, we used calming procedures. Proprioception was provided by tight swaddling in a blanket with hands near his face. This encouraged self-calming by way of hand-sucking and provided sensory feedback. (Most drug-exposed infants have an increased oral drive, which may be mistaken for hunger.) Vestibular stimulation was provided by slow rocking while being held firmly with deep touch pressure. This is optimally done in a dimly lit room to provide environmental inhibition. Visual stimulation was provided with the use of black-and-white contrast pictures; and auditory stimulation was provided by voice or with a soft rattle.

Follow-Up

Brian was discharged to home with his parents. One of the conditions that needed to be met was obtaining occupational therapy on an outpatient basis. Brian's mother was strongly encouraged by the physician and social worker to enroll in a drug-treatment program. On Brian's first visit to our clinic, a Brazelton exam was performed to obtain a baseline. At the time of the examination, Brian was 39 weeks corrected gestational age.

Motoric Processes: Worrisome

Brian had increased flexor tone in his right upper extremity and increased extensor tone in his lower extremities. "Scissoring" was noted with his right leg. He exhibited a high-intensity suck, and required a pacifier for calming.

Interactive Processes: Low Average

Brian was able to focus and follow with his eyes horizontally for at least a 30° arc. Because he was aversive to lights, we needed to dim them in order to obtain focusing. Auditorily, he had alerting and shifting eyes to sound. His head turned toward sound source on the left only.

Organizational Processes—State Control: Average

As is common with many cocaine-exposed infants, Brian had difficulty modulating his states. He alternated between an alert state and an irritable one. He was unable to calm himself without intervention.

Organizational Processes—Response to Stress: Average

Brian had tremulousness that was seen in several states. He required swaddling to assist with organizational skills.

Treatment

Initially, Brian received occupational therapy two times a week on an outpatient basis. He was very irritable, and would calm only when swaddled and/or fed. He had a decreased quality of alertness, and he became overstimulated very easily. ROM exercises were provided, along with visual and auditory stimulation. Parental instruction was given to encourage carryover at home. Calming techniques were suggested to the parents. When Brian continued to be irritable in our clinic, a home visit was made. There, Brian's state control was noticeably improved. He was able to interact both visually and auditorily, and the natural light of his home did not appear to upset him. In subsequent visits to our department, treatment was done in a softly lit room without extraneous stimulation.

At three months CGA, Brian is able to perform the following skills:

Cognitive: Turn his eyes and head to the sound of a hidden voice; play with his own hands; quiet to his mother's voice; localize sound with eyes; follow a dangled ring vertically up, down, and at 180°.

Expressive Language: Brian is now crying when hungry or uncomfortable, and he has begun to laugh and squeal. He is beginning to make sounds with cooing.

Gross Motor: Brian is starting to roll from his back to his side, hold his head steady in supported sitting, and hold his chest up in prone. His extremities remain in a flexed pattern, but he can move out of it with position change.

Fine Motor: Brian is able to bring his hands to midline in supine, look from one object to another, use ulnar palmar grasps, and hold his hands open or closed loosely.

Social/Emotional: Brian socializes with strangers, enjoys social play, responds with smiling when socially approached, and vocalizes in response to talking and smiling.

In summary, Brian is performing at an age-appropriate level for three months CGA, using *Developmental Screening Inventory–Revised* and the *Hawaii Early Learning Profile* as guidelines. (These both are structured exams, and therapists treating drug-exposed infants and toddlers need to observe them also in an unstructured setting.)

We remain concerned regarding Brian's overall tone and will continue to see him on a follow-up basis.

Conclusion

The above case study demonstrates the importance of early intervention with these children. Therapists working with this population need to include the family, caregiver, home environment, and social services to ensure the child's continued well-being.

Reference

Tjossem, T. 1976. *Intervention strategies for high-risk infants and young children.* Baltimore: University Park Press.

Readings

Hanft, Barbara. 1988. The changing environment of early intervention services: Implications for practice. *American Journal of Occupational Therapy* 42:724.

Howard, J., L. Beckwith, C. Rodning, and V. Kropenske. 1989. The development of young children of substance-abusing parents: Insights from seven years of intervention and research. *Zero to Three* 9(5):8-12.

Hyde, A., and S. Trautman. 1989. Drug-exposed infants and sensory integration: Is there a connection? *Sensory Integration Special Interest Newsletter* (American Occupational Therapy Association) 12(4):1-6.

Ramm, Patricia. 1983. The OT process in specific pediatric conditions: Neonatal flow chart. In *Willard and Spackman's occupational therapy,* 6th ed. Edited by H. Hopkins and H. Smith, 123-125. Philadelphia: J. B. Lippincott.

Silberzahn, Mary. 1983. Sensory integration theory. *Willard and Spackman's occupational therapy,* 6th ed. Edited by H. Hopkins and H. Smith, 101-105. Philadelphia: J. B. Lippincott.

Appendix B

Toys for Special Infants

Cordelia H. Puttkammer, M.Ed., OTR/L

Children who have been exposed to drugs need appropriate toys at least as much as their drug-free peers. This section contains an overview of appropriate toys and activities at various ages and stages of development through a child's first four years.

Infants and children learn through play, and they become bored with the same toys. Change or rotate their playthings every few weeks. Take note, though, that a drug-affected child may be fascinated by a toy beyond the age when it seems appropriate. As much as possible, let each child play according to individual needs and wishes. Some modifications may be useful or necessary, particularly as the affected infant progresses from visual to motor involvement or if the infant has severe or complicated limitations. For specific information or instruction, parents and caregivers may want to get involved with special-needs library programs and toy-lending programs. Supervisors of these programs are skilled at teaching adults how to use toys creatively and therapeutically.

Just about anything can be a toy for a child if you make certain that a few basic safety rules are followed. Many disposable toys and some lasting ones can be homemade if they meet certain criteria based on simple observation and practical knowledge.

1. Every toy for infants must be mouthable. Anything smaller than 1¼ inches can be swallowed or can present a choking hazard.
2. Inspect toys for any detachable parts or sections. Toys that have parts or pieces that can be pried, unscrewed, or bent challenge inquisitive infants.
3. Make sure the construction material is nontoxic, that it won't peel or chip, and that it is colorfast.
4. Avoid toys and equipment that are made of vinyl-clad metal. The vinyl covering is all too easily chewed and eaten.
5. Toys must be easy to clean—hand washable, machine washable, or dishwasher safe.

Toys for Newborns

Almost from birth, infants focus visually, if only on a field of limited depth. An optimal distance is about eight inches from the eyes. Strongly contrasting colors attract attention; soft pastels, including the ever-present pink and powder blue, have not proved to interest babies and young children. Simple black-and-white designs placed so the baby can see them are best for newborns. A black marking pen can be used on a white paper plate to draw a simple face, a checkerboard, or a bull's eye. Foam balls, painted or drawn on with a black marking pen and suspended with string from a hanger, make a great mobile.

A great advantage of these homemade things is that they can be discarded and changed easily. Last week's checkerboard design gives way to this week's stripes; the foam balls are hung in a different pattern every few days. Even newborns are refreshed by a change of scenery! The neonate sees only the closest side of the toy, while the adult—who can move around—will view it from different perspectives. Remember, though, that the toy is for the infant's benefit.

Discovery Toys produces a line of visual stimulators called Eye Catchers™. Phone your local Discovery Toys distributor (listed in the Yellow Pages) or contact the Discovery Toys headquarters at 2530 Arnold Drive, Martinez, CA 94553 (1-800-426-4777).

For many ideas on making baby's toys from virtually nothing, refer to *Smart Toys for Babies from Birth to Two–77 Easy-to-Make Toys to Stimulate Your Baby's Mind,* written by Kent Burtt and Karen Kalkstein and published in 1981 by Harper & Row.

Other sensory systems besides the visual are becoming acute during the first weeks of life. Newborns need gentle stimulation of the senses of touch and hearing. Blankets with various textures may be useful. Use soft rattles that attach to the infant's wrist. Playskool, Fisher-Price, and Chicco make these.

3 to 6 Months

During these months, infants begin to use their hands and feet in a more purposeful manner. They practice reaching and grasping. They are sharp observers, watching their hands and feet and any moving, dangling, or flashy items. We all know that long hair, glasses, earrings, and necklaces are very attractive to inquisitive babies!

Things that can be mouthed and chewed are especially useful at this age. Things with different textures are fascinating. Toys that move when touched, and others that make noises—bells, rattles, jingles—are appropriate. Balls, rattles, and cuddly animals are standard equipment at this age. Gerber's Happy Elephant™ mirror and rattle are recommended, and the Fisher-Price® Play Gym™ provides visual interest, sound, and touch stimulation.

6 to 9 Months

Now the infant is gaining more strength and motor ability, and can move by rolling or scooting to get to a toy placed a short distance away from reach. The baby is still practicing reaching and grasping, and is fascinated with things that cause an action. Light switches are favorites, as are the controls on television sets, tape recorders, the vacuum cleaner, and anything else within reach. Thus, toys that produce action are a source of delight—pop-ups, a jack-in-the-box, busy boxes, pushbuttons, and toys that make a noise when squeezed.

Also at this age, the baby is beginning to understand that a thing can exist even if you can't see it. Peek-a-boo is an absolute favorite game. The game of hide-a-toy is a good variation: leave the toy partly visible, then find it and pull it out.

Teething toys, colorful things, dolls, and blocks are appropriate at this age. So are bright things, lights, and mirrors—the last particularly because babies are endlessly interested in themselves. Placing a mirror overhead so that babies can admire themselves while on the changing table helps to prevent squirming and rolling over during diapering.

9 to 12 Months

During this stage, the urge to explore is very strong. Children observe older family members, and they begin to move in an upright posture. They feel challenged to get their hands on everything. Household accidents are common from this stage onward. Children get hold of cleaning supplies by opening cabinet doors, or they use their newly acquired dexterity to explore electric plugs and sockets.

Good toys for this age will engage and keep the baby busy and, one hopes, out of trouble. A busy box (perhaps in the crib), stacking rings, shape sorters, buckets of animals or blocks, and wind-up music boxes all hold the attention of young explorers. Containers full of "collections"—for example, a small plastic bucket filled with tops and lids from assorted jars and containers—can be fascinating. The busy and budget-conscious mother can provide some toys by looking around the kitchen for clean, mouthable plastic items (too big to choke on!)—spatulas, ladles, measuring spoons, margarine tubs. Many of these are useful for water play, too.

For the little imitator, first books are valuable. There are vinyl-covered books for infants, and others made of heavy paperboard with a glossy, wipe-off finish in bright colors. *Baby's First Cloth Book* (nontoxic and washable) by Random House is a favorite.

12 to 15 Months

By this time, most children are becoming truly mobile. A trip to the playground is a great excursion for a toddler. Children of this age enjoy push-pull carts, pull toys, and the popular "lawnmower" that produces bubbles. One-year-olds benefit from shape-sorting toys; they can distinguish circles from squares from triangles in more purposeful fashion. They can do simple puzzles of two or three pieces. They like pots and pans, measuring cups, and other things that nest together.

Books for the very young are enjoyable. *Pat the Bunny* features things for the toddler to do—pat the furry bunny and put a finger in the circle. *Goodnight, Moon* is within the child's understanding. And if the fiberboard and vinyl books from the first year have survived all the chewing and dropping and tossing, the child may be able to point to a picture or respond to a word or two: "Kitty!" "Uh-oh!"

Babies who have passed the first birthday are developing finger skills and coordination of a higher order. They can–and should–pick up finger foods, tear up paper, and figure out latches and knobs. Water play is still great fun.

15 to 18 Months

Children of this age are attracted to small details. They are truly fascinated by little toys, and they require a great deal of supervision because they still put toys (and anything else) into their mouths. Toddlers left to themselves on the lawn will put leaves in their mouths, and they must be discouraged from eating the sand in the sandbox. Keep an eye on the cat food and dog dish, too!

Imitation and make-believe are important play patterns at this stage. Thus, dolls, animals, and other figures featuring details are appropriate toys. It may well become important to the toddler that the toy farm has cows and horses and chickens, and that the tiny car is parked near the house–not in the barn. Identifying and naming things are important now. Items to unwrap, images to point to (picture books are useful), and toys with details are interesting. ("Look! the horse's ears! Nose! Tail!")

Drawing and other art materials can be introduced at this age if the tools and materials are suited to very young children. An ordinary sheet of paper is too small for a child under two, but shelf paper or a roll of wrapping paper is just fine for drawing and "writing." Similarly, crayons and markers should be large and easy to grasp. (Washable markers!) Modeling clay is an appropriate material for fun and creativity from this age through adulthood. Good nontoxic clay can be made in the kitchen by mixing two parts peanut butter, two parts powdered milk, and one part honey.

18 to 24 Months

Children at this age continue to explore. It is very important for them to use their whole bodies. Experiences should include play on slides, in wading pools, with ride-on toys and vehicles with push pedals. Fine motor development is occurring, too. Finger paints may be appropriate now. Books may well include pictures of children doing things such as dressing, bathing, playing, eating. These help toddlers to make sense and order of the world. Toys that say words when you pull a string or set a pointer are appropriate now that the child can use a few words.

24 to 30 Months

Children at this age can "join in" at play groups and participate in more formalized day-care programs. Intervention programs may include bringing the child to a group setting. Use of toys and equipment can be expanded into simple games.

Favorite action songs are "The Wheels of the Train Go 'Round and 'Round," "Itsy-Bitsy Spider," and body-part songs such as "Ten Fingers" and "Head, Shoulders, Knees, and Toes."

Perhaps *rituals* is a good word to describe these games; the procedures are always very simple, noncompetitive, and nonthreatening. They serve to introduce the concept of a group.

Useful toys for this age group include finger paints, water colors with paint brushes, and large chalk for sidewalk drawing. Two-year-olds like cars, trucks, dolls, and toys that simulate adult equipment, such as child-size brooms, dustpans, and garden rakes. Little ones do a lot of developing through imitation. Blocks, things for building, and toys to manipulate can be introduced.

Two-year-olds may enjoy books featuring the simplest of stories. (A kitten wanders into the garden next door, chases a butterfly, and makes friends with another kitty.) Toddlers entering a group can be given unbreakable dishes and spoons; by this age, they will have had a lot of practice in feeding themselves and will be able to function fairly independently in a group setting.

30 to 36 Months

Children learn a great deal at this age. They continue to develop their gross motor skills, such as throwing, catching, and jumping. Their mental grasp of many concepts is growing rapidly. Children approaching the third birthday can use various shape sorters that involve five or more shapes, identify some colors, and learn a bit about numbers. (Two cars!)

Almost-threes enjoy books with real stories. *The Little Engine that Could, The Cat in the Hat,* and *I Can Do It Myself* are likely to be favorites.

36 to 48 Months

It is in this fourth year that most children in the United States begin to attend a group or school of some description. They may attend a Head Start program or a preschool. They still do a great deal of "parallel play"; that is, they "do their own thing" right next to other children without much interaction. But by now they seek out other children more and more often for interactive play. Important skills for functioning in a group can be mastered now. Three-year-olds can follow simple rules such as sitting in a circle, listening for their names to be called, or lining up for an activity. They can listen to stories, either alone or in groups. The misadventures of Curious George and the lessons learned by Brother Bear and Sister Bear are of great interest.

Three-year-olds are ready for some board games, including Candy Land® and Chutes and Ladders.® Very simple crafts, such as lacing cards, may interest them. Toys to manipulate often command sustained interest; building logs, blocks, and interlocking train tracks that can be laid down in a different pattern every day all have a high play value.

Candy Land® and Chutes and Ladders® are registered trademarks of Milton Bradley Co.

Ready for games, ready to be knit into a group of children—three-year-olds have come a long way from infancy and total dependence. They are independent at home, too. They may enjoy creating their own space with a blanket draped over a big chair or small table, and they may take great delight in beginning to perform household chores.

And through these eventful years of growing and learning, some children have gone to sleep every night with their arms around the same brown bear or stuffed elephant or rag doll. This toy may have been the favorite when the infant could do no more than look at it. It has been dragged everywhere and worn to rags. It should be washed, but never "rotated" or retired. It is cherished by the child as a source of security and comfort. Medical and psychological professionals agree that this is developmentally appropriate even beyond age four. Parents and caregivers should find the habit a source of satisfaction, because it's one more thing that normal, healthy children do.

Readings

Abrams, B., and N. Kauffman. 1990. *Toys for early childhood development: Selection guidelines for infants, toddlers, and preschoolers.* West Nyack, NY: The Center for Applied Research in Education.

Burtt, K., and K. Kalkstein. 1981. *Smart toys for babies from birth to two: 77 easy-to-make toys to stimulate your baby's mind.* New York: Harper Colophon Books.

Crowley, R. J., and J. C. Mills. 1989. *Cartoon magic: How to help children discover their rainbows within.* New York: Imagination Press.

Musselwhite, C. R. 1986. *Adaptive play for special needs children: Strategies to enhance communication and learning.* Austin, TX: Pro-Ed.

Rappaport, L. 1986. *Recipes for fun: Play activities for young children with disabilities and their families.* Washington, DC: The Joseph P. Kennedy, Jr., Foundation.

Schwartz, S., and J. Miller. 1988. *The language of toys: Teaching communication skills to special needs children.* Rockville, MD: Woodbine House.

Drugs and Babies: A Dangerous Mix*

Jean Gardner Cole, M.S.

Dear Parents and Other Caregivers,

Drugs and babies are a dangerous combination. Any illicit drugs taken during pregnancy have affected the baby. Cocaine may be the most dangerous drug of all for the developing fetus, but all drugs are dangerous for babies and affect their growth and development.

Some babies have a difficult time getting over the effects of drugs. This pamphlet is to help you understand how the baby's behavior has been affected and what you can do to help in the baby's recovery.

All babies are different, so some of this information will describe your baby and some won't. However, the suggested interventions are appropriate for all drug-affected babies.

Some babies who have been exposed to cocaine tend to be sleepy, unresponsive babies. They stay "shut down" to protect themselves from stimulation. Babies affected by heroin or other opiates are very irritable, frantic babies. They have great difficulty shutting out stimulation, and they overreact to light, noise, handling, and movement. They are very hypertonic (*their limbs are stiff and tight*), are difficult to console, and cannot deal with interaction; they find it too stimulating.

The baby's behavioral cues can be used as a guide to help you—the most important person in the baby's life—provide the kind of care and interaction your baby will need to grow and develop well.

*This material is published by Boston City Hospital, Boston. Printing of the pamphlet is supported by a grant from March of Dimes. Reprinted by permission.

The pamphlet is available through Cole Consultants, 78 High Street, Leominster, MA 01453.

How Can You Tell If Your Baby Has Been Affected by Drugs?

- Color change, pale or flushed, nostrils pale or flared, mouth puckered and pale, mottling of skin
- Rapid irregular breathing patterns, brief pauses
- Uncoordinated eye movements, rolling or jerky movement, "sun-setting" eyes (*the eyes drop downward*).
- Irritable behavior, difficult to console; or excessively sleepy, rarely awake. Sleeps all night during first weeks of life.
- Legs and arms are tight and stiff, hands are fisted, movements are jerky.
- Tremors (*shaking*) and startles (*jumping*) to handling, movement, and noise.
- Poor sleeping and feeding.
- Sneezing and yawning often.
- Easily overstimulated. Overreacts to sound. Cannot sustain eye contact, looks away (*averts eyes*).
- High cry that is not sustained (*cocaine*) or frantic crying that is difficult to console (*heroin*).

How Can You Tell When Your Baby Has Recovered from the Effects of Drugs?

- Healthy color
- Relaxed tone and posture with smooth movements
- Relaxed facial expression
- Good sleeping and eating patterns
- Longer times in quiet-alert state
- Baby interacts without difficulty. Baby will look at you and listen to your voice calmly.
- Good strong cry, and easily consoled

Coping Strategies Babies Use to Avoid Overstimulation

- Avoiding eye contact, looking away
- Sneezing or yawning (*This gives them a rest from interaction.*)
- Sucking on hands or fingers. Sucking is a powerful soother and a baby's technique to quiet himself/herself
- Getting into a drowsy or sleepy state to shut out stimulation
- Fussing to signal overstimulation or fatigue

These are clever behaviors babies use to get away from stimulation (*too much noise, light, looking, handling, etc.*). It is the baby's way of telling you she/he has had enough and needs "time out" (*quiet time to recover*).

How You Can Help Your Baby

- Provide "time out" when your baby appears to be overstimulated. Hold baby quietly, or swaddle baby in a blanket, wrapping firmly. Don't interact until baby is calm.
- When baby is awake, try interacting in a quiet, low-keyed way. Look at baby quietly without talking. If baby can deal with this without becoming upset, then begin speaking very softly and slowly. If this is too much, the baby will fuss and turn away. Give baby some "time out" and try again later.
- Let baby sleep on her/his tummy or side. Swaddle baby firmly with a blanket, and put a small rolled blanket at the baby's feet and side. This helps the baby feel more secure, and she/he will sleep more soundly. Or hold baby snuggled on your chest.
- If your baby has difficulty eating, try keeping all feedings quiet, with no noise or talking during the feeding. Swaddle baby firmly. Shield the baby from light. Sometimes there is just too much going on around the baby, and she/he gets over-stimulated. This affects the feeding.
- If you use a swing to console your baby, keep the motion gentle. Do not swing your baby vigorously. Vigorous swinging keeps the baby in a state of overstimulation. An overstimulated baby does not learn to console herself/himself, and will depend on vigorous stimulation every time she/he is upset.

How Babies Communicate: Reading Behavioral Cues

Your baby's behavioral cues are her/his way of "talking" to you. When you understand what the baby is telling you, then the baby's cues will help guide you in taking care of her/him. Some babies recover quickly, others need a longer time, but usually by one month the worrisome behaviors are gone. If they do continue, call your doctor. If we at Boston City Hospital can be of any assistance, call us.

Best of luck!

Jean Gardner Cole, M.S.

For further information about babies and the effects of alcohol and other drugs, contact your local March of Dimes Birth Defects Foundation Office (call 1-800-458-0039).

How to Take Care of Your Baby before Birth*

If you want your baby to be strong and healthy . . .

There are many good things you can do right now to keep yourself healthy. These things can help your baby grow strong and healthy, too.

- Visit your doctor at least once a month for the first seven months, and more often after that.
- Eat right. Include plenty of milk, fish, meat, fruits, vegetables, whole wheat bread, and cereals.
- Take time to exercise, rest, and get enough sleep.
- Learn all you can about taking care of your baby. Look for childbirth classes in your community.
- Tell your problems to your doctor, your school counselor or religious leader, or the librarian in your neighborhood.

While you are pregnant . . .

Don't use alcohol and other drugs. When you use drugs, so does your baby. Alcohol and other drugs can harm your baby.

- Don't drink beer, wine, wine coolers, or liquor.
- Don't smoke cigarettes or marijuana (pot).
- Don't use crack/cocaine, heroin, inhalants (such as gasoline or ammonia), or drugs sold on the street.
- Don't even take drugs you can buy in a store (such as aspirin, laxatives, or vitamins) unless your doctor says it is okay.

If you use drugs or drink alcohol now, your baby might have health problems later. Using drugs can make your baby sick, small, or slow to learn.

---

*This material is published in pamphlet form by the Office for Substance Abuse Prevention, and distributed by the National Clearinghouse for Alcohol and Drug Information, Washington, DC. U.S. Department of Health and Human Services (DHHS) Publication No. ADM/91-1557. Printed 1987, revised 1991. Reprinted by permission.

If you are drinking alcohol or using other drugs . . .

Stop Now. It's not too late to quit. Don't drink any more alcohol or use any more drugs. If you stop drinking alcohol or taking drugs now, you can give your baby a better chance to be born healthy.

If you want to quit taking alcohol or other drugs . . .

Talk with a doctor or nurse. They can help you or tell you how to get help. Dial 911 for the telephone number you need. Here are some groups that can help:

- Health department or clinic
- Alcoholics Anonymous (AA)
- Narcotics Anonymous (NA)
- Church groups

Call 1-800-662-4357 (a free call) if you want to talk to someone about a problem with alcohol or other drugs.

You can help your baby to grow strong and healthy . . .

- Visit your doctor regularly.
- Take care of yourself. Eat good food, exercise, and get enough sleep.
- Talk to somebody you trust about problems.
- Learn all you can about babies.
- Take childbirth classes.
- Remember that alcohol and other drugs can make your baby sick.
- Get help from a clinic, organization, or support group.

To learn more, call or write:

National Clearinghouse for Alcohol and Drug Information
P.O. Box 2345
Rockville, MD 20852

1-800-729-6686 (free call)

Esta publicación está disponible en español.

Please feel free to be a "copy cat," and make all the copies you want. You have our permission!

Universal Precautions for Prevention of HIV and HBV* in a Health-Care Setting

Universal precautions apply to:

- Blood
- Semen
- Vaginal secretions
- Cerebrospinal fluid (spinal cord)
- Synovial fluid (joint)
- Pleural fluid (lung)
- Peritoneal fluid (abdomen)
- Pericardial fluid (heart)
- Amniotic fluid
- Breast milk

"Body fluids" to which universal precautions do not apply unless there is visible blood. Use gloves, if possible. Wash hands with soap and water.

- Urine
- Feces
- Tears
- Sweat
- Vomitus
- Sputum
- Nasal secretions
- Saliva (except in dentistry or when saliva contains blood)

Universal blood and body fluid precautions:

- Consider all clients as potentially infectious.
- Use appropriate barrier precautions routinely.

Reasons for precautions:

- To prevent the spread of infection from client to client.
- To protect clients from infection carried by health-care workers.
- To protect health-care workers from infection carried by clients.

Wash hands before and after assisting others in personal, sick, or injury care.

Wear gloves if there is likelihood of exposure to blood and certain body fluids. Wash hands before and after wearing gloves.

Cuts, scratches, and other skin breaks should be covered and gloves are to be worn.

* Hepatitis B

Use mask and eye protection if splashing is likely to occur.

Spills of blood or bodily fluid must be cleaned up promptly. Wear utility-type gloves for cleanup.

Freshly made household bleach solution (1 part bleach to 9 parts water) is the best disinfectant for cleanups. Leave solution on for 20 minutes.

For venipuncture, use only disposable vacutainers and multiple-draw needles. Do not recap needles. Wear gloves for all venipunctures.

Discard entire vacutainer and needle assembly immediately into a puncture-proof hazard container.

Universal precautions are used to prevent transmission of blood-bone infectious agents, particularly HIV and HBV.

Please use these precautions routinely. Take no risk!

Appendix F

Resources

Organizations

Clearinghouse for Drug-Exposed Children
Division of Behavioral and Developmental Pediatrics
University of California–San Francisco
400 Parnassus, Room A203
San Francisco, CA 94143-0314
(415) 476-9691

Education/Training/Research Associates
Network Publications
P.O. Box 1830
Santa Cruz, CA 95061-1830
1-800-321-4407
Ask for catalogs regarding pregnancy and substance abuse resources.

National Association of Perinatal Addiction, Research and Education
11 E. Hubbard Street, Suite 200
Chicago, IL 60611
Contact: Nancy Lodl, Information Specialist
(312) 329-2512

National Clearinghouse for Alcohol and Drug Information
P.O. Box 2345
Rockville, MD 20852
(301) 468-2600
1-800-729-6686
Provides information for Office of Substance Abuse Prevention (OSAP), National Institute on Drug Abuse (NIDA), and National Institute on Alcohol Abuse and Alcoholism (NIAAA).

Office of Substance Abuse Prevention (OSAP), National Resource Center for the Prevention of Perinatal Abuse of Alcohol and Other Drugs
9300 Lee Highway
Fairfax, VA 22031-1207
(703) 218-5700
(703) 218-5701 (Fax)

Drug Abuse Hotlines

Drug Abuse Information Line
1-800-552-5353

Child Abuse and Prevention Information
1-800-342-7472

Poison Control Center
1-800-336-6997

National Hotline
1-800-COCAINE (1-800-262-2463)

National Institute on Drug Abuse (NIDA)
1-800-662-HELP (1-800-662-4357)

Books and Articles

Arendt, R., S. Minnes, N. Diffenbacher, G. Davis, and H. Nagusky. 1991. Cocaine-exposed infants and their mothers: An interdisciplinary model of service and research. *The Child, Youth, and Family Services Quarterly* 14(4):2-4.

Baumeister, A. 1991. Cocaine-exposed infants: A complex problem awaiting coherent policy. *The Child, Youth, and Family Services Quarterly* 14(4):8, 9.

Chasnoff, I. J. 1989. Cocaine and pregnancy: Implications for the child. *The Western Journal of Medicine* 50:456-59.

Creighton, L. 1991. Grandparents: The silent survivors. *U.S. News and World Report.* Dec. 16:80-89.

McKelvey, C. 1991. Mother–Don't write off drug babies. *Attachments* 4(3):1, 3.

______. 1991. Parenting cocaine/crack babies. *Attachments* 4(3):3.

Scafidi, F., and T. Field. 1991. An intervention program for adolescent mothers and cocaine-exposed infants. *The Child, Youth, and Family Services Quarterly* 14(4):4-5.

Singer, L. 1991. Cocaine-exposed infants and children. *The Child, Youth, and Family Services Quarterly* 14(4):1, 2.

Smith, I. 1991. Intervening with substance abusing pregnant and post partum women: Policy, practice, and advocacy. *The Child, Youth, and Family Services Quarterly* 14(4):6-7.

Stokes, L. 1991. A congressional viewpoint of substance abuse and children. *The Child, Youth, and Family Services Quarterly* 14(4):10, 11.

Substance abuse during pregnancy. 1991. *Pediatrics Annals* 20:523-70.

U.S. General Accounting Office. 1990. *Drug-exposed infants: A generation at risk.* Report to the Chairman, Committee on Finance, U.S. Senate. Washington, DC: GAO Document No. GAO/ARD 90-138.

Bibliography

Compiled by Jean Gardner Cole, M.S.

Als, H. 1982. Toward a synactive theory of development: Promise for the assessment and support of infant individuality. *Infant Mental Health Journal* 3(4): Winter.

Brazelton, T. B. 1984. *Neonatal behavioral assessment scale.* 2d ed. Philadelphia: J. B. Lippincott.

Chasnoff, I. J., Guest Editor. 1991. Chemical dependency in pregnancy. *Clinics in perinatology* 18(1).

Chasnoff, I. J., D. R. Griffith, S. MacGregor, K. Dirkes, and K. A. Burns. 1989. Temporal patterns of cocaine use in pregnancy: Perinatal outcome. *Journal of the American Medical Association* 261(12):1741-44.

Cole, J. In press. *Indices of neurobehavioral dysfunctioning in Infants/INDI.* Boston: Boston City Hospital.

_____. *Drugs and babies: A dangerous mix.* Boston: March of Dimes pamphlet published by Boston City Hospital. Available for $2.00 from Cole Consultants, 78 High Street, Leominster, MA 01453.

_____. 1991. High risk infants: Prenatal drug exposure, prematurity, and AIDS. In *Readings in child development,* edited by Nancy Lauter-Klatell. Mountain View, CA: Mayfield Publishing.

D'Apolito, K. 1991. What is an organized infant? *Neonatal Network Journal* 10(1):August.

DeStefano-Lewis, K., B. Bennett, and N. Hellenger Schmeder. 1989. The care of infants menaced by cocaine abuse. *Maternal Child Nursing* 14:324-29.

Dixon, S. D., K. Bresnahan, and B. Zuckerman. 1990. Cocaine babies: Meeting the challenge of management. *Contemporary Pediatrics* 7(6):70-92.

Flandermyer, A. 1988. A comparison of the effects of heroin and cocaine upon the neonate. *Neonatal Network Journal* 6(3) December:42-48.

Gawin, F., and H. Kleber. 1985. Neuroendocrine findings in chronic cocaine abusers: A preliminary report. *British Journal of Psychiatry* 147:569-73.

Hadeed, A. J., and S. R. Siegel. 1989. Maternal cocaine use during pregnancy: Effect on the newborn infant. *Journal of Pediatrics* 84(2):205-10.

Heagerty, M. 1991. America's lost children: Whose responsibility? *Journal of Pediatrics* 118(1).

Howard, J., L. Beckwith, C. Rodnig, and V. Kropenske. 1989. The development of young children of substance-abusing parents: Insights from seven years of intervention and research. *Zero to Three* 9(5):8-12.

Mirochnick, M., J. Meyer, J. Cole, T. Herron, and B. Zuckerman. 1991. Circulating catecholamines in cocaine-exposed neonates. *Journal of Pediatrics* 88(3) September:481-485.

Nuckels, C., and J. Greeson. 1989. Cocaine addiction: Assessment and intervention. *Nursing Clinics of North America* 24(1) (March):33-43.

Russell, F. F., and T. A. Free. 1991. Early intervention for infants and toddlers with prenatal drug exposure. *Infants and Young Children* 3(4):78-89.

Schneider, J. W., D. R. Griffith, and I. J. Chasnoff. 1989. Infants exposed to cocaine in utero: Implications for developmental assessment and intervention. *Infants and Young Children* 2(1):25-36.

U.S. General Accounting Office. 1990. *Drug-exposed infants: A generation at risk.* Report to the Chairman, Committee on Finance, U.S. Senate. Washington, DC: GAO Document No./ARD-90-138.

Van Baar, Anneloes. 1991. *The development of infants of drug dependent mothers.* Amsterdam/Lisse: Swets and Zeitlinger B.V.

Zuckerman, B., D. A. Frank, R. Hingson, H. Amaro, S. M. Levenson, H. Kayne, S. Parker, R. Vinci, K. Aboagye, L. E. Fried, H. Cabral, R. Timperi, and H. Bauchner. 1989. Effects of maternal marijuana and cocaine use on fetal growth. *New England Journal of Medicine* 320(12):762-68.

Appendix G

Score Sheet for Neonatal Drug Withdrawal Symptoms*

Howard University Hospital
Department of Pediatrics and Child Health

		Day #			Day #			Day #			Day #			Day #		
Symptoms	**Mild Moderate Severe**	**N**	**D**	**E**	**N**	**D**	**E**	**N**	**D**	**E**	**N**	**D**	**E**	**N**	**D**	**E**
Excessive movement	½ 1 2															
Persistent crying or high-pitched cry	½ 1 2															
Skin abrasions	½ 1 2															
Coarse tremors	½ 1 2															
Diarrhea	1 1 1															
Vomiting	1 1 1															
Excessively smacking lips or sucking hands and fingers	1 1 1															
Frank convulsions	5 5 5															
	Total															
Sleep pattern	Indicate with a + or – whether or not the infant is sleeping ≥ 2 hours at a time.															
TLC response	Indicate with a + or – whether or not the infant is calmed with TLC.															
	Initial and title															

Howard University Developmental Assessment Profile (HUDAP)*

Mitzi A. Parks, Ed.D., and Merceline M. Dahl-Regis, M.D., M.P.H.

Name of child: ______________________ Date of birth: __________

Name of examiner: ______________________ Date of testing: __________

Site: ______________________

Description of testing area(s): ______________________

____

____

____

Description of child's level of alertness: ______________________

____

____

____

____

____

____

TASKS	YES	NO	OTHER	COMMENTS
Lifts head when held				
when on stomach				
when sitting				
Crawling movements when on stomach				
chest up with arm support				
rocks on hands and knees				
drag-crawls				
creeps				

(continued)

TASKS	YES	NO	OTHER	COMMENTS
Rolls body side to back				
back to side				
stomach to back				
back to stomach				
Sits head drooping				
head erect				
with support				
without support				
pulls self to sitting				
pivots while sitting				
Stands bearing some weight				
bearing most of weight				
bouncing				
holding onto object				
holding hand of other				
alone				
Walks with both hands held				
holding onto object				
one hand held				
alone				
Tracks object to midline				
past midline				
Rattle held when placed in hands				
grasps				
Dangling object reaches for, attains stationary				
reaches for, attains moving				

(continued)

TASKS	YES	NO	OTHER	COMMENTS
Blocks or small toys holds two				
picks up two				
pushes one				
removes one from cup				
places three in cup				
Picks up raisins or cereal with fingers raking				
with finger and thumb				
Feeding sucks bottle				
mouths objects				
eats finger foods				
licks lollipop or ice cream				
Another person regards				
makes response to				
reaches for				
Smiles responsively				
spontaneously				
to mirror image				
laughs				
Plays with feet				
with hands				
peek-a-boo				
pat-a-cake				
Looks at object directly				
in direction of fallen object				

(continued)

TASKS	YES	NO	OTHER	COMMENTS
Toy, rattle, bell bangs				
squeezes				
shakes				
rings				
Responds to rattle				
tone of voice				
name				
"no-no"				
familiar words				
Locates voice				
rattle				
other sounds				
Makes sounds crying				
cooing				
gurgling				
squealing				
babbling				
Vocalizes to self				
mirror image				
other persons				
Communicates with single syllables				
double syllables				
gestures				
jargon				

Utilize practical information in your therapy with these products . . .

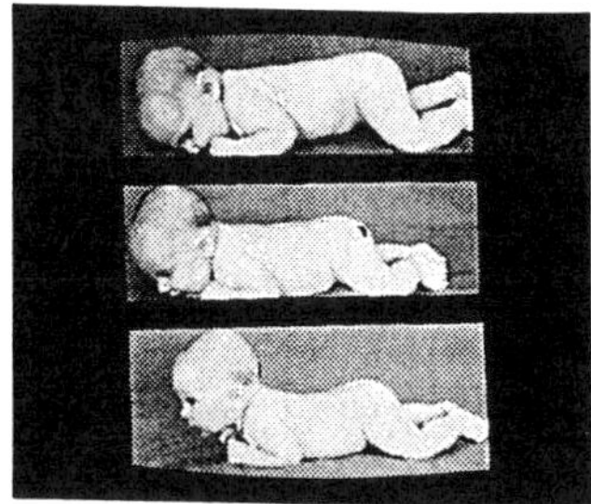

INFANT MOTOR DEVELOPMENT
A Look at the Phases
by Kerry Goudy, OTR, and Joan Fetzer, M.S., CCC-SLP

This 20-minute full-color VHS videotape provides you with a complete look at normal development from birth through 12 months. You'll be able to identify components of movement and specific skills that are acquired during the four phases of development—Infantile, Preparation, Modification, and Refinement. **Catalog No. 4141-YTS**

DEVELOPMENTAL HAND DYSFUNCTION (Second Edition)
Theory, Assessment, and Treatment
by Rhoda P. Erhardt, M.S., OTR, FAOTA

Take advantage of up-to-date theory, assessment, evaluation, and treatment of prehension. Three case studies of children with cerebral palsy show the importance of their hand skills. Use the EDPA to measure and score prehension development. Plus, you'll have explicit instructions for implementing innovative treatment techniques. **Catalog No. 4313-YTS**

NORMAL DEVELOPMENT OF FUNCTIONAL MOTOR SKILLS
The First Year of Life
by Rona Alexander, Ph.D., CCC-SP, Regi Boehme, OTR, and Barbara Cupps, PT

Gauge the functional motor levels of children with this resource. Focus on normal development during the first year of life. You'll find this an effective tool in planning treatment of infants with neurological involvement. Each developmental stage includes a summary chart for quick record-keeping that outlines postural control, gross and fine motor, vision, reach, respiration/phonation, and oral-motor/feeding.

Catalog No. 4187-YTS

NORMAL DEVELOPMENT COPYBOOK
by Marsha Dunn Klein, M.Ed., OTR/L, Nancy Harris Ossman, B.S., OTR, and Barbara Tracy, B.S., PT

Completely reproducible, you'll find all your favorite pictures from the *Normal Development Poster Set.* Each page features a developmental age, skill illustration, and space for you to suggest "Helpful Hints." Individualize pages by writing at-home activities for reaching goals. As a special plus, 24 "Developmental Sequence" pages illustrate skill acquisition in a glance. On one convenient page you'll have pictures and steps showing a task through completion—a great overview for parents!

Catalog No. 4732-YTS

HELPING BABIES LEARN
Developmental Profiles and Activities for Infants and Toddlers
by Setsu Furuno, Ph.D., Katherine A. O'Reilly, PT, MPH, Carol M. Hosaka,. M.A., Takayo T. Inatsuka, OTR, and Barbara Zeisloft Falbey, M.S., CCC-SP

Show parents how to help their children realize their fullest potential. Provide parents with reproducible activities to integrate all aspects of development. Plus, parents learn how their child is doing with six developmental charts summarizing normal skills development.

Catalog No. 7898-YCS

PARENT ARTICLES FOR EARLY INTERVENTION

Edited by Marsha Dunn Klein, M.Ed., OTR/L

Provide parents with pages of practical information on therapeutic ways to interact with their child who has special needs. Written in clear, everyday language for parents of children ages birth through three who have physical and communication disorders. Articles include normal development, therapeutic handling, and daily living activities. **Catalog No. 7549-YCS**

PREPARING PARAPROFESSIONAL EARLY INTERVENTIONISTS (PPEI)

by Samera Baird, Ph.D., CCC-SLP

Save time in your early intervention program by training paraprofessionals to make home visits! Use this complete curriculum to train those serving infants and toddlers birth through 2 years. **Catalog No. 7972-YCS**

For current prices on these practical resources, please call toll-free 1-800-228-0752.

ORDER FORM

Ship to:

Institution: ____________________

Name: ____________________

Occupation/Dept: ____________________

Address: ____________________

City: __________ *State:* ______ *Zip:* ____

Please check here if this is a permanent address change.

Telephone No. ____________ ☐ *work* ☐ *home*

Payment Options:

☐ *Bill me.* ☐ *My check is enclosed.*

☐ *My purchase order is enclosed. P.O. #* __________

☐ *Charge to my credit card:* ☐ *VISA* ☐ *Master Card* ☐ *American Express*

ard No. ☐☐☐☐☐☐☐☐☐☐☐☐☐☐☐

ion Date: Month ________ *Year* ________

____

Qty.	Cat. #	Title	Amount

Prices are in U.S. dollars. Payment must be made in U.S. funds only.

- If your account is not currently listed as "tax exempt," applicable destination charges will be added to your invoice.
- Orders are shipped by United Parcel Service (UPS) unless otherwise requested. If another delivery service is required, please specify.
- For regular delivery service, your order will be charged 5% handling plus actual shipping charges.
- We occasionally backorder items temporarily out of stock. If you do not accept backorders, please tell us on your purchase order or on this form.

Money-Back Guarantee

You'll have up to 90 days of risk-free evaluation of the products your ordered. If you're not completely satisfied with any product, we'll pick it up within the 90 days and refund the full purchase price! **No questions asked!**

For Phone Orders

Call 1-800-228-0752. Please have your credit card and/or institutional purchase order information ready. Monday-Friday 7am-7pm Central Time.
Voice or TDD 1-800-723-1318
FAX 1-800-232-1223

Send your order to:

Therapy Skill Builders

a division of The Psychological Corporation

555 Academic Court / San Antonio, Texas 78204-2498